D1287014

DICK HERN

THE AUTHORISED BIOGRAPHY

DICK
HERN

THE AUTHORISED BIOGRAPHY

Peter Willett

Hodder & Stoughton

Copyright © 2000 by Peter Willett

First published in Great Britain in 2000
by Hodder and Stoughton
A division of Hodder Headline

10 9 8 7 6 5 4 3 2 1

A CIP catalogue record for this title is available from the British Library

ISBN 0 340 79263 9

Typeset by Rowland Phototypesetting Ltd,
Bury St Edmunds, Suffolk
Printed and bound in Great Britain by
Clays Ltd, St Ives plc

Hodder and Stoughton
A division of Hodder Headline
338 Euston Road
London NW1 3BH

This book is dedicated to Sheilah Hern,
Dick's devoted wife for forty-one years,
whose insistence that the details of his life
should be recorded was its inspiration.

CONTENTS

ACKNOWLEDGEMENTS

I owe thanks to many people without whose help this book could not have been written: first and foremost to its subject, Dick Hern, whose autobiographical notes, compiled before the work was undertaken, were a fertile source of material. He also showed marvellous powers of recall during numerous interviews, answering with patience and good humour streams of questions many of which, no doubt, were fatuous. Elizabeth Brown, a friend of Dick and Sheilah for many years and now Dick's 'dame d'affaires', gave unflagging assistance, and her knowledge of documents and photographs in the Hern archive was invaluable. Sheilah's cousin Giles Blomfield also was generous with his time and contributed many recollections besides access to his comprehensive cuttings books. Marie Hamilton performed the vital task of transcribing Dick's notes from the tapes. Ian Balding, a staunch friend and a man of extraordinary moral courage, threw a revealing ray of light on a dark phase of Dick's life. Among many others who contributed useful information Brian Holmes, Lord Halifax, Willie Carson, Jimmy Lindley, Neil Graham, Julian Seaman, John Gallimore and Marcus Tregoning deserve special mention. I am deeply grateful to them all.

PHOTOGRAPHIC ACKNOWLEDGEMENTS

The author and publisher would like to thank the following for permission to reproduce photographs:

Associated Press, Gerry Cranham, Provincial Press, Sport & General.

All other photographs are from private collections.

FOREWORD

by Major M. B. Pope MC

Dick Hern and I have been the greatest of friends since we first met as greenhorn subalterns in the North Irish Horse during the Second World War. This friendship was clearly enhanced by our mutual love for the horse in every shape and form. Various battles in North Africa and Italy did not deter us from reminiscing about equine events in the past or from planning horse ventures for the future. So I was delighted to be invited to write a Foreword for his biography.

When hostilities ended Dick returned to the Porlock Vale Riding School where, as a very able horseman, he became a highly qualified instructor. I returned to my home in the Berkshire Downs, where my wife and family had been slaving to prepare a small stableyard in readiness for me to start my training career. My father, meanwhile, had been equally busy leaning on racing pals to extract promises of horses for me to train.

In the autumn of 1952 I asked Dick to join me as my assistant; not that I could teach him very much about racing, as I was still working on a trial and error basis myself. In fact he had forgotten more about horses, riding and stable management than I should ever know. Dick undoubtedly longed to become fully involved in the racing game but needed to learn the tricks of the trade.

For over five years we had wonderful sport and, surprisingly enough, quite considerable success. Dick rode a few winners over fences on a great little horse called Sir John IV owned jointly by my father and Lord McAlpine. Out of the blue Major Lionel Holliday appeared wanting a replacement trainer at his Lagrange Stable in Newmarket. With the most glowing of references, away went Dick to embark on a brilliant career training top class winners internationally, and in the course of time had many victories for H.M. the Queen at her West Ilsley Stables in Berkshire.

Sadly in December 1984, when out with the Quorn Hunt, Dick had a horrendous fall and broke his neck but, after three months in Stoke Mandeville Hospital, he was able to return home and start training again. After a slow start he had a good year, winning the King George VI and Queen Elizabeth Stakes with Petoski. Three years later he had a serious heart operation when a metal valve was inserted in his heart, and at the same time he had to endure worry and uncertainty over his lease at West Ilsley. Everyone admired the fortitude with which he confronted and overcame these problems. He was back in action in 1989 and, with the loyal support of his devoted wife Sheilah and wonderful backing from the Maktoum family, went on to produce the classic winner Nashwan and many other top class winners.

In order that Dick could continue training after the termination of the lease at West Ilsley, Sheikh Hamdan Al Maktoum very generously built Kingwood House Stables at Lambourn where he trained until his retirement at the end of the 1997 season after holding a licence for forty years.

INTRODUCTION

Dick Hern holds a unique position among the great English trainers of the twentieth century. His distinction does not rest on any such common method of assessing a trainer's performance as a count of his Classic winners. Indeed his score of English Classic winners, sixteen, was exceeded by Henry Cecil, who had twenty-two and was still going strong as he passed the millennium; by the Manton wizard Alec Taylor, with twenty-one, and by Noel Murless and Fred Darling, with nineteen each. Nor did it rest on a record number of years as champion trainer. Using stakes earnings as the criterion, he was leading trainer in Britain four times, a splendid achievement, but surpassed during the twentieth century by Cecil, Taylor, Murless, Frank Butters, Darling, Sir Cecil Boyd-Rochfort, and Sir Michael Stoute – the three first-named all being top trainer at least twice that number of times.

So Dick Hern's uniqueness cannot be a numbers game. To some extent it is a matter of being multi-talented, of being not only an exceptionally skilful trainer of racehorses and a horseman in the American sense of someone connected with horses, but also a horseman in the English sense of a master of equitation. Dick was an instructor of Olympic Games standard, and would in all probability have ridden in the British Olympic team if he had not been barred as a professional; and he rode with success in point-to-points and steeplechases. None of his peers among

1

the great trainers of the twentieth century could compare with him as an all-round horseman. Noel Murless rode a few winners under National Hunt Rules, but it was only necessary to see him sitting long-legged and splay-footed on his hack on Newmarket Heath to realise that he could never have been an elegant horseman or an Olympic team instructor. Fred Darling, small and light compared to Hern and Murless, rode a few winners on the flat while apprenticed to his father, but never became a full jockey. Dick's involvement with other activities, with soldiering in the Second World War and afterwards with equitation, meant that he took to training relatively late in life, and only a special flair for the job enabled him to train as many Classic winners and gain as many trainers' championships as he did.

This many-faceted involvement with the Horse did not constitute his only claim to uniqueness. Darling and Murless suffered from bad health during the later part of their careers, but neither they nor any of the other great twentieth century trainers had to contend with such a severe physical handicap as Dick Hern. A fall while taking part in his favourite recreational activity, foxhunting, at the age of sixty-three resulted in a broken neck, a long spell in hospital and confinement to a wheel-chair for the rest of his life. Only a man of exceptional strength of character and dedication to his profession would have thought of carrying on in the circumstances. Dick did not hesitate; nor was he deflected from his chosen course by major heart surgery four years later, rising above a multitude of problems that would have overwhelmed a less single-minded man to supervise the training of Nashwan, his third Derby winner.

Dick has a number of natural gifts that helped to put him at the forefront of the training profession. He has an inborn empathy with horses, honed by his close contacts with them from his earliest years: that is one of the most precious assets that a trainer can possess. He has self-confidence. Training is no job for anyone tormented by self-doubt but Dick, when faced by the daunting appointment of private trainer to one of the most formidable of owner-breeders, Lionel Holliday, as his first venture in the profession, never entertained the slightest doubt about his ability to get the best out of high class horses. He is a disciplinarian with men and horses, and nobody can exploit the potential of a large stable successfully without tight control of his human and equine resources. He is absolutely honest and he is a great communicator; many owners, sickened by the devious ways and lack of information from some other trainers, found having horses with Dick an immensely refreshing and enjoyable experience. He has good spirits and a sense of humour; though sometimes seeming dour, even taciturn, with strangers, he can be the best of fun in the company of friends, while his love of a sing-song and his fund of popular and often bawdy ditties are legendary. While he was training he was always meticulous in his dress; his single-breasted grey suits with two vents, his brown trilby hats and freshly shined shoes perfected the image of a well turned-out English racing and hunting man. His physical appearance matched his turn-out. He is good-looking, was tall and very slim in his youth, and kept his figure well into middle age. His features are symmetrical, his jaws wide, his nose prominent and broad, his forehead also broad and rising to a thatch of dark brown hair which has thinned only slightly, even in his late seventies. His eyes are wide-set, his gaze straight. The dominant feature has always been the nose which seems as if, in some inexplicable fashion, it was put in place first and the rest of the face modelled round it. It is a face which has always radiated honesty and sense of purpose.

For all the forty seasons that he held a trainer's licence one of his greatest assets was his wife Sheilah, whose tiny frame encompassed, among many other qualities, an intense capacity for steadfast support of his interests in every eventuality. She was a marvellous hostess, which is so important in the wife of a trainer who has wealthy and demanding patrons, and she had a natural sparkle and a sunny temperament which kept everyone around her happy.

His ability to run a well-drilled and disciplined establishment has often been attributed to his war service in the army. His retention of his army rank and the tendency to refer to him as 'The Major' have encouraged that opinion, but it is not necessarily correct. Success as an officer may be due to a person's natural authority and power to command rather than training, and that may very well have been true in the case of Dick Hern. One lesson that life in the wartime army certainly does teach is how to understand and get along with people from many different walks of life, and it is a lesson that was not lost on Dick.

One aptitude that was missing from Dick's catalogue of talents was a shrewd appreciation of business matters, and a lack of application to this side of his interests denied him the accumulation of wealth that accrued to some other trainers who may have been less scrupulous and without doubt were less well versed in the art and science of training the racehorse. Dick has always been a countryman through and through, a hunting man who never lost some of his innocence in the world of finance If he had been a hard-headed man of business, he would have been a different person, not the person who earned the respect of the racing community and of many people who knew of him only through his well-publicised tribulations.

The principal sources of income for a trainer are training fees, the trainer's percentage of prize money earned by horses in the stable and a percentage of the sums realised by horses when they are sold out of the stable. For most of his career, until the Queen bought West Ilsley Stables in 1982 and he became a tenant, Dick was a salaried employee and so training fees did not enter his financial equation; this was probably an advantage, because training fees seldom cover overheads. Also for most of his career, percentages of prize money were a variable factor. When he retired the percentages were laid down by the British Horseracing Board, deducted from the owner's prize money by the stakeholders and credited directly to the trainer's account; a few years later they ranged from 5.66 per cent in the case of Pattern race winners to 6.6 per cent in the case of races for which there was no fourth prize money. Before the authorities took a hand the percentages were a matter of negotiation between owner and trainer. 'Major Holliday paid something, but not very much,' said Dick. Nor did many of his owners pay a percentage of the sums for which their horses were sold. Dick Hollingsworth was an exception; he was generous when good horses like Longboat were sold out of the stable as stallions. Otherwise Dick profited from the grant of breeding rights to good horses he had trained when they retired from training and went to stud. Sir Arnold Weinstock gave him breeding rights in Troy and Ela-Mana-Mou, Mrs Etty Plesch gave him a breeding right to Henbit and Sheikh Hamdan gave him breeding rights to Unfuwain, Nashwan and Dayjur.

Although numbers are only one of the factors, and are not the ultimately determining factor, in assessing Dick's proper place among the most famous British trainers of the twentieth century, there is one achievement in which he takes special pride: he is the only man, apart from the greatest of Irish trainers Vincent O'Brien, to have trained the winners of all five Classic races in both England and Ireland. In England he won the 2000 Guineas with Brigadier Gerard and Nashwan, the 1000 Guineas with Highclere and Harayir, the Derby with Troy, Henbit and Nashwan, the Oaks with Dunfermline, Bireme and Sun Princess and the St Leger with Hethersett, Provoke, Bustino, Dunfermline, Cut Above and Sun Princess. In Ireland he won the 2000 Guineas with Sharp Edge, the 1000 Guineas with Gaily, the Derby with Troy, the Oaks with Shoot A Line, Swiftfoot and Helen Street and the St Leger with Craighouse and Niniski. It is a record that will stand for ever because the Irish St Leger, having been opened to older horses in 1983, is no longer a Classic race in the traditional sense of a championship race for three-year-olds.

The Irish St Leger was just one of the changes, and far from the most epoch-making change, that affected racing in Dick's time. When he began to train at Newmarket in 1958 Sir Cecil Boyd-Rochfort was champion trainer, holding first place for three out of four seasons. The names of British-born owner-breeders like the Queen, Lord Rosebery, Lord Howard de Walden, the Astors, Sir Victor Sassoon, Jim Joel and Dick's employer Major Holliday were usually high in the appropriate winning lists. Forty years later, when Dick retired, Sir Cecil's stepson Henry Cecil had been champion trainer ten times, but was coming under increasing pressure from Saeed Bin Suroor, who relegated him to second place in 1996. The challenge of Saeed Bin Suroor and the Maktoum-owned Godolphin operation symbolised the change that had revolutionised the British racing scene during Dick's training career – the advent of the Arabs, primarily the Maktoum family of Dubai, and their accession to and consolidation of the position of prime movers in British racing.

Dick was one of the beneficiaries of this revolution. His first Arab owner, Sheikh Mohammed Bin Rashid Al Maktoum, joined the stable in 1983, when the total roll of horses at West Ilsley was ninety-nine, fourteen of them owned by the Queen. Four years later the roll had risen above the century mark, to a hundred and five, and four members of the Maktoum family – Sheikh Maktoum Al Maktoum, Sheikh Hamdan Al Maktoum, Sheikh Ahmed Al Maktoum and Sheikh Mohammed – accounted for twenty-five of them and were, collectively, much the biggest owners in the stable, while the number owned by the Queen remained static. Sheikh Hamdan was the owner-breeder of Dick's last two Classic winners, Nashwan in the 2000 Guineas and the Derby and Harayir in the 1000 Guineas, and was his benefactor by buying and modernising the Kingwood Stables for his occupation when he left West Ilsley. The reverse side of the coin was that races had become much harder to win with moderate horses; a horse that had cost millions or was the produce of a stallion and a mare worth millions might be encountered in an insignificant race on the least prestigious course. With the intense competition of the Arabs and prize money obstinately low, the lot of the small owner was not a happy one.

The Arab domination of British racing was only one aspect of the growing internationalisation of racing in the last thirty years of the twentieth century, a process in which Dick not only participated but of which he was a pioneer. His raids on big races in France captured the Prix Vermeille with Highest Hopes, the Prix Robert Papin with Sun Prince, the Prix du Moulin with Sallust and, as a climax, the Prix de Diane with Highclere.

There were other fundamental changes during the forty years that Dick held a trainer's licence. In the first place there was a colossal increase in the volume of racing, from under 2500 to well over 4000 races a year. On the organisational side, central planning of the national racing programme was rudimentary, if it existed at all in 1958. A few elementary rules controlling, for example, the distances over which races should be run, were laid down, and racecourse executives had to submit their programmes to the Jockey Club for approval, but whether the programmes were ever subjected to critical scrutiny is another matter. The question of who was responsible for the vetting process was debated at a Jockey Club meeting in 1965, and the outcome was inconclusive. Major David Gibson wound up the debate with the statement: 'There is in fact a committee. I cannot remember what it is called. It has not functioned much yet, but it will function.' This state of farcical ignorance was a far cry from the rigid centralised control of the nineteen-nineties.

If the organisation of programmes generally was loose, it was no stricter in respect of the provision of opportunities for quality horses. Such high-class races as did exist, like the Classic races, the King George VI and Queen Elizabeth Stakes, the Ascot Gold Cup, the July Cup and the Princess of Wales's Stakes, were the products of tradition and the enterprise of individual racecourses. This chaotic situation began to change with the report of the Duke of Norfolk's Pattern of Racing Committee in 1965, which enunciated the doctrine that 'the

Turf Authorities must ensure that a series of races over the right distances and at the right time of the year are available to test the best horses of all ages'. This doctrine was the seed from which the Pattern race system, with its division of top quality races into three groups or grades according to their importance, grew and became the model adopted in every racing country in the world. Combined with the International Classifications, which collated the ratings of the best horses in the principal racing countries, the Pattern provided an enormous boost to an integrated international racing programme. Dick freely acknowledged the benefits of the system: 'The Pattern made it much easier to plan the programme of a good horse, and was a great help to owners and trainers by ensuring that prize money for the best races was as adequate as possible,' he declared. The Benson and Hedges Gold Cup, which Dick won with Relkino and Troy – though the race was less happily the occasion of the only defeat of Brigadier Gerard – was an example of a new race introduced to enhance the opportunities for top-class horses which Dick was able to exploit.

Other major changes in Dick's time were the advent of evening racing and the introduction of the five-day entry system. As a ratio of all racing, evening racing reached its peak in 1968, when 115 out of a total of 848 flat meetings were evening fixtures. However, evening programmes were designed mostly for the lower categories of horses and involved relatively few of Dick's horses. Nor did the five-day entry system make much difference to Dick's entry procedures. The entry forms were issued in *The Racing Calendar* three weeks in advance of the date of closing – for example *The Calendar* of 6 April would contain entry forms for races due to close between 26 April and 1 May – and Dick made his running plans, which were subject only to last-minute revision, as soon as they were received. Lacking the full use of his hands following his hunting accident, he had the forms cut out and pasted on a board which was placed in front of him.

For much of his training career his relationship with many members of the press was uneasy. He never denied this. He attributed his wariness of the press to an incident soon after he had arrived at Newmarket to hold a licence for the first time as private trainer to Major Lionel Holliday. A pressman telephoned asking whether he could come round for an interview, with a view to writing a profile for his paper. Dick replied that he would rather leave it until he had had a little time to settle in, and maybe train a few winners. The pressman then said: 'Well, my editor has told me to write the article, so if you will not see me I shall have to make most of it up.' Dick thought that revealed an unacceptably low standard of authenticity and fair dealing.

Much later, when he was training at West Ilsley, he had a fancied candidate for the Derby. A journalist rang up at eleven o'clock one night, when Dick and Sheilah were in bed, to ask after the horse's welfare. Sheilah took the call and, to save Dick aggravation at a late hour, said that he was not available. She then heard a voice in the background say: 'Try him every hour.' 'That won't do you any good, because I am going to leave the phone off,' she said. It was Dick's firm belief that a trainer, whose day begins early and who works long hours, should be disturbed after ten o'clock at night only in cases of dire emergency.

His coolness did not extend to all members of the press. A few of them, notably Peter Scott of *The Daily Telegraph* and Michael (Mikey) Seely of *The Times*, not only enjoyed his confidence but were also close friends. In character they were poles apart. Peter, always soberly dressed in a dark suit, had the earnest air of an Anglican curate. In fact he was a Catholic convert devoted to his faith, and regularly attended 9 a.m. Mass at the Church of Our Lady of Mount Carmel in Kensington Church Street. He had a profound knowledge of the racing programme and the Pattern, and was a student of racing history and of defunct and obscure racecourses. The journey to Salisbury races might well include a pilgrimage to the elder-clad ruins of the

Bibury Club stand at Stockbridge, where the last meeting was held in 1898; and he was lucky to escape from a savage guard-dog on a voyage of exploration to the course at St Pierre-Sur-Dives, a small market town deep in the Norman countryside which held one meeting a year. He was an active member of the Richard III Society, dedicated to the rehabilitation of that monarch who had been much maligned as the alleged instigator of the murder of the little princes in the Tower; he was an eager researcher into the history and ethos of boys' public schools, preferably minor public schools; he enjoyed nothing more than an evening at Ronnie Scott's jazz club; he was a voracious reader of Agatha Christie and Charles Dickens, whose works loaded his shelves; and he loved cricket and was a keen if indifferent golfer. He had an endearing capacity for hero-worship of objects both equine and human; the unbeaten Ribot, winner of the Prix de l'Arc de Triomphe twice and the King George VI and Queen Elizabeth Stakes, was his idea of the sublime race-horse, and the tennis star Billie-Jean King attracted his intense admiration not for her physical charms but for her gutsy will to win. To balance his immensely wide range of interests, serious and semi-serious, he had a sly sense of humour and a taste for good champagne.

As a racing journalist Peter was enormously conscientious. His style was precise and factual, and he eschewed flights of fancy. By contrast Michael Seely gave the impression of perpetual disorganisation. He was an alcoholic whose addiction was strictly controlled by implants; but if by an oversight the implants were not renewed at the due time his backsliding was immediate and sometimes spectacular. His other addiction was to the telephone; he was always seemingly convinced that just one more call would yield the vital information to complete the story he was pursuing at the time. He was chronically untidy. The exterior of his car was always coated with motorway grime and sported a number of dents, while the interior seemed to contain about half the belongings of himself and his wife Pat, which had been stirred with a gigantic spoon. He procrastinated and he dithered. To listen to him and Pat planning their moves for the next few days was to be reminded of T. S. Eliot's vacillating Prufrock:

'In a minute there is time
For decisions and revisions which a minute will reverse.'

For years before he joined *The Times* he had worked on *Race-form* and *Chaseform*, and the peculiar shorthand of those publications (b.b.v, blkd, j.b, p.u, swvd, u.str.p, and so on) could be regarded as the worst conceivable training for a fluent style of writing. Yet fluency, readability and masses of inside information were the hallmarks of his articles. The fluency must have been due, in part at least, to a natural flair for language. He had a deceptively casual air; in fact he was extremely industrious, and when publication of *The Times* was suspended for a year he took on four minor jobs to keep his hand in and the cash-flow going. He was a skilful if idiosyncratic bridge player – 'Three no trumps is the quickest way to game' was his favourite dictum – and an enthusiastic windsurfer.

Despite their enormous differences, Peter and Mikey had a number of qualities in common that appealed to Dick. They were unusual characters, they were never dull, they loved racing and understood its intricacies, and they were men of integrity for whom a confidence was sacrosanct. They were always liked and trusted at West Ilsley because those qualities mirrored Dick's own. Some other racing writers found Dick brusque, taciturn and unhelpful at times. They did not appreciate his old-fashioned view that his obligations to his owners and his horses took priority over his obligations to disseminate information to the public. He had no patience with the ignorant or the impertinent question. It was not until later life, when he was perceived as the victim first of misfortune and later of injustice, that he earned the sympathy of the press as a whole, and his fortitude earned their respect and affection. Against the odds, he outlived both Peter and Mikey by a comfortable margin.

Nobody ever impugned his professionalism. His steadily mounting score of Classic winners, the way he structured and developed the career of the great Brigadier Gerard and extracted the best from top-class fillies owned by the Queen, like Highclere and Dunfermline, constitute irrefutable proof of his supreme ability to train racehorses at the highest level. What has really set him apart from other trainers who have been equally, or even more, successful in purely statistical terms is the immensely wide range of his activities and his experiences, and the invincible spirit with which he has confronted and overcome seemingly catastrophic setbacks.

Every trainer needs to have guiding principles – a philosophy of training if you will. Sir Cecil Boyd-Rochfort, who like Dick trained Classic horses for the Queen, once remarked that trainers could be divided into two broad categories: hard trainers and soft trainers. That of course is an oversimplification, because it ignores the infinite nuances that divide one trainer's methods from another's. The early two-year-old specialist Jack Berry did not train horses in the same way as the ultimate hard trainer Sir Jack Jarvis; and Jack Jarvis did not train in the same way as Fred Darling, the master of the art of preparing a horse for the Derby. In his memoirs, *Riding Recollections*, Henry Custance, who rode the horse in the Derby and the St Leger, recalled that a few days before the St Leger in 1864 Lord Lyon, then a yearling, was given his first trial, failing by a head to beat Jezebel, a two-year-old winner of two recent races, who was conceding him only 7lbs. That would not have been Dick Hern's way of preparing a horse to win the Triple Crown, though Dick did make a practice of finding out which of his two-year-olds, even the backward ones, had speed at an early stage of the season; after that he could put them away and bring them along gradually. Patience, he believed, was an essential virtue in a trainer. Years after he had retired he wrote:

12

I have trained some really good horses in my time, and I'm sure the secret is to give them plenty of time; let them come on their own and don't be in too much of a hurry. High-class horses that are running in Pattern races don't want to run too often because they get a hard race every time. It is important to keep them sweet.

A trainer must be with his horses as much as possible. He must see them walk out, do their work, and walk in again afterwards. It is very informative to see the way they walk home. If they are getting stirred up, you may have to keep the soft pedal down. You must study their temperaments. Like people, they are all different.

Dick was naturally observant, and after his hunting accident his eye became even keener. At the age of seventy-nine he could detect an impending drip from a salad-dressing jug at the far end of the dining-room table, and issue a timely warning. Translated into racehorse terms, the drip might be an incipient leg problem or the state of being slightly off colour. His powers of observation were matched by an attention to detail that was an equally important part of a trainer's armoury of talents. A young man about to start up as a trainer once asked Norman Bertie whether he could, from his vast experience, give him one piece of advice that would help him in his career. Norman Bertie had been head man to Fred Darling for many years before setting up on his own and winning the Derby with Pinza. He pondered the question with care, puffing at the cigarette sagging from his lower lip and narrowing his eyes against the clouds of smoke and ash, while the young man waited expectantly for a pronouncement on the work that should be given to a Classic horse, or the like. After a long pause Norman handed down this lapidary verdict: 'Watch the dungs, watch the dungs.'

Dick would have echoed Norman's opinion. It is one of his cardinal beliefs that to give a high priority to this kind of unglamorous detail is an essential part of a conscientious and responsible trainer's craft, just as vital to success as anything that happens on the gallops. In training the racehorse this attitude differentiates the true professional from the amateur.

ONE

BOYHOOD

Dick Hern was born in Somerset and resided in the county until he was thirty-one years old. He was as much a man of Somerset as any member of the Somerset Stragglers, the county's amateur cricket club, though Dick's concern was with horse and saddle, not bat and ball. Happily, for a horseman, he was living in the right county.

Topographically speaking, Somerset is one of the most diverse of the English counties. Its heart is occupied by Sedgemoor and the Levels, former marshland of which little is more than a few feet above sea level, where the rivers Brue and Parrett, fed by scores of streams and drainage channels called 'rhynes', wind sluggishly across the flat plain. By contrast with the Levels there is an immense variety of uplands: the grass and heather-clad expanses of Exmoor, whose northern edge drops steeply to the Bristol Channel; the adjacent wild Brendons; the wooded combes of the Quantocks; the limestone plateau of the Mendips with their caves and gorges: and the gentle hills along the Dorset border with landmarks like Corton Beacon and the outlying stone-age fort of South Cadbury, held by oral tradition to have been King Arthur's Camelot. Even the Levels are incongruously bisected by the long ridge of the Polden Hills rising to more than 150 feet above the plain, while the curious green cone of Glastonbury Tor dominates their south-eastern end.

Most significantly for the horseman, Somerset is England's

premier dairying county. Dairying requires a region that is predominantly grassland and pasture, and grassland is an essential ingredient of good hunting country. In the 1930s, when Dick was in his teens and his love of the horse and hunting was burgeoning, very little of the county was arable. Moreover topographical diversity was matched by the variety of the demands made on horse and rider. Exmoor, the location of the Devon and Somerset Staghounds, was all uphill and downhill galloping. The West Somerset Vale, where Dick hunted most frequently in his boyhood, was mostly banks, with open water obstacles in its marshy eastern extremity. The Mendips featured stone walls, and the Levels were criss-crossed by the rhynes. The Blackmore Vale (the B V), the cream of West Country packs, was famous for its hairy banks in the Blackmore Vale proper which runs south and south-westwards from Wincanton, straddling the county boundary with Dorset. The B V proper was a little out of reach of Dick's home near the coast of the Bristol Channel, but he had days from Millfield in the Sparkford Vale which formed the north-western part of the B V country. The Sparkford Vale comprised 8 square miles of a fast rider's paradise, bounded to the north by the Babcary brook and to the south by the hump-backed ridge of Camel Hill, with a triangle of compact coverts – Wheathill, Annis Hills and Yarcombe – and neat fly fences and big ditches. Fields in the Sparkford Vale, the B V's Tuesday country, were swelled to more than 200 by an influx of eager and highly competitive young officers from the garrisons on Salisbury Plain and, in such company, Dick had days to remember.

Altogether two packs of staghounds (the Devon and Somerset, and the Quantock), six packs of harriers and nine packs of foxhounds were contained within, or partly within, the county boundaries of Somerset in the 1930s. Between them they provided sporting opportunities for the hunting man for nine months of the year. The Staghounds hunted stags in April and from August to mid-October, by which time the cubbing season was nearly at an end and foxhunting was about to take over until March. The hind-hunting season ran concurrently with foxhunting. Between them the Somerset packs offered an ideal environment for a boy who was brought up to ride and conceived a passion for horses and hunting.

William Richard Hern, Dick as he was always known, was born on 20 January 1921 at Holford, a village at the foot of the eastern slopes of the Quantock Hills. His father and mother, Roy and Winifred, had rented a cottage there, the last one up Butterfly Combe, while they were waiting to move into Wick House in the hamlet of Wick, four miles away on the far side of Stogursey. Dick was their second son; their first, William John Roderick, born on 5 October 1918, had died of acute laryngitis when only sixteen months old. Two more sons, Rupert and Michael, were born in 1922 and 1925 respectively.

The Herns were a West Country family, coming originally from around Ashburton and the fringes of Dartmoor in Devon. However, the three sons of William Hern, who died in 1832, decided to break free from the bonds of country life in Devon, and all entered branches of the medical profession. William, Dick's grandfather, opted for dentistry and gained distinction in both its academic and practical aspects. He published a work on 'Fractures of Maxillae and Treatment' in the *British Journal of Dental Science*, and became a lecturer at the Royal Dental Hospital in London. As a dental practitioner he became one of the most famous of his day, and his patients at his house and consulting rooms at 7 Stratford Place, a cul-de-sac off the north side of Oxford Street, included King Edward VII. Nevertheless he did not abandon country pursuits, and shooting, fishing and golf were his principal recreations. His eldest child William Roderick, known as Roy, was born in 1893 and became the father of Dick.

Roy Hern was educated at Rugby. It was intended that he too should go into the medical profession, and consequently he went as a student to the Middlesex Hospital. However, he hated it, and the call of the countryside soon became too strong for him to resist. In a complete change of tack, he went as a pupil to a farmer named Sheldon at Stragglethorpe near the Fosse Way in Leicestershire, and found life on a farm much more to his liking. Sheldon bought him a hunter, and he used to go out with the Quorn on the forest side, developing a love of hunting which remained with him all his life. He rode the same horse when shepherding the sheep down by the Trent and never needed to open a gate, as he was a brilliant timber jumper. On the outbreak of war in 1914 he jumped on the hunter, rode into Nottingham and enlisted in the South Notts Hussars at the Black Boy Hotel, while the horse was bought into the army as a charger. Later Roy was commissioned in the Glamorganshire Yeomanry, but transferred back to the South Notts Hussars, went abroad with them and saw service in the Struma Valley, leading north from Macedonia into Bulgaria, during the futile Salonika campaign in 1916.

Roy Hern and Winifred Mullens were married on 27 October 1917 at Chedzoy just outside Bridgwater on the Somerset Levels, when they were both twenty-four years old. Winifred was one of six daughters of George Mullens, the rector of Chedzoy. George Mullens was no impoverished country parson. The family lived in some style with domestic staff, a large and beautiful garden and grass courts where tennis parties were held during the summer months. George Mullens took his parochial duties very seriously, taking care of both the spiritual and the material needs of his parishioners. The whole family joined in taking meals to the sick and old, and George Mullens had the village hall built at his own expense. He was really the squire as well as the rector and if a girl got into trouble, he made sure that the boy concerned married her. During the war Winifred volunteered for the VADs and was posted to a big hospital at Wandsworth which was full of wounded soldiers back from the western front in France. The hospital work involved a traumatic shock for a young woman brought up in the sheltered environment of a country rectory; one of her first jobs was to carry an amputated gangrenous leg from the operating theatre and put it in the incinerator.

Until he left the army at the end of the war, home for Roy and Winifred was Chedzoy rectory, but they then moved first to Holford and then to Wick House. That part of Somerset is remote and full of historical associations. The name of Stogursey, the larger village a little over a mile south-west of Wick, is a corruption of 'stoc' meaning place and 'Courcy', the owner of the land in Norman times. Stogursey boasts the ruins of a Norman castle and is reputed to have been the lair of the ruthless Fulke de Breaute who terrorised the surrounding countryside in the twelfth century. Happily there have been no such disruptions in recent times, and in the 1930s the area was well-suited to the pursuit of such peaceful occupations as riding and hunting.

Wick House was a solid stone building with stables and a hundred acres of grass, perfect for a horse-mad family. Only Winifred, who was kept busy looking after her husband and sons, did not ride, but she was adept at driving a pony and trap. When he was grown up Dick could never remember a time when he could not ride. However, his development as a horseman was not without interruption. One day when he was four he was sitting on an old bay pony with a short tail that was used in the trap, waiting to be led out for a ride. Roy went back into the tack room to fetch something he had forgotten, and the pony started to walk off down the lane towards the field where he was turned out. Dick was terrified. Roy followed, but the faster he walked the faster the pony walked and eventually broke into a trot. After about 300 yards Dick threw himself off, fearing that the pony was going to go right down the lane and out to sea. Dick was so badly shaken that for a long time he got a tummy ache whenever it was suggested that he should ride.

To the immense credit of a man who lived for riding and naturally wanted his sons to enjoy riding too, Roy never tried to force Dick, and gradually he began to feel that he wanted to have another go. About that time Roy bought a pony mare called Maggie, who was used in the governess cart and could trot into Bridgwater on shopping expeditions, a distance of 8 miles, in forty minutes. She was always kept in and clipped during the winter, and was practically the family's only means of transport until about 1930, when Roy bought his first car. She was also Dick's first pony, and was a marvellous performer. She could jump almost anything a big horse could jump, and she loved it. In the early 1930s, when Dick and Rupert were ten or eleven, Roy had a scratch pack of hounds registered as the Bridgwater Harriers that used to hunt the country east of Bridgwater and north of the river Parrett. This country included Sedgemoor, Winifred's family home at Chedzoy and the village of Weston Zoyland, the site of the last great battle on English soil in July 1685, when the cavalry of the army of James II cut down the ill-armed followers of the rebel Duke of Monmouth. Roy's predecessor as Master had been Joe Hawkins, who had a milk round in Bridgwater and was a genuinely eccentric character. He owned an American trotter stallion that he used to drive round the neighbourhood in a sulky, stopping at various farms to cover mares. Sometimes, to save time, the stallion would cover a mare while still between the shafts of the sulky.

That part of the county is entirely low-lying grassland south of the Poldens and drained by rhynes. Native hares and foxes were scarce, so Roy had some sent down in boxes by train from Scotland, and then released them on the Levels. The supplier used to notify despatch of a consignment by means of a coded telegram which read: 'Goods to Hand'. They provided wonderful sport for a boy mounted on a pony that could jump water, as Maggie loved to do. There were never more than about half a dozen people out, and that was when Dick really learnt to enjoy hunting. The hunters had to go as much as 14 miles to the meet and as far back again at night, but Dick was spared that tiring ride, as Maggie was led to the meet and he was driven there by car. Maggie was extremely durable, and after Dick had grown too big for her she carried both his brothers to hounds.

Once when Rupert was riding her hounds ran right away to the Brendons after a spring stag and killed him at Brompton Ralph on the south-east side of the hills, 20 miles from home by road. Someone gave Rupert and Maggie a lift into Taunton in their horsebox, Maggie was stabled for the night and Roy drove over to collect Rupert. The next day Dick went over to fetch Maggie. She was a bit stiff when she was first led out of the box, but that soon wore off, and Dick mounted her and they got home without trouble.

The development of the riding skills of the Hern boys was not left to chance. Roy took an immense amount of trouble teaching them to be good horsemen, putting them through the mill just as if they were soldiers. Dick always acknowledged that his father had taught him so many things about horses that had been useful to him all through his life, and few days passed when he did not think of him with gratitude. He used to say, 'If you've got a difficult horse there is always something you can do', and Dick believed that that was absolutely true, because the human brain could always think of some ruse to outwit the recalcitrant animal. The Herns lived well, but they were always short of cash not only for clothes – as Dick grew out of his clothes they were passed down in succession to Rupert and Michael – but to buy horses, and they were forced to acquire animals that other people had found unbreakable and therefore were cheap. One was a cart mare called Blossom that Roy got for nothing as a four-year-old because her previous owner found her unmanageable and she was going to be shot. Roy got her going, and she earned her keep doing the haymaking.

Dick was not cut out to be a schoolboy, and in later life did not look back at his days either at his prep school, Norfolk House at Beaconsfield, or his public school, Monmouth, with nostalgia. 'I could never understand boys who said that they enjoyed going back to school and that their schooldays were the best time of their lives,' he wrote. 'I always think what a miserable time they must have had when they were at home for the holidays.' The first thing that Dick and his brothers did when they arrived home was to run into the stables and kiss their ponies on the nose. They would then go into the house to see their mother. 'You've been to see the ponies before me, haven't you?' she would chide them, but she did not really mind. In those days before television the Hern boys used to make their own fun, and with ponies, ferrets and other country activities their time was full. One of the neighbours, a smallholder called Albert Dulborough, often used to accompany them on ferreting expeditions, and they had a lot of fun with him. Hinkley Point, later the site of a power station, was a mile to the north across Wick Moor. At low tide in the autumn a shelf of rock was exposed, and the boys would poke long hazel sticks into the holes in search of conger eels. 'You would feel something just giving and keep at it until out would come a conger – some of them very big. We would have a log or a club in the other hand and knock him down. Sometimes we got half a dozen good ones and Mother used to cook them for us in milk. I always think anything tastes good if you have had to work for it,' wrote Dick.

There was plenty to be done with the ponies besides hunting. When they were small and the hounds were nearby, Winifred would take the boys out in the governess-cart. If there was a shower of rain, Dick and Rupert would get down on the floor under a mackintosh rug and look out through the dashboard to see what was going on. If the hounds and the field were coming in the opposite direction, Dick would jump out and stand proudly at the pony's head on the verge until they had passed. There were not many gymkhanas, but the Hern boys always went to the one at Lord St Audries's seat, Fairfield Park near Stogursey. They used to go in for all the events – musical chairs, potato and bucket and the local jumping. Once Dick rode a big hunter mare of Roy's called Bracken. She was 17 hands and Dick was a tiny boy, but she took him round safely. Besides the mounted events there was all the traditional fun of the fair –

swingboats and skittling for a pig. They would let a greasy pig go and if anyone could catch the pig they could have it.

They also had a go at playing polo with sticks that Roy had cut down for the purpose, with keenly contested matches against the Baron family on the ground at Orchard Portman near Taunton racecourse. The teams were the Baron father, his daughter Kitty and two sons against Roy and the three Hern boys. The boys also attended Pony Club rallies at Orchard Portman which meant a 20-mile ride each way from Wick, so the ponies were tired by the time they got home.

However, it was hunting that really preoccupied Dick as a boy, and he used to echo the immortal declaration of Surtees's Mr Jorrocks that ''unting is all that's worth living for – all time is lost wot is not spent in 'unting'. When he and Rupert arrived home for the Christmas holidays the ponies were all clipped out and ready to go, Roy having got them fit by leading them from a big horse and cantering them round Wick Moor. Dick went out mostly with the West Somerset Vale and the Quantock Staghounds, two days a week with each. The West Somerset were usually hunted by the Master Sir Dennis Boles, who was by then an old man and, in consequence, a slow huntsman and reluctant to jump more fences than he could help. In this he was not dissimilar to his contemporary 'Hodge-Podge' Hodgson, the Master of the Sparkford Vale, who adopted a stylised ritual, with loud vocal accompaniment, to wind up himself and his horse on the rare occasions when he decided that there was nothing for it but to become airborne. Dick was a lot happier when hounds were hunted by the kennel huntsman Charlie Taylor. Taylor was a character, a north countryman, and was scathing about Boles as a huntsman and about the hunt horses, which were mostly very rough and common. He once said to Roy: 'I were 'untsman to Lord Ribblesdale's Book'ounds. He were a gentleman, 'e were. 'E gave us 'osses to ride, not these 'ere boogers.' On one occasion when Boles was hunting hounds in Wick Park and was cheering a hound by name, Taylor – who was on point –

commented scornfully: ' 'Ark at 'im cheering that 'ound. Its been dead ten years.' Boles's defects were all the more regrettable as the vale was first-rate hunting country, glowingly described in *Baily's Hunting Directory* as a tract in which 'every variety of fence – banks, fly fences, timber and open water – is encountered; a very clever and handy horse is required'. The Cannington Brook was a particularly formidable obstacle, and Dick was proud of having jumped it.

Dick dated his life-long love of hunting from the day Charlie Taylor blooded him as a little boy of five on a leading-rein. He described his feelings graphically: 'I always jumped out of bed with alacrity on a hunting morning. I well remember Dad coming into my room at 4 a.m. with a candle, lighting mine and saying: "Time to get up my boy". We had to get up as early as that when we went cub-hunting with the Bridgwater Harriers.'

The large majority of the farmers in the vale welcomed riders and the hounds, but there were exceptions like the Stacey brothers who lived about a mile west of Wick at Shurton. One day a friend of the Herns, Mervyn Vernon, jumped into one of their fields and found himself facing one of the brothers armed with a gun. 'I'll shoot 'ee, I'll shoot 'ee,' shouted Stacey. Vernon sat quietly on his horse and said: 'Go on then, shoot me.' That called Stacey's bluff, and he stood there nonplussed. Vernon just turned his horse and walked off unharmed.

The Master of the Quantock Staghounds, Mrs Wimbush, was an elderly lady who neither hunted hounds nor rode with the hunt, but was a great sportswoman. Instead she went out in a car driven by a chauffeur in very smart dark green livery with boots and gaiters. Somehow she always managed to keep in touch with hounds and at the end of the day dispensed drinks to the followers of the hunt from a big basket carried in the back of the car. After a long, hot day's staghunting in August Dick found a glass of lemonade very refreshing before beginning the ride home.

It was also hard work for the horses galloping up and down the steep Quantock hills, but the work did not always fall on Dick's ponies as he was sometimes mounted by Harold Worrall, the head of a well-known west country family, who often hunted hounds until the first whipper-in, Gilbert Sloley, took over. Dick had great admiration for Sloley as a huntsman. Sometimes when there had been a kill and Sloley paunched the deer he would give a piece of the liver to Dick and Rupert. When they got home Winifred would cook it while they did the ponies, and it made a delicious meal.

Harold Worrall had two sons, Ted and David, who were both good horsemen, went well to hounds and were close friends of Dick's. When the Second World War broke out Ted went into the Somerset Light Infantry, but lost a leg fighting with the Eighth Army at the battle of the Mareth Line on the borders of Libya and Tunisia. He was never able to ride again, as he had no knee and it is impossible with a completely stiff artificial leg. David was in the North Somerset Yeomanry, so both brothers fought in Somerset regiments. Before the war David invited Dick to the Yeomanry sports where there were tent-pegging competitions. Dick practised a lot at home, but found that the horses got terribly hotted up.

Sunday was a rest day for the ponies, and if it was a fine morning the Hern family would walk over the footpath to Stogursey Church, a distance of a mile and a half. When they got home after the service a joint of beef would be ready-cooked in the oven. In the evenings before bedtime Roy would often read stories to the boys; *Jock of the Bushveldt* was a particular favourite.

Prep-school terms interrupted Dick's riding activities, but his grandfather William Hern lived nearby and Dick was able to go out to lunch with him after attending the service at Penn parish church on Sundays. Before he was allowed out he had to recite the collect of the day to the master on duty but, unlike some of the other boys, Dick found no difficulty in memorising it. The first intention had been that Dick should follow in Roy's footsteps and go to Rugby, with William paying the fees; but as the time for public school approached William decided that cash was short and the Rugby fees were too expensive, so Dick was sent to the smaller and cheaper Monmouth School instead.

The alumni of Monmouth included the distinguished cavalry commander General Sir Jakes Harman, and afterwards Dick expressed moderate approval of its educational standards when he wrote: 'I suppose that from the academic point of view we learnt all that was necessary – enough to pass the School Certificate anyway.' More satisfactorily from a recreational point of view, he made friends with Will Coldicutt who farmed at Troy about 2 miles from Monmouth and also had a son at Monmouth School. In the spring Dick used to go to Coldicutt's farm to work a point-to-point horse he owned called R.O.R. When he arrived at the specified time, which was early so that he could get back in time for school, Dick would find no sign of life and had to chuck a handful of gravel at his bedroom window to wake him up. Coldicutt would then put his head out of the window and tell Dick how many times to work the horse round Troy meadows. Gaps had been made in the fences to gallop through, and Dick must have given R.O.R. plenty of work because he was fit enough to win the Llangibby Members Race first time out. Dick went to the meeting with the Coldicutt family and had a few shillings on. The win kept him in funds for some time, and was very welcome as Roy gave the boys a pound note each when they went back to school, and that was supposed to last the whole term.

At home Dick's point-to-pointing career was about to begin, and he was only seventeen when he had his first ride on Happy Days in the Hunt Race at the West Somerset meeting held at Dyche, near his birthplace Holford. In later life he felt that young race-riders were at a disadvantage at that time in that there was no television to enable them to study how the good jockeys rode, and they had to develop their skills by experience. In the weighing room before the race Dick must have been looking nervous, because Ted Worrall offered him a glass of sherry, which Dick declined, not knowing what effect it would have; sherry seems a strange kind of jumping powder, and a glass of brandy would surely have been more appropriate. Happy Days was a very hard puller, jumped off in front and went like the wind for a mile and a half, but then made a mistake at the open ditch and Dick fell off, exhausted by his attempts to hold him. Ted Worrall, who was following, sportingly called out to ask whether Dick was all right while he was still on the ground. Fortunately he was unhurt and later in the afternoon got round safely to finish second in the Farmers Race, so the day ended better than it had begun. The next season, 1939, he rode Happy Days in several races. By then he was stronger and could hold him, but he still pulled hard and did not really stay three miles. When the war broke out Roy had him bought in as a charger with the North Somerset Yeomanry, and he went to Palestine with the First Cavalry Division. He was a thoroughbred and a brilliant hunter. Throughout his life Dick believed firmly that thoroughbreds are the best horses to ride out hunting or in any other equestrian discipline because they are only cantering when half-bred horses are galloping flat out. Although they tend to be frightened of water when they first see it, they jump it better than anything once they have taken to it.

Of all the horses that passed through their hands between 1930 and 1939 Dick was specially fond of a white-faced gelding called Rock whom Roy bought as an unbroken four-year-old from a farmer on the Brendon Hills. His original name was Shamrock, but Roy said it was ridiculous to call a horse bred in England by such a name; as it was considered unlucky to change a horse's name, it was simply shortened to Rock. Dick described him as one of the bravest horses he ever sat on; whatever obstacle you pointed him at he would jump it, and he was a marvellous ride over a big fence in cold blood. He was very impetuous and hated to queue up at a jump, but Dick could always manage him. He was a superb jumper of water, and once jumped over the daunting Horsham brook and back again, which was the first time it had been jumped at all for a long time. All the Hern horses were trained to jump the rhynes on the Levels. They began by jumping them over the grips, or small water courses, and then progressed until they would jump a rhyne in their stride. 'To have a fast hunt over the water is a terrific thrill if you have a good water jumper between your knees,' Dick declared.

The family plan was for Dick to go into the army, but this was scotched when he failed the entrance exam – a failure which called in question his endorsement of the standards of tuition at Monmouth, because passing into the army in the summer of 1938 was not a mountain to climb and Dick, though no scholar, was equally no dunce. Of course learning was not top of the list of priorities of a boy who had embraced with enthusiasm the philosophy of Mr Jorrocks, and it must be assumed that while he was working Mr Coldicutt's point-to-pointer some aspects of his academic work had to lapse. It was clear that Monmouth had nothing more to give him, and accordingly he left at the end of the summer term and went to Millfield when the autumn term started in September.

There was already a connection with Millfield, as Roy had acted as the riding instructor there since the school opened, and had bought the horses for the school, where riding was one of the sporting activities available for the pupils. The 1930s were a time of numerous pioneers in the public-school system, like Kurt Hahn of Gordonstoun, and R. J. O. Meyer, who founded Millfield at Street in Somerset, was one of the most remarkable of them. Jack Meyer was a first-class cricketer and would surely have played for England as an all-rounder if he had not wasted ten years in India in an attempt to make a career as a cotton-broker. His schoolmaster's duties limited his appearances for Somerset mainly to the month of August, though he did captain the county for the 1947 season. His prowess as a batsman is attested by the fact that he once made 202 not out for Somerset against Lancashire, and as a bowler by the fact that his scalps included Collins, Ponsford, Macartney and Bradman, all 'greats' among Australian batsmen. A tall, wiry figure, he specialised in a wily mixture of spin, swerve and flight at slow-medium pace. He once said of his bowling: 'It works but, like the earlier models of the motor-bike, it needs a lot of attention.'

Meyer's own proclivities convinced him of the character-forming value of sport and prompted him to give encouragement to boys who showed promise in a full range of sporting activities from cricket to riding. As a result Millfield turned out numerous boys destined to become prominent sportsmen. Meyer also took many boys in need of special coaching, for example Dick for the army exam. Classes were small in the 1930s, never more than six or seven, so there was plenty of individual tuition. He believed in cultivating a sense of responsibility, and used to send Dick on foraging missions to buy hay from local farmers, which helped him to develop an idea of his own worth and of the relationship between fodder and cash, a lesson which served him well in later life. The school owned horses on which Dick could go hunting, and he had days to conjure with in the Sparkford Vale.

During his time in India Meyer had met a number of the Indian princes, who proceeded to send their sons to Millfield. Two days before the Grand National in 1940 Meyer, known to the boys as 'The Boss', called Dick into his study and said: 'Would you like to go and see the Grand National, Dick?' 'I certainly would,' he answered. 'Well,' Meyer said, 'you can go and have all your expenses paid if you take the Jhalah brothers with you.' Surendra and Birenda Jhalah were Indian princes, fifteen and sixteen years old. Their English was rudimentary, and no accommodation had been booked. However, they made their way up to Liverpool by train, and then Dick, who had never been there before, had to find somewhere to stay the night. This proved difficult, but eventually they managed to book into a very seedy hotel and took two rooms, one for Dick and the other for the two brothers. The sheets looked as if they had been slept in several times, so Dick just wrapped himself in a blanket and left the sheets for the next occupant. They left early the next morning because Dick was determined to walk the course, taking the reluctant Indians with him to look at the fences, whose size filled them with awe. At that time the fences, then devoid of the aprons of later times which made them so much more inviting for the horses to jump, stood starkly upright, and the unreconstructed Becher's Brook, with its big drop, looked a fearful obstacle from the landing side. The day was fine and clear for the race which was to be the last Grand National for six years. Bogskar was a long way behind the leaders when they passed the stands after the first circuit of the course. He then began to make up ground steadily, but at Valentine's he was still a dozen lengths behind the ultra-safe Scottish-trained jumper Macmoffat, who had been second to Workman the previous year. However, Macmoffat was having trouble from the attentions of a loose horse, and in order to shake him off Ian Alder kicked Macmoffat on sooner than he would have liked. As a result Macmoffat tired in the closing stages and Bogskar, who was in close touch at the last fence, was able to outpace him on the run-in to win by 4 lengths.

For Dick the result was appropriate, because Bogskar was owned by Lord Stalbridge, a great supporter of steeplechasing in Somerset and the West Country. The whole expedition was an enjoyable part of Dick's education, as it was of the education of the two princes, and he had taken charge of the operation in a thoroughly responsible manner. They got back to Millfield without incident the same evening. The venture was a typically successful example of Meyer's methods. Dick responded equally well to the Millfield teaching regime. He was confident that he would pass the army exam, and naturally was crestfallen when it was cancelled after war broke out on 3 September 1939.

The 1938–1939 hunting season was the last of peacetime, and the last in which Dick was able to hunt from the cosy and intimate family base of Wick House, because Roy went out to

Palestine with his regiment at the end of 1939. The Somerset of Dick's youth was worlds away from the Somerset of the millennium, not merely through the span of years, but in style and custom. There was innocence and purity of vision in the 1930s countryside of empty roads and empty skies, a countryside more akin to the spirit of *Cider With Rosie* than the spirit of *The Archers*, where TV was unknown and the wireless, as radio was called, crackled and was still something of a novelty in the majority of homes. It was a rural Somerset of seemingly permanent agricultural depression to which people had adjusted their lives in a variety of ways, and learned the local news 'by reading it on the Western', as *The Western Gazette* was familiarly known. Drug-taking, if perhaps practised surreptitiously in the cities, was unheard of as a spur to crime or as a threat to the moral fibre of the nation. Every village cricket team included at least three players, mighty hitters usually, in tweed caps, thick black trousers and braces, and the outfield was grass 6 inches high and dotted with cowpats. The veleta was danced at village hops. The cloakrooms of middle-class houses were redolent of saddle soap and leather polish; most importantly, hunting was an unchallenged and integral part of country life, and a point-to-point was a social gathering of the locals of all classes, bearing the name of the relevant hunt and not the course where the races were run, enlivened by a flow of home-made sloe-gin and dignified by the elegant few who rode side-saddle against the thoroughly modern girls who rode astride with short stirrup leathers in the ladies' race. That way of life never fully returned, and by 1946 the Somerset of the 1930s was subtly but permanently changed.

TWO

THE SECOND WORLD WAR AND WAR SERVICE

WITH THE ARMY EXAM CANCELLED, Dick returned to Mill-field at the beginning of the autumn term in 1939. However, the war was in progress and, against a background of dire news from the front in Poland, it was difficult to settle back into the routine of school life. He and another boy called Peter Dalton-White, who had also been cramming for the Sandhurst exam, chafed at the prolongation of their school days and decided to form up to 'The Boss'. They found him in his study, smoking his pipe with a little smile on his face, and told him that they wanted to join up. Meyer said that it was a very good idea, and that if they went to Bristol they could join up there, adding, typically of his policy of encouraging initiative, 'I'll lend you the car'. As Dalton-White had just passed his driving test they jumped at the offer and drove up to Bristol. There they were able to join an organisation called a Reception Unit, for which the qualifications were having the School Certificate and Certificate A in the Officer Cadet Corps, and passing a medical examination. Successful candidates, who included the two Mill-field boys, were considered officer material and were called to do their basic training when required.

The call-up was slow during the so-called 'phoney war' which lasted throughout the first winter of the war and, as he was not required straight away, Dick stayed at Millfield until the end of

the Lent term, which made his trip to the Grand National possible. There was still no sign of his call-up, so he went up for
two terms to Jesus College, Cambridge, where his Mullens
grandfather had been in the 1880s. The only course available
was engineering, a subject in which he had little interest, so Dick
was able to devote most of his time to more congenial activities.
Jesus had a great rowing tradition and, as he had done some
rowing at Monmouth, he joined the college boat club. He got
into the Jesus boat and made friends with his fellow crew
members who, as usual with rowing men, were a convivial bunch
who used to meet frequently at The Volunteer in Green Street,
a pub kept by Joe and Clara Mullens. Joe had been a professional
boxer, and behind the bar there were numerous photographs of
him in his heyday. He had a fist the size of a small leg of mutton,
and had no trouble in keeping order if things looked like getting
out of hand. Many undergraduates were awaiting their call-up
that winter, and few took their studies very seriously, concentrating instead on the hedonistic use of their remaining leisure time.
Every term the Jesus Boat Club used to have what was called
a Boat Club Blind. All the furniture was taken out of someone's rooms in college and a barrel of beer and numerous
tankards were brought in. The beer flowed freely and games like
Cardinal Puff, which involved copious drinking, were played.
There was also a lot of singing, mostly bawdy songs. At a later
and more sedate age Dick commented: 'We probably behaved
very badly, but it was great fun at the time.' More responsibly,
Dick joined what afterwards became the Home Guard and was
then called the Local Defence Volunteers, known as the LDV
for short, and when he was at home he transferred to the local
branch.

By then the phoney war was over, France had fallen, Great
Britain stood alone against a rampant Germany in Europe and
the Home Guard assumed much greater importance in the
defence structure. They used to meet at The Greyhound in
Stogursey. There was a desperate shortage of weapons of all

kinds. The local Home Guard was issued with Lee-Enfield 303s which had been packed in grease since 1918. Over the years the grease had congealed, and it took hours of work with paraffin to get it off. When at last the rifles were clean Dick called on his OTC experience to instruct the squad in their use. The men of his platoon were relatively well-armed. Other Home Guard recruits in the summer of 1940 were armed with shot guns, axes, heavy sticks and even pikes, a weapon last wielded in anger in England at the battle of Sedgemoor three centuries earlier, with which they would have been expected to confront elite formations of German parachutists had the expected airborne invasion materialised. Their uniforms, where any were issued at all, were denim overalls. Altogether they bore little resemblance to Captain Mannering's well-armed and battledressed men as portrayed in *Dad's Army*. If, equipped so primitively, they had been called upon to honour Churchill's undertaking to 'fight in the fields and in the streets' and 'fight in the hills', they would have been massacred.

One day the Home Guard of all the villages in the area paraded at Nether Stowey. They were formed up in a hollow square and given a pep talk by Field-Marshal Lord Birdwood, who had commanded the Australia and New Zealand Army Corps at the Gallipoli landings in 1915 and afterwards the Fifth Army in the final victorious advance on the Western Front. By 1940 he was seventy-five years old and somewhat out of touch, but Field-Marshals never retire. The Home Guard were deadly serious about the part they had to play in the defence of the nation. Dick and Rupert, as owners of 12-bore shotguns, were issued with ball ammunition and told that they could fire at anything at their discretion. They decided that they had better try it out, so they set up a sheet of corrugated iron against a big oak tree in one of the fields at home and practised firing at it, and were gratified to find that it made a big hole. They were under orders to do dawn and dusk mounted patrols along a 5-mile stretch of the coast north of Wick. If they saw anything suspicious, they were to ride into Stogursey and telephone Taunton, where a company of the Somerset Light Infantry, the only regular troops in the area, was stationed. Fortunately they never needed to do so, nor did they have the scary experience of Eric Westman and his standing patrol on Knowle Hill between Exmoor and the Brendons. Westman recorded this account of the incident:

> Always alert to the possibility of parachutists, imagine our alarm when we suddenly heard footsteps coming towards us on the grass . . . scrunch . . . scrunch . . . scrunch. Paralysed with fear, we didn't know what to do and just stood back to back – my mate clutching the 12-bore, which he didn't know how to use, and me the bandolier, which I could hardly hold. The footsteps got nearer and nearer. 'Christ – the bloody Germans are on us!' I said, and was shaking like a leaf. Just then a large cow loomed out of the darkness.

Dick's call-up finally came in December 1940, when he was ordered to report to the 55th Armoured Corps Training Regiment at Farnborough. Recruits were not allowed out of camp for the first six weeks during which they were given plenty of square bashing. At the still tender age of eighteen Dick was surprised by the amount of bad language used by the drill instructors, which he had never come across before. When they were allowed out they all went to the Theatre Royal in Aldershot where Phyllis Dixie was appearing nude on stage. This was another first for Dick, as he had never seen a naked woman before. In those days naked women on the stage were not allowed to move in the sight of the audience. The curtain would rise to reveal her in a certain pose, then fall and rise again to reveal her in a different pose. Each new pose was greeted by wild applause.

After several months he was posted to an Officer Cadet Training Unit (OCTU) right beside the racecourse at Lanark. Soon after arriving there he felt very ill and reported sick, only for the

MO to send him straight back to duty. Later that day he felt even worse and reported sick again. This time jaundice was diagnosed and he was admitted to hospital, where he spent several very boring weeks in isolation without even a gramophone to amuse himself with. Eventually he was passed fit and sent home on leave. His next posting was to an OCTU at Perham Down near Tidworth on Salisbury Plain. The camp was on top of a hill and all the accommodation was in Nissen huts which were bitterly cold. Racing was severely restricted at the time, and Newbury and Salisbury were the only two courses at which meetings were permitted in the south of England. Jack King, a friend in Dick's troop, had a car, and they used to go racing at Salisbury as often as possible when they had enough petrol. After racing they would stop at the Cathedral Hotel to complete an enjoyable outing with a few drinks before going back to camp.

At that time Dick was booked to go into the 13th/18th Hussars if he passed his course, but that came to nothing when the commanding officer, who apparently was the only person who knew anything about him, went out to the Middle East and, within a few days of his arrival, was captured when out on reconnaissance. Happily Gordon Russell, who was on loan to the OCTU from the North Irish Horse, a yeomanry regiment formed at the end of the Boer War, heard of Dick's predicament and invited him to join the regiment, which he was pleased to do. That was a seminal event, because two of the North Irish Horse officers were the Pope brothers, Michael and Barry, who shared his love of horses and became great friends.

The regiment was at Westbury on the west side of Salisbury Plain when he joined. They had some old Valentine tanks, but they were not much use because they spent most of the time breaking down when they took them out on the plain for training. From Westbury they moved to Didlington near Thetford and were able to train on the Stanford Practical Training area.

The land was very poor sandy soil, what might be called 'rabbit land', and more or less useless for agriculture. The few inhabitants had been moved away and exercises with live ammunition were permitted. Thetford was within easy reach of Newmarket, where in 1942 there was a ration of twelve days racing restricted to horses trained in the town except for fourteen important races, including the Classic races, which were open to horses trained in the southern and northern regions. Dick and other officers in the regiment used to go racing at Newmarket whenever training permitted. As in 1999, when the Rowley Mile course was closed for the re-building of the stands, all the wartime racing at Newmarket was on the July Course because the Rowley Mile had been taken over by the RAF. Dick was there to see the dramatic finish of the substitute Derby in 1942, when Watling Street, ridden by Harry Wragg, turned the tables on Big Game, a horse of brilliant speed who had beaten him by 4 lengths in the 2000 Guineas. Big Game, who started at 6–4 on, exhausted himself by refusing to settle for Gordon Richards in the early stages. He was in front with 2 furlongs to go, but then failed to stay and dropped back to finish sixth, while Watling Street, carrying the 'black, white cap' colours of Lord Derby, who had previously won the Derby with Sansovino and Hyperion, got up in the last 50 yards to win by a neck from Hyperides, carrying the 'primrose and rose hoops' of Lord Rosebery, who had won the Derby with Blue Peter – all names whose renown was to be echoed by horses and owners associated with Dick Hern's stable in years to come.

Roy was invalided home in 1940, but the Empress of Britain in which he sailed was torpedoed and sank. He and all the other passengers were rescued, but he never liked to talk about it much. The one thing that really rankled with him was that he lost a practically new pair of Maxwell boots. He spent the rest of the war in Northern Ireland in the Claims Commission for the counties of Tyrone and Fermanagh. As Dick also was in the army and Michael joined the RAF, Rupert stayed at home with

Winifred and ran the farm. In accordance with wartime regulations a lot of the farm, which had been all grass, had to
be ploughed up to grow cereal crops, and Rupert taught
himself to do it with an old tractor and a plough. Dick had some
marvellous short leaves at home with the family. He and Rupert
would go out flighting for duck and once, when Roy too was
at home for a few days, they went down to Steart on the west
side of the Parrett estuary in the hope of shooting duck. Instead
a flight of swans came over and they managed to shoot one.
Luckily it was a young one, and they had it roasted for dinner,
finding the flesh dark and tasty. As there was no petrol Maggie
was drafted back into harness, and Winifred used to drive her
into Bridgwater once a week to do the shopping. The old pony
did not really show her age, and she was as sound at the age
of twenty as she was when Roy bought her as a four-year-old.
She was a wonderful character, and had some quality; they
thought that she was by a thoroughbred horse out of a Dartmoor
pony.

The North Irish Horse did not go overseas until January 1943,
and then it was to join the First Army in North Africa. The First
Army, in conjunction with American forces and under the overall
command of General Ike Eisenhower, had taken part in the
Torch landings on the Algerian coast the previous November,
and had then advanced rapidly eastwards into Tunisia, only to
be blocked short of Tunis by the German Fifth Panzer Army
under Von Arnim which had been hastily airlifted to the country
to prevent the entire North African coastline falling into Allied
hands. After some hard fighting the situation settled into something like stalemate on the Tunisian front for some weeks, while
the German-Italian forces were steadily squeezed by the British
Eighth Army advancing from Libya after their decisive victory
at El Alamein at the beginning of November. That was the state
of play into which the North Irish Horse were introduced. The
North African campaign, and the Italian campaign which followed, have been, and indeed still are, subjects of controversy.

Their critics argue that they were costly sideshows which distracted effort from the urgent necessity of concentrating on a second front against the Germans in north-west Europe; their advocates, of whom Churchill was the leader, maintained that the North African campaign enabled the Allies to engage the Axis powers on land long before a cross-Channel invasion of the Continent was feasible, and that the Italian campaign knocked Italy out of the war and tied down large German forces. What is certain is that both campaigns involved some bitter fighting, and that the North Irish Horse, and Dick, were at times in the thick of it.

The regiment embarked at Liverpool in a big liner, the Duchess of York, which carried 4000 troops in very cramped conditions. In order to avoid U-boats the convoy nearly crossed the Atlantic before turning back to enter the Mediterranean via the Straits of Gibraltar, which extended the duration of the voyage to ten days. The weather was rough, and on the troop decks conditions were appalling. The men were all in hammocks and terribly sea-sick, just leaning over the side and vomiting onto the deck. As the ship rolled the vomit rolled back and forth like a wave and the smell was indescribable. The orderly officer had to stay down there to stop panic in case the ship was torpedoed. However, the voyage was uneventful as far as enemy action was concerned, and Dick was able to play a good deal of poker. He played in the same school every day; but by the time they reached Algiers they were practically all square, so little money changed hands.

On disembarkation they had to march 17 miles to a big French colonial farm, where they spent the night in a wine vault lying on concrete. They only had what they stood up in, plus a groundsheet and a gas cape, so the discomfort was extreme; and as rats were very numerous, squeaking and running noisily over the gas capes, nobody got much sleep. The next day they were taken back to the docks by truck to disembark the tanks, which had been all greased up for the voyage. Once on land they were loaded on to flat rail-wagons and sheeted down, while the men travelled in the notorious old French trucks marked 'Hommes 40/Chevaux 8'. For several days they trundled slowly across Algeria, with the train making frequent unscheduled stops in open countryside at which they would hurriedly jump down to relieve nature and get back on again before it moved on. Occasionally some of the men would be left behind and would have to make a run for it to catch up the train, causing a great deal of amusement.

The destination at the end of the 450-mile journey was Le Kef, a picturesque small town just over the Tunisian frontier with a hilltop Kasbah overlooking fertile agricultural land. They were there for only a few days, training and preparing the tanks for action under the command of David Dawnay. A former 10th Hussar, Dawnay was a first-class polo player and was in the English team at the Berlin Olympics, and after the war held the post of Clerk of the Course at Ascot for several years. He soon had the opportunity to exercise command in action. The North African campaign was entering a crucial phase. General Erwin Rommel, the charismatic commander of the Panzer Armee Afrika facing the Eighth Army, in mid-February switched his Panzer divisions to attack the American forces in central Tunisia, while further north Von Arnim attacked the Free French and the British. Both attacks made rapid initial progress though, fortunately for the Allies, their timing was badly coordinated because no love was lost between the two generals: between Rommel, whose instinct to attack at all costs was tempered by a strong dose of cautious realism, and Von Arnim, who was not quite good enough to judge what was and what was not militarily feasible. If they had acted in concert, the situation of the Allies collectively and of the North Irish Horse in particular would have been much more perilous. To help contain the northern thrust, the North Irish Horse had to undertake a 50-mile night march from Le Kef to Beja, a market town and road centre in the Medjerda valley which was the principal supply route to the forward elements of the First Army. If Beja, which was the objective of the German offensive, had fallen, the whole front would have been in danger of crumbling, and the North Irish Horse had a crucial role in defending it.

'A' squadron, with Dick in temporary command, because the Squadron Leader had been killed when his tank had been hit by an anti-tank gun and the second-in-command Robin Griffith had not arrived to take over, was ordered by Dawnay into Hunt's Gap to cover the town. Hunt's Gap was a natural defensive position in a bowl in the hills some 400 yards across, and any enemy attack would have given them a good shoot as they came over the ridge in front of the position. For two days nothing much happened, and Dick decided that the time had come to show some initiative. He gave the following description of what followed: 'I got out of my tank to have a look over the crest of the hill and see what I could see. Well, just over the top there was a Tiger tank quite close with the turret traversed sideways on, exposing the thin side of its armour. I ran back, got in my tank, crept back over the hill and got in one shot, which luckily pierced the turret and knocked it out. I then reversed back over the crest to my original position.' This was an achievement against all the odds. The North Irish Horse were then mounted in Churchills, heavy tanks weighing 40 tons but seriously undergunned with a six-pounder. The Churchill was outclassed by the Tiger, which had the deadly 88mm, formerly an anti-aircraft gun but converted into a high velocity anti-tank weapon, and a stabiliser which enabled it to fire accurately on the move. In any normal encounter the Tiger would always be expected to be the winner, but Dick had subtracted one from the total of fifteen Tigers with which Von Arnim began the offensive. A few days later the German advance was finally halted by a very heavy British artillery bombardment.

Dick was not left to enjoy his triumph for long. The next day he was sitting in his tank with the turret flaps open when it was hit by a shell. He was very lucky not to have his head blown off, but he sustained severe concussion and had his eardrums badly damaged. His hearing never recovered fully. Ever since he has been completely deaf in his left ear, but fortunately his hearing in his right ear is good with the help of a deaf-aid. He was evacuated to hospital in Algiers, and when he was discharged he spent a short time convalescing on a French farm. The colonial French were very friendly, and his stay improved his French no end because the farmer's daughter was attractive and Dick wanted to be able to chat her up. They used to go out shooting quail in the vineyards and Dick was at pains to avoid being on the left of the line; they all had old hammer guns which they carried over the crook of the arm so that if you were on the left of the line you had quite a few guns pointing straight at you.

When Dick rejoined the regiment he was at first attached to Headquarters Squadron until he was declared fully fit to go back to 'A' Squadron. The Quartermaster, Frank Marks, was a former 17th/21st Lancer and full of amusing reminiscences. He and Dick discovered a little restaurant run by some monks where they had congenial dinners and bought some of the liqueur which the monks made and was similar to Benedictine.

By that time the German attacks had been firmly repulsed and the Allies were closing in for the final assault on Tunis. The Eighth Army under Montgomery had occupied the southern two-thirds of Tunisia and had reached the mountains at Enfidaville, 60 miles south of the capital. It could make no further progress, but two of its divisions and a corps commander, Horrocks, were brought round to take part in the assault. Before that could be launched it was necessary to secure the so-called Longstop Hill which dominated the Medjez El Bab–Tunis road and the valley which was to be the launching pad for the main attack. Longstop had been the scene of fierce fighting in the early weeks of the campaign and had changed hands several times before ending up in the possession of the Germans. Now the North Irish Horse had a vital role in the plan to capture it.

It had been accepted that it was impossible to get tanks up the steep and rocky sides of the almost impregnable peak at the eastern end of the range, but Michael Pope gave the lie to that idea, manoeuvring his tank to the top in support of the Buffs and taking large numbers of prisoners, a feat for which he was awarded the MC. With Longstop at last in Allied hands, the infantry attacked straight up the valley under furious air and artillery bombardments, the German line broke and the British armour passed through to complete the victory. The North Irish Horse had the honour of being the first tanks to enter Tunis, after supporting in turn four different infantry divisions. By 13 May 1943 the last vestiges of Axis resistance in North Africa had been cleaned up, and the North Irish Horse had played no insignificant part in that result. For the men of the regiment it was an exhilarating experience to drive through the city to a tumultuous welcome from the inhabitants, who swarmed round the tanks handing up bottles of wine and shouted and cheered from the balconies. They camped by the shore on the far side of the town and got plenty of swimming in the beautiful warm sea.

While they were at Tunis Dick took the opportunity to revisit the Hunt's Gap battlefield and study it from the other side of the hill. The tank he had knocked out was still in position with a dead member of the crew lying beside it. Dick noted that he was in an advanced state of decomposition, but had a beautiful set of teeth, while the French liaison officer accompanying him wrinkled his nose, sniffed the air and remarked: 'Dead Boche – wonderful smell.' On a less macabre note, they also had time to do some sightseeing. One day they visited the old Roman provincial city of Thuburbo Majus, 40 miles south-west of Tunis, and noticed such telling features as the ruts worn by chariot wheels in the paving stones of the city gateways which were strangely evocative of the way that ordinary citizens went about their daily business in the Roman world. However, their most lasting impressions were of the sophisticated public loos which had water running beneath them as a kind of natural flush. The old native guide had clearly picked up a few words of vernacular English. Asked what the building was, he replied with relish: 'Shithouses.' They were also impressed by the loos in the palace of the Bey of Tunis, which had seats made of green plush.

The winter of 1943 was spent under canvas in a forest of stunted cork oaks near Bone, a small port 150 miles west of Tunis, waiting for shipping to be available to take them to Italy. In January 1944 they were shipped across to Naples and, after a spell there, moved to Foggia where they took part in combined exercises with the 1st Canadian Infantry Division. The Allied advance had stalled on the Gustav Line 40 miles north of Naples and 60 miles south of Rome, to which Cassino, dominated by a sixth-century Benedictine monastery, was the key, and at the Anzio beachhead created by an Allied seaborne landing between the Gustav Line and Rome. Repeated attacks on Cassino and the monastery on Monte Cassino above the town had failed, and it was not until a well-coordinated offensive was launched on 11 May 1944 that the Gustav Line was finally breached and the monastery was captured by Polish troops. The Germans retreated up the Liri valley to a prepared fallback position, the Hitler Line, which was where the North Irish Horse were sent into action in support of the Canadian Infantry with whom they had trained. The fighting centred on the two small towns of Pontecorvo, on the Liri river, and Aquino, 3 miles to the north, where the German defences were covered by extensive minefields and incorporated Panther tank turrets mounted on concrete emplacements covering fields of fire where the trees had been cut down. Each turret incorporated a 75mm anti-tank gun, a machine gun and a rocket launcher, and was supported by a pair of self-propelled armoured vehicles mounting a 75 or 88mm anti-tank gun. The North Irish Horse were shown aerial photographs of the defences before the attack, but they were so well camouflaged that the mysterious black dots which appeared on the photographs were not interpreted as tank turrets, and their immense fire power took the regiment by surprise.

Although the defences were clearly very strong, the North Irish Horse were ordered into a head-on attack in support of the Canadian infantry who were held up by uncut wire and machine-gun fire. Dick's troop was in the lead, and had to advance through a belt of trees to the edge of the Germans' tank-killing ground where the trees had been cleared. Dick gave this account of the action which followed: 'My Troop Sergeant was in front and I was about 25 yards behind him, with my Troop Corporal another 25 yards behind me. As soon as we emerged from the wood and were visible to the enemy guns my Troop Sergeant, Jack Best, was hit and his tank set on fire. All the crew were killed as they tried to get out. My Troop Corporal's tank blew up on a mine. Luckily for me the squadron second-in-command Tony Finch-Noyes put down smoke and I was able to reverse into the minefield and, luckily again, I didn't hit a mine.' The whole area was subjected to a torrent of artillery and anti-tank fire, and the regiment suffered heavy casualties, thirty-four officers and men being laid to rest in a special section of a Canadian cemetery.

The Hitler Line was turned by Moroccan Goums of the Free French forces who advanced through the practically roadless Aurunci mountains between the Liri and the coast, but before that happened the Canadians, supported by the North Irish Horse, had taken their objectives and broken the line. The gallant performance of the Canadian infantry won Dick's admiration. The admiration was mutual, and after the battle the North Irish Horse were awarded the Maple Leaf as a battle honour, and wore it proudly on uniform sleeves. However, Dick's lasting impression of the battle was that it demonstrated the futility of tanks making frontal attacks on well-organised and mined-in enemy positions without adequate preparation.

The Hitler Line was the last big battle for the North Irish

Horse, and thereafter they were involved only in sporadic fighting as the Germans retreated up the boot of Italy, until hostilities finally came to an end on the Po the following spring. The regiment's progress was not without incident. One day Dick noticed the wreck of a car in the burnt-out remains of a haystack that had been ignited by tracer fire, and deduced that the Italian peasants made a habit of concealing objects of value in haystacks. He decided that it was always worthwhile giving a haystack a prod, and once recovered a double-barrelled 12-bore shotgun which came in handy for shooting guinea fowl on the abandoned farms. The farmers used to remove all the stock they could, but could not catch the guinea fowl which used to roost in the trees. They made a welcome change from army rations. On another occasion when Dick was with the regimental transport the cooks unearthed the neck of a large glass jar when they were digging a trench for the cooker. They asked what to do, and Dick told them to dig it up. It was full of eggs, so that night the tank crews got omelettes, another welcome change of diet.

Dick had one fortuitous meeting in the last autumn of the war in Italy. At Millfield he had been friendly with an Australian, Bob Barr-Smith, whose father owned an enormous station called Mount William about 150 miles from Melbourne. His father had been in the Lifeguards during the First World War and Bob joined the Lifeguards during the Second World War. One day Dick was driving in a column of vehicles when they met another column coming in the opposite direction. Dick described what happened next: 'We both stopped and I looked across and there, sitting in the front seat, was Bob Barr-Smith. We jumped out and danced round like a couple of dervishes. After the war we used to exchange Christmas cards and on two occasions we went to stay with them in Australia. He had four daughters who all married horsemen, either racing or polo. When he died each daughter inherited a quarter of the station. Even so, they all got plenty.'

When the war was over Dick's regiment was stationed at Rimini on the Adriatic, where the narrow coastal strip opens up into the broad, flat expanses of the plain of Lombardy. At that time the commanding officer was Tony Llewellen Palmer, formerly of the King's Dragoon Guards. He was a first-rate soldier and everyone thought the world of him. He took the initiative in collecting some horses. The first three or four were taken over from the KDGs when they were posted away from Italy to Greece where a civil war was raging. Makeshift stables were constructed in some bombed-out buildings on the front at Rimini; doors were sawn in half and some boxes were quickly knocked up. Michael Pope's brother Barry, Paddy Lavery and Dick were sent to Padua to escort 500 men and 1500 horses and mules, the remnants of a German Pack Transport Unit, to a POW camp at Cesena, a distance of about 100 miles. Dick was expecting them to be all pack animals, and was pleasantly surprised to find that there were a number of riding horses among them, obviously mounts for the officers, some with enough quality for what they had in mind, which was to get some army racing going. They covered about 15 miles a day, and Dick would go ahead to pick a place where they could stop the next night. He would then commandeer a field of lucerne and put some of the prisoners to work with scythes to cut it for the horses. Once that was done Barry and Dick would ride a number of the horses to decide which were suitable for racing, and those that were chosen were sent down to the regiment in a three-ton lorry that Michael Pope, then the Adjutant, provided for the purpose.

The North Irish Horse had taken over the Grand Hotel close to the Adriatic seafront at Rimini, which had a beautiful wide sandy beach ideal for working horses. The stables that had already been constructed were supplemented by some pens inside a bombed-out building which were perfectly adequate, and nice and cool. They set about getting the horses fit on the beach, and even put up some flights of hurdles, though these had to be removed after use else they would have disappeared by the following morning. The stables were run by Basil Cooper, who performed the functions of a head lad in a racing stable. He then had a full head of hair. In the 1970s Dick was on holiday in South Africa and went racing at the Capetown track, Kenilworth. He saw a man coming towards him with a completely bald head and a patch over one eye. The man stopped as Dick approached and said: 'You're Dick Hern, aren't you?' 'Yes, I am,' said Dick, 'but I'm afraid I don't know who you are.' 'I'm Basil Cooper,' he answered. Dick felt that he could be excused for not recognising him. Tragically Basil, who trained with considerable success for a time in South Africa, eventually lost his sight altogether. His brother Tom was a brilliant judge of a horse and became a very successful bloodstock agent with the BBA (Ireland).

While at Rimini Tony Llewellen Palmer decided to run a regimental race meeting on the old trotting track at Ravenna 35 miles further north, which had suffered severely from war damage. The regiment's main job was to guard a cage full of German prisoners a few miles north of Rimini, but this boring chore had the advantage that the camp provided sappers to clear the mines with which the trotting track had been sown, a reservoir of labour to work on the track – and a blacksmith. No iron was available except the reinforcement from a blown-up pillbox, but the blacksmith was able to use it to make some beautiful shoes. Once the mines had been cleared a harrow was needed for the dirt track, which had been badly compacted because it had been used as a park for German heavy lorries. This was achieved by welding a number of pick-heads to a bar and towing it behind a truck. It worked extremely well, and by alternately harrowing and rolling a satisfactory dirt surface was produced. In addition Dick supervised the building of two immaculate steeplechase fences on the outside of each side of the track using juniper, which grew in profusion in the region. The track was only 4 furlongs round and in the flat races, which were run on the inside, anyone who could jump off in front and go the shortest way had a big advantage.

Dick and Barry Pope decided to stay in Ravenna for a while to prepare the track. They set up their camp beds in the stands and used to have dinner and a bottle of wine every night at a little bistro called the Albergo Capello. They were happy days. For anyone who loved horses as much as Dick did, it was marvellous to be with them again. He had two for his own use – Birdcatcher and Victoria. Birdcatcher was about 15.2 hands and a very safe jumper. Victoria was excitable and usually ran over 5 furlongs because she really had only two paces – stop and go. Michael Pope used to ride in races on Farina, a grey mare with a short tail, probably caused by having a tail bandage put on too tightly. She had the royal crest branded on her cheek and had been extracted somehow by the KDGs from the King of Italy's stables. She was well-made and very sound. Training for the races proceeded apace, but there was a nasty scare one day at Rimini. They were working the horses on the sand just above the tide line when they noticed a big mine with spikes being washed up on the shore. They kept on at full speed and, when they had gone about 200 yards, it hit the beach and blew up, fortunately without hurting anyone.

A lot of time was spent foraging for food for the horses, which was in very short supply. The regiment had a store of civilian clothing taken from German prisoners, and Dick set off from Rimini with it in a 3-ton lorry to engage in some barter. North of Ravenna there was a stretch of marshy land with scattered farms, which Dick knew well because they had spent much of the last winter of the war there. Dick planned to reach it by a Bailey bridge that had been in place over a canal, but when he got there he found that it had been removed. Instead there was an antiquated ferry which had probably been used for donkey carts before the war. They got the lorry across on it, visited some of the farms and exchanged the clothes for sacks of oats. The oats weighed a good deal more than the clothes had done, and on the return journey some of the boards of the ferry cracked and creaked ominously, but luckily held. Afterwards Dick remembered thinking at the time: 'I hope God's in his heaven today, because if this truck goes in the drink I'm going to have quite a bit of explaining to do.'

One of the regular riders at the Ravenna race meetings was Lionel Vick, the son of a trainer in Sussex. Dick went to a farmhouse looking for a billet for him and found a place where he had stayed before. The woman came out of the house, and when Dick had explained what he wanted she said, 'That's OK as long as it's Tenente Vick', so evidently he had made a good impression on her. After he had been demobbed Lionel turned professional and rode with some success in the north until he broke his back in a fall. When he was in Stoke Mandeville and was trying to walk he kept falling over, and eventually they managed to persuade him that he never would be able to walk again. He then showed amazing determination in carving out a new career for himself. Although he had left school at the age of fourteen, he trained and qualified as an accountant – no ordinary accountant, but a brilliant one. He did the accounts for many people prominent in the racing world, including Dick while he was training at Newmarket. Dick used to take him round the yard in his wheelchair to see the horses, and he loved it.

The first army race meeting was held at Ravenna on 12 July 1945. Brigadier David Dawnay was Senior Steward, and Dick had a winning double on Birdcatcher and Victoria, while Michael Pope won a race on Farina. British forces in other parts of North Italy and Austria were not slow to follow the example of the North Irish Horse. At various times meetings were held at Aiello and Treviso in Italy and Spittal, Klagenfurt, Graz and Vienna in Austria. Except for Treviso and Vienna, all the courses were laid out and built by the army. Although it lacked the picturesque setting of Klagenfurt and Graz, Aiello was the fairest because it was a flat, galloping course with a straight 5 furlongs. The horses, which were owned by and represented their regiments or other units, were a motley collection. The majority, like those of the North Irish Horse, had been captured from the Germans, who had used vast quantities of horsed transport. A smaller number were English hunters which had arrived in Italy with the Veterinary Corps via the First Cavalry Division in Palestine; and there were a few second-rate thoroughbreds bought out of Milan racing stables. In view of their diverse origins, they provided surprisingly competitive racing in mixed programmes of flat races and steeplechases. There was Tote betting, and the administration attained a considerable degree of sophistication, with a *Racing Calendar* on the English model containing results and notices. The racing authorities at home decreed that these meetings should not be regarded as 'unrecognised meetings', which was just as well as if they had been so regarded all those who had taken part would have been warned off the Turf. The results would have been far-reaching, as Dick was not the only participant destined for distinction in the regular racing world; others included his brother officer Michael Pope, later a successful trainer, and Tim Rogers, whose trend-setting methods were instrumental in transforming the Irish breeding industry.

During the summer of 1945 Dick and the Pope brothers took some horses to run at Aiello, which was situated in the extreme north-east corner of Italy near the walled town of Palmanova and not far from the frontier of what is now Slovenia. They stayed in a little pub and stabled the horses in a farm for a few days before the meeting. While riding out on the course one morning they fell in with a man riding a little grey Arab-like horse which turned out to be a Tunisian or Moroccan Barb. The rider was George Rich, a squadron-leader in The Queen's Bays who had been responsible for making the course. When he went home eighteen months later George took the little grey with him. He was a brilliant jumper, and after George had married, his wife Jill won the Queen Elizabeth Cup at the White

City on him – a wonderful feat for a horse found running about loose on the south side of the Po. They met George again the next day and were invited back to his mess for a drink. That was the beginning of a great friendship for Dick. George was a wonderful person and a clever mimic, and was always entertaining company. His sense of humour was sometimes mischievous. One day he was out riding near Aiello with a friend, 'Crash' Keyworth, a man of more courage than sense. The road ran between fields in which vines were trained along horizontal wires. 'I wonder whether that horse of yours jumps wire,' George asked Keyworth. 'I don't know; I'll go and find out,' he replied, turning his horse into the vineyard while George rode straight ahead. Half a mile down the road Keyworth caught up, his horse bleeding from several nasty cuts and his clothing plastered with clods of earth. 'It doesn't,' he said.

The North Irish Horse had little joy from their runners at Aiello. The galloping course did not suit the handy Birdcatcher, who was much better round the sharp turns at Ravenna. Nor did Michael do any good on Red Sails, though she was full of quality, probably seven-eighths thoroughbred, and the best they got out of the column of captured horses. At the end of the summer the regiment moved up to Graz in Austria, and in October a race meeting was organised at Vienna. The meeting was run by General Dick McCreery, who had commanded the Eighth Army in the final stages of the Italian campaign and was then in command of the British Forces of Occupation. He was an accomplished horseman and former amateur rider who had won the Grand Military Gold Cup at Sandown on Annie Darling in 1923 and Dash o' White in 1928. The North Irish Horse party set off to Vienna in three 3-ton lorries without proper tailboards, so that at night stops on the way the lorries had to be backed up against muck heaps so as to unload the horses. On arrival at Vienna they had to pass through a Russian check-point, which seemed to take an age; but once they were in the city they found that McCreery, the most meticulous, professional and mild-mannered of generals, had organised things perfectly. The horses were stabled at the Vienna racecourse at the Freudenau, and Dick and his colleagues stayed at a hotel in Vienna. The hotel had been stripped of its furniture and other facilities, but they had brought their campbeds so there was no accommodation problem.

Some bombs had fallen on the Freudenau, but the craters had been filled in and the course, with its capacious stands and buildings, was a cut above the other courses on which military meetings were held in Austria and Italy. The North Irish Horse runners did not do particularly well at the meeting, only Birdcatcher, ridden by Dick in a 3-mile chase, running into a place. General Konev, the Russian High Commissioner in Vienna, was sent an invitation to the meeting, which he accepted on the condition that a red carpet was laid out for him. Dick McCreery invited him to present the cup for the winner of the steeplechase which was the big race of the day, but a mistake by the interpreter led Konev to believe that he was being asked to give a cup. An ADC was hastily dispatched to get one, and returned with a huge and hideous red glass vase full of half dead flowers filched from the Imperial Hotel. The race was won by McCreery's own horse Jumbo, ridden by Joe Hartigan, the son of Frank Hartigan who had trained Shaun Goilin to win the 1930 Grand National, Red Sails having been pulled up lame by Michael Pope before the last fence. Konev presented the red vase to McCreery as owner of the winner, and Hartigan received the attractive silver vase which McCreery had provided. No doubt Konev went away convinced that the result had been fixed.

After the races McCreery invited all those who had brought horses to run at the meeting to a party in Schönbrunn Palace, the Hapsburg rival to the splendours of Versailles, on the outskirts of the city. It was a magnificent party in civilised surroundings which contrasted with the squalid condition of the Russian soldiers with whom Vienna teemed. Their uniforms consisted of kapok jackets well stained with grease down the front where they had spilled their food. Many of them had Mongolian features and were not house-trained, relieving themselves wherever they felt like in the houses where they were billeted, and there were innumerable cases of rape on Viennese women.

Dick McCreery took Jumbo back to England and hunted him with the Blackmore Vale, of which he was Joint Master. Subsequently his son Bob, who was to become a leading amateur rider and a prominent thoroughbred breeder, qualified Jumbo with the Royal Artillery Harriers on Salisbury Plain, and gained his first racing success by winning the Members Race on him. He was a fine, big, blood-like horse, but his origins remained a mystery. Bob inherited the 'Konev Vase', and kept it in his house at Stowell Hill in Somerset.

When the time came to set out on the return journey the North Irish Horse party were approached by a little Hungarian lad who wanted to get out of the Russian zone and work for them in the stables, and they agreed to take him. They got him through the Russian check-point by hiding him under the straw in one of the lorries, but after they arrived back in Graz he quickly disappeared and was never seen again.

Army racing was not the only form of equine activity in which Dick was involved while at Rimini and Ravenna. He got to know a trotting trainer at Ravenna called Zotti, and he and the Pope brothers used to go to the trotting races at Bologna with him on Sundays. Most of his own horses had been at it for a long time and stood around in their boxes heavily bandaged. However, he knew the form and used to mark their cards; and he was usually right. There also were show jumping competitions at Bologna and Dick sometimes took part, generally riding a little grey horse called White Cloud. There was not much serious soldiering to be done, and the horses helped to pass the time pleasantly.

From Graz the North Irish Horse moved to Germany. They were not allowed to take the horses, which were handed over

… and Winifred in 1917, after
… r wedding at Chedzoy Church.

…dzoy Rectory in the 1920s,
…re Dick's mother Winifred was
…n and her father was rector.

Roy with Jezebel. Salonika Campaign, 1916.

The Bridgwater Harriers in 1930. Roy Hern (*right*) on thoroughbred mare, Cynthia. Joe Hawkins (*left*) Whipper In and Kennel Huntsman.

opening of a bridge on the farm at Wick House. Roy and Winifred (*top left*), Michael on girl's lap *tom left*), Rupert (*centre foreground*), Dick (*right foreground*). 1931.

ert on Angeline and Dick on Autumn ready for a day's hunting, 1936.

Tanks of the North Irish Horse on Longstop Hill, 1943.

Mick Pope (*left*) on Farina, and Dick on Birdcatcher dispute the lead at the last fence at Ravenna in the summer of 1945.

Dick on Happy Days III at the first fence at the West Somerset point to point, 1938.

Roy Hern on Happy Days III on the polo ground at Weston-super-Mare, autumn 1939. In the background is Colonel Spence, C.O. of the North Somerset Yeomanry and father of Christopher Spence, the Senior Steward of the Jockey Club at the end of the century.

Dick on White Cloud receiving a prize for show jumping at the Bologna Show, 1945.

Dick on King Willow in April 1950, jumping the water at Badminton.

Dick on Tollbridge, before the dressage at Badminton, 1951.

Dick on Starlight at the Staff College and RMA Show at Camberley, 1951.

Dick schooling Fitz at Porlock before Badminton in 1952.

Dick on Fitz in 1952, during a clear round of the show jumping at Badminton.

to the 16th/5th Lancers. Dick knew that regiment well, as they had 25-pounder field guns and he had done an attachment with them during the last winter of the war to learn about gunnery. He had shared a tent with John de Burgh and became friendly with him. The 16th/5th were out of the line, so they were able to play poker every night, and Dick had one of those golden periods when he held good cards all the time, with the result that he ended up well in pocket. When the war was over the 16th/5th were stationed near Klagenfurt and John took a prominent part in the racing. After he was demobbed John, who had commanded a squadron and was awarded an MC, went as a pupil to the famous trainer Ivor Anthony, whose many well-known horses had included the great stayer Brown Jack. He rode a certain amount as an amateur before retiring to Ireland, where he showed great shrewdness in building up a successful stud at Naas. He and Dick always kept in touch, and used to see each other sometimes at the sales.

In Germany the North Irish Horse were stationed in a big barracks near Wuppertal, a dreary town in the industrial Ruhr. To pass the time Dick took up skiing, but was forced to give that up when he strained the ligaments in his knee. The Popes had departed, Michael to go home and Barry to join the Royals. Consequently Dick was far from sorry when the time came for him to be demobbed and the regiment to be disbanded in the autumn of 1946.

For Dick Hern, like so many of his British contemporaries, the Second World War was a mixture: of boredom, discomfort and occasional acute danger, but compensated for in large measure by the pleasures of comradeship, the interest of travel to places which he might otherwise never have seen, the experience of meeting men from many different walks of life – and, when the fighting was over, of renewed association with the horses that he loved so much. Unlike many of his contemporaries, Dick made two close friendships during his years in the army which were to have a profound influence on his future life:

with Michael Pope, who was to be instrumental in launching him on a career as a trainer, and with George Rich, who was to be his eager collaborator in much of the fun he was to derive from horse and hound in the Shires.

THREE

PORLOCK AND POPE

THE URGE TO COMPENSATE for the wasted years was almost universal among the men and women demobbed from the Services after the Second World War. However, they were divided into two clear-cut camps – those who had definite ideas about the way they wanted to go, and those who lacked any real sense of direction for the rest of their lives and drifted into one job or another. Dick Hern was in the former camp. He had no doubts. He was absolutely determined to be with horses.

There was one other certainty: there could be no return to the close-knit pre-war Hern family life of Wick House, for that life was in the process of disintegration. Rupert, who had held the fort there with Winifred during the war, had moved to Wales and taken a farm near the shores of Cardigan Bay. Thence he moved again to Totnes in Devon and reared sheep and cattle. Michael had spent the war in a state of frustration, as he had joined the RAF yearning to fly but had failed the eyesight test. He was also left permanently lame as a result of injuring a hip in a motor-cycle accident. He was with Rupert in Wales for a time, but then went to Canada where he achieved his ambition of learning to fly, and worked for some time flying uranium prospectors to Alaska. On one of those flights the plane crashed and they spent several days marooned in a canyon before they were rescued. In Canada he met and married an Australian girl called Beryl. They moved to Australia, where he made a living in real estate, buying houses, improving them and then selling them on.

Roy and Winifred separated after more than thirty years of married life. As a boy Dick had been close to both his parents. 'Father showed me sport, and mother taught me how to behave,' he recalled in later years. Winifred went to live in Wales to be near Rupert, and then moved to Devon, where she had a cottage in the village of Cornworthy 5 miles south of Totnes close to the Dart estuary. Gallantly, at the age of eighty, she took to the air for the first time and flew to Canada to attend Michael's wedding. Roy stayed at Wick House until he died of cancer at the age of seventy-five. Dick alone lived to see the millennium.

Within the general certainty that he must work with horses Dick had serious problems to solve. Two factors limited his options: he had no capital, and he had no pre-war job to which he could return. He chose the most obvious option in the circumstances. Before the war Roy, who was a Fellow of the Institute of the Horse (FIH), besides instructing at Millfield had taught two days a week at the Porlock Vale Riding School founded by Joe Collings at the foot of Exmoor on the north Somerset coast, 20 miles west of his home at Wick. Joe Collings's son Tony, also an FIH, had been a brother officer of Roy Hern in the North Somerset Yeomanry, and had re-opened the riding school after the war. For this reason it seemed natural for Dick to enrol on the three-month equitation course and endeavour to qualify as an instructor.

Equitation had been a much neglected art in nineteenth-century England, when any kind of riding not directly related to crossing country behind a pack of hounds or to steeplechasing was deemed to be wimpish and alien. The hunting seat was neither elegant nor effective, with the rider's toes usually pointed at the ground and what a French jockey of a later era described as 'beaucoup de sitback', or 'mode ancienne' as Dick's friend George Rich called it. Attempts to improve English standards of horsemanship had to await the foundation of the Cavalry

School by General (later Lord) Baden-Powell as Inspector General of Cavalry in the first decade of the twentieth century. Baden-Powell is better remembered as the defender of Mafeking against the Boers in the siege of 1899–1900 and as the creator of the Boy Scout and Girl Guide movements, but he was also in a true sense the father of English equitation. He saw the need for a centre of equitation based on the principles of the continental schools like the French Cavalry School at Saumur, and successfully translated this conviction into practice. The School opened at Netheravon, but moved to Weedon in Buckinghamshire after the First World War as a joint venture of the cavalry and the gunners. The Weedon School of Equitation became firmly established as the centre for the development of correct principles in training man and horse. From Weedon the same ideals spun off into civilian riding. The Institute of the Horse was formed by retired cavalry officers after the First World War, and in 1929 introduced an exam for an Instructor's Certificate in Equitation, Training the Horse and Stable Management based on Weedon methods. The Pony Club was founded the same year, and by the outbreak of the Second World War nearly every hunt had a branch under the control of a district commissioner and dedicated to teaching children the same principles. The Institute also sponsored civilian riding schools, of which Porlock was one of the most prominent.

In the late 1940s Porlock was still a sleepy village in the valley between Dunkery and Selworthy Beacons, though it attracted a fair number of tourists during the summer months. The A39 from Minehead wound through the narrow streets, past the red sandstone church with its curious truncated spire, and then turned south and up a hill with a 1 in 4 gradient onto Exmoor. A minor road ran due west from the village to Porlock Weir, and a mile and a half along that road stood Porlock Ford House, where Joe Collings had started the school. After the war Tony quickly built it up into the finest residential riding school in the country, still following the Weedon principles and using the two army manuals, *Animal Management* and *The Manual of Horse Mastership*. He had as a partner Captain Chris Leyland, who had been in the Household Cavalry before the war and was in the Mounted Police in London during the war. He was a good horseman and helped with the instructing, while his wife Violet was very kind and hospitable to the younger instructors and instructresses. Dick described her as 'a very nice person but a very nervous rider'. Tony also took Arthur Owen as a sleeping partner, and Owen and Leyland both put money into the business.

Porlock Ford House, where Joe Collings still lived, was used to house the short-term pupils who came on weekly courses and as the site of the big covered school. The other pupils, mostly girls, lived in a big house in the village called The Gables. The tan yard and the school office, a paddock with a lot of jumps in it and a loose-lane where pupils could ride with arms folded and their irons crossed, were also in the village. Dick had lodgings in a house with a window overlooking the road up onto the moor. Farmers and their sons from the moor used to ride down into Porlock to drink at the pub, and Dick's peace was sometimes disturbed late at night when they were turned out of the pub and cantered home, their horses' hooves clattering loudly on the tarmac surface.

Dick passed his course, obtained his certificate and became one of the first recipients of the diploma introduced after the amalgamation of the Institute of the Horse and the British Horse Society. He was asked by Tony Collings to stay on as an instructor, an invitation which he was pleased to accept. The standards of instruction were enhanced by outside equitation experts like Harry Asselberghs of Antwerp, who used to take dressage courses at Porlock in the 1930s and returned to do so again in Dick's time. Asselberghs was well-known in Britain, as he had given demonstrations of dressage and directed the display by the British Riding Club at the International Horse Show at Olympia in 1939. He was quite an old man by the time he was instructing at Porlock, but was a great character and used many striking phrases to illustrate the points he wished to make. In order to explain the correct position in the saddle he would say: 'When you have ze wind you should blow it out forwards and not backwards,' meaning that the rider should tuck his tail under him. Another of his favourite expressions was: 'A spur on ze heel of an untrained man is like a razor in ze hands of a monkey.' Dick had great respect for him and acknowledged that he learned a lot from him. The respect was clearly mutual, because at one time he offered Dick a job riding a high-school horse in a circus in Belgium. Dick was not tempted by the offer, but was amused by the thought of himself going into the ring with a white buckskin saddle and bridle and doing the Spanish walk and the passage two or three times a day, besides helping to put up the big top.

When Dick first went to Porlock it was very difficult to get enough food for the horses. Oats were in very short supply, but ex-Army biscuits were freely available; they were soaked in hot water with some chaff and fed to the horses with plenty of hay, and the horses thrived on it. Many essential things, not only food, were rationed. To save petrol they used to coast down all the hills, a very dangerous procedure on the steep hills around Porlock. It was nearly impossible to get tyres, and they used to run them right down to the canvas and then try to get them re-treaded. Dick had a terrible old Standard 9 which he had bought in 1940, and had to nurse it along to keep it on the road. Daylight was visible through the floorboards in one place, and on flooded roads water would spurt up through the hole.

Dick got along very well with Tony Collings, who did not pay much but was generous in allowing Dick time off for hunting and point-to-pointing. Dick's first post-war point-to-point riding was on Jubilee Star, a black gelding by the good stayer Noble Star who had won the three big long distance handicaps, the Ascot Stakes, the Goodwood Stakes and the Cesarewitch. Jubilee Star had inherited plenty of stamina.. Roy had bought him at the beginning of the war from Frank Cundell, who had ridden him to win on the flat at Lewes in 1938. He was sent down from Aston Tirrold to Bridgwater by train, where Dick met him. Dick gave the following account of his arrival: 'I don't think he had had a saddle on him for some time, but I made him ready in the railway box and led him out. He never put his back up and I led him round the station yard, jumped on him and rode him back through the town. He behaved beautifully for a horse that had just come out of training and had probably always been out with a string.' Rupert, and Dick at odd times when he was home on leave, got him jumping, and Dick rode him in a point-to-point for the first time in 1946 when he was eleven years old. He ran a very good race to be second in the South and West Wilts Open Race, where he was narrowly beaten by a horse owned and ridden by Harry Freeman-Jackson called Iloilo, with the rest of the field a mile behind. Iloilo went on to win the Foxhunters Cup at Cheltenham, so that was top-class point-to-point form. Unfortunately Jubilee Star got a leg in that race and, although he was fired and given plenty of time to recover, he would never really let himself go in the way he had done before. He was an excellent hunter, and Roy rode him to hounds for many years.

Dick rode nine point-to-point winners from Porlock and also served the sport as Honorary Secretary of the Point-to-Point Committee of the Devon and Somerset Staghounds. His most prolific winner was Shanrahan, owned by Chris Leyland, on whom he won three point-to-points in 1949: the Minehead Harriers Members and Farmers Race, the Adjacent Hunts Moderate Race at the West Somerset and the Members Race at the Devon and Somerset. Bertie Hill, the leading West Country point-to-point rider of the post-war years, had great respect for Dick's ability, paying tribute to the horsemanship which enabled him to get the best out of all sorts of horses.

Some of Dick's most enjoyable days hunting from Porlock were with the Mendip, where he used to go with Tony Collings with two horses each. They would join up with Duggie Baker, who lived there, had served with Tony in the North Somerset Yeomanry and had married his sister Joyce. An immensely enthusiastic hunting man, Duggie would urge them on with cries of 'come on boys, it's half a crown for a fall and a pound for a pounding'.

Although the instructing was serious business, those were happy-go-lucky days and there was plenty of social life. Dick became very friendly with Norman Kenneally who had a farm right up against the moor beyond Wootton Courtenay 4 miles south-east of Porlock. Kenneally shared Dick's love of hunting and went out regularly with the Staghounds. One day he lost his bowler hat during a good hunt and declined to run the risk of missing the best of it by stopping to pick up his hat. Dick and some of Kenneally's other friends, without his knowledge, put an advertisement in the *West Somerset Free Press* which read: 'Bowler hat wanted. Age immaterial but still serviceable. Norman Kenneally, Holt Ball Farm, Luccombe.' When they saw him ten days later he said: 'I don't understand it. People keep coming to deliver bowler hats, and they are arriving by every post.' They hoped that one or two were the right size.

Several girls had stayed on at the school as instructresses after qualifying. They were Molly Coleridge-Smith, Sue Thompson, Pat Pope and Pat Wykeham-Fiennes. Molly used to run the yards in company with 'Mr' Fitch, who was always so-called – nobody knew his first name. He used to show the students how to muck out, tack a horse up and clean tack. He was a first-class stableman and a great asset to the whole establishment. He was much missed when he went as Master of the Horse to Lucy Jones, a former pupil who lived on the Mendips and had several good point-to-pointers which used to be partnered by the leading rider John Daniel.

Dick and Pat Wykeham-Fiennes fell in love. They went out together a lot, often to Norman Kenneally's Farm or to Pat's aunt Mrs Binney, who lived at Wootton Courtenay, for supper.

They had some wonderful evenings. They would certainly have got married if Dick had had any money and they had had somewhere to live. Pat was a dare-devil rider and, together with Di Holden, accompanied Dick to Anna Griffiths' and Roy Beddington's engagement party in Sherborne, a north Dorset town renowned not only for its glorious abbey church and boys' and girls' public schools but as a centre for the Blackmore Vale country whose Digby Hotel was a haven for visiting riders to hounds until it was converted into an additional house for the boys' school. Anna was an excellent rider and secretary to the leading National Hunt trainer Fulke Walwyn, and Roy was a talented painter of equine subjects and one-time Master of the Tedworth Hounds. After the party they all, including the engaged couple, were invited back to Vicky and Bill Brake's house at Limington in the vale close to Yeovilton Fleet Air Arm station. Bill was a member of a well-known Blackmore Vale farming, hunting and point-to-pointing family. The party continued until the early hours of the next morning, when they all went out preparing to go home. Dick gave a graphic account of what followed:

> We were all in a very giggly state and certainly none of us would have passed the breathalyser test. It was a brilliant moonlit night, almost as light as day. Bill Brake exclaimed: 'I've been waiting for a night like this all my life to have a moonlight ride.' We all agreed that it would be a wonderful thing to do. Bill directed us to the tack room to get a saddle and bridle and choose a horse, saying that they were all good rides. We each made a horse ready, brought it out into the yard and mounted. Anna was wearing a billowy lace dress and had a big diamond brooch on her bosom, an engagement present from Roy. Shouting to us to follow him, Bill set off on a tantivy round the farm, with the others strung out behind him. The horses all jumped beautifully, we must have jumped twenty fences, and the only person who had a fall was Roy Beddington who had taken off his trousers and was riding in his long johns. He was thrown off into a coil of barbed wire

but was unhurt. I can still see Anna's dress which had worked up right under her armpits. We returned to the yard, put the horses away and got back to Porlock just as dawn was breaking. Of course we were all young in those days, and when you are young you can do that sort of thing and still do a day's work later. But I wanted an early bed the next night.

In the end Pat left Porlock to take a job in Ireland, and Dick lost touch with her for many years.

This re-enactment of the moonlight steeplechase was Dick's most spectacular exploit at Porlock, but there were many other leisure activities to enjoy. There were bathing parties at the secluded, unfrequented Bossington beach on Porlock Bay just north of the village, and sometimes they would hire a boat from Porlock Weir and go down the coast for a picnic. However, the work became ever more demanding as Tony Collings was increasingly preoccupied with training horses and riders for Badminton and the Olympics. Many of the leading riders used to come down to Porlock to train and practise. One of them was Colonel Harry Llewellyn who was a member of the British show jumping team that won a gold medal in the Helsinki Olympics in 1952 in spite of his great horse Foxhunter having three fences down in the first round. Llewellyn took Foxhunter and his other top class show jumper Kilgeddin to train in the school at Porlock before the 1948 Olympics in which both horses were in the British team which won a bronze medal. Dick noticed that Llewellyn rode both horses in a Market Harborough – a type of draw-rein invented by a nagsman at Market Harborough which consists of two straps running from the breast-ring through the bit-rings and fastening on to 'Ds' set on the rein; it can be adjusted to permit the head whatever degree of elevation is desired. Dick realised at once what a useful gadget it was, as it saves horses getting sore places inside their cheeks which make them pull even harder. He had one made and used it on all sorts of horses, even racehorses in their slow paces if they had a tendency to carry their heads too high.

Although eventing had been included in the Olympic equestrian programme since 1912, Tony Collings was largely responsible for its development in England after the Second World War and, with the enthusiastic support of the Duke of Beaufort, for the foundation of the Horse Trials at Badminton. The first three-day event held at Badminton in 1949 was won by John Shedden, but the following year Tony gained a well-deserved victory on Remus. Remus had been one of the horses in training for the 1948 Olympics, but in the end neither he nor George Rich, who had become one of the finest horsemen in the country, was selected – because, it was said, George could never remember the correct sequence of movements in the dressage test.

Dick himself rode at Badminton four years running from 1950 to 1953. In 1950 he rode a little horse belonging to Millfield called King Willow, who stood only about 15.1½ hands but was strong and a marvellous jumper. He gave Dick a wonderful ride in the cross-country and was in front on time until he reached the last fence, when he had got a little bit tired, clipped the top and toppled over. Dick remounted to finish without time penalties but his chance of winning, which was enhanced by an excellent display in the dressage, had vanished and he had to be content with eleventh place overall. He rode King Willow, on whom he also had several days with the Blackmore Vale and jumped the famous Babcary brook, again at Badminton in 1953, when he finished fourteenth. King Willow's trouble was that he was not very accurate at his show jumping and always knocked down a few of the fences. In the meantime he rode Tollbridge, who was withdrawn on the final day, in 1951, and Fitz, on whom he was tenth in 1952 after good performances in the dressage and the show jumping but sustaining a fall on the cross-country.

Tony Collings and Dick were debarred from riding in the Olympics because they were professional instructors, though it is possible that the British authorities were over-scrupulous in conforming to the rules; the best rider in the winning German team at the 1936 Olympics had been specially promoted from the ranks because participation was restricted to officers, so the rules could be bent. Instead they were given the responsibility of training the horses and riders short-listed for the 1952 Olympics on an extended course at Porlock, the riders including Bertie Hill, Laurence Rook, Reg Hindley, Michael Naylor-Leyland, John Oram and, for a time, George Rich. Hill was the youngest member of the team. He had ridden scores of point-to-point winners in the West Country, many of them over banks, and Tony Collings had the vision to see that he was a born rider with the scope to get right to the top when his natural ability had been honed. He had little experience of dressage and was handed over to Dick to be taught. Dick spent many hours passing on to him the skills he had learnt from his father and Harry Asselberghs, and he responded so well to the tuition of Tony and Dick that he became one of Britain's greatest horsemen.

As for the horses, Dick was mainly concerned with Starlight XV, who was obtained from Gerard Balding's stable at Weyhill and had run four times over fences without distinguishing himself in the least. He was handed over to Dick for training as a three-day event horse as soon as he arrived at Porlock. He was a brilliant natural jumper, very accurate and with a terrific spring. It was with him in mind that Dick remarked: 'The thoroughbred horse will do anything a half-bred horse will do, and a bit better; but of course they take a bit more schooling and require a first-class man on their backs; they are never mugs' companions.' Starlight XV was not an easy horse in his box and kicked a lot, but he was looked after by a girl groom called Joyce Whitaker who was very patient and got on with him as well as anyone could. Dick alone rode him from the time he arrived at Porlock and spent many hours schooling him in elementary dressage, following the old maxim of not trying to do too much on one day and always ending up on a high note. He was convinced that you can teach a horse anything if you are content to make slow progress, and proved it with Starlight XV. There was a piece of marshy ground in the Porlock Vale, usually under water in winter but with lovely springy old turf in summer, where Dick would take him for schooling; and Sheilah Davis, who had stayed on as the first working pupil after completing her riding course and shared a little cob-walled cottage at West Porlock with Pat Pope, would walk down with her gramophone so as to get him accustomed to music. It was with Starlight in mind that Pat Pope (afterwards Pat Salt) said of Dick: 'He was marvellous with rogue horses. He willed the bad points out of them and made them come good.'

It was soon obvious that Starlight XV was going to be a star, and Dick began to take him to small shows and competitions. The next stage in his progress was taking part in the one-day event at Guisburn Park, Reg Hindley's place in Lancashire. It was a tedious journey in those days before the building of motor-ways, and it took them two days in Tony's old pre-war Vincent horsebox with two horses – Starlight XV for Dick and Banbridge Boy for Laurence Rook – and Joyce Whitaker to do them both. On arrival they were billeted comfortably with a friend of Reg Hindley, where they dined well and slept in bedrooms with coal fires and the flames playing cosily on the ceiling. The next day Starlight XV behaved really well and won the competition easily to round off a successful expedition.

The Guisburn Park victory produced an invitation to ride Starlight XV at the 1951 Badminton, but Dick had already accepted an invitation to ride Tollbridge, on whom he had clocked a very fast time at the Larkhill one-day event, and decided that he must honour that commitment. Afterwards he chided himself for not going to Arthur Owen, the owner of Tollbridge, and explaining what had happened. 'I'm sure he would have been only too pleased to let me off. That's what I should have done, and that's what I would have done if I had been a little more mature,' he said when he reflected on the circumstances which may have deprived him of a victory at Bad-minton. He was replaced on Starlight XV by Colonel Duggie

Stewart, who had no time to get to know the horse and went much too slowly. 'He didn't realise what a good horse he was sitting on,' said Dick.

Laurence Rook rode Starlight XV in the Helsinki Olympics the next year, and only bad luck robbed them of a medal. They were going extremely well when Starlight XV put his foot in an invisible drain, turned over and gave Rook a bad fall and mild concussion. Rook remounted and completed the course, but in his semi-conscious state he went the wrong side of a marker, with the result that he and the whole team were disqualified. In the individual placings Bertie Hill was seventh on Stella and Reg Hindley was thirteenth on Speculation. They received some consolation at the European Championships the following April when the team won the gold medal and Starlight XV proved what a brilliant horse he was by winning the individual gold. In this way Starlight XV vindicated Dick's high opinion and justified all the hard work Dick had put into training him.

By the time of the Helsinki Olympics Dick's time at Porlock was coming to an end. He had been there for five years and had held the post of deputy chief instructor while Tony Collings concentrated on training the Olympic team, and he felt that it was time to move on. Moreover he was never going to earn enough money at Porlock to be able to afford to get married or buy a house. Fortuitously the opportunity for a change arrived when his old North Irish Horse friend Michael Pope, who had been training racehorses ever since he was demobbed, asked him to join him as assistant trainer to replace his brother Barry. So, while it was a wrench to leave Porlock, where he had enjoyed many happy days, he had no doubt that it was right to accept Michael's invitation.

From an equally early age Michael had shared Dick's passion for horses and hunting. He had always had an ambition to train racehorses, and it was not difficult for him to fulfil it because his father Alec was a wealthy London estate agent and funds to finance a training operation were not lacking. By the time he arrived home after the war some old cattle stalls at Wood Farm, Streatley, across the river from Goring-on-Thames, had been converted into a makeshift stable yard with a dozen boxes, and he was ready to go. Streatley stands below the eastern extremity of the Berkshire Downs, no more than 8 miles as the crow flies from West Ilsley, where Dick was to train for a quarter of a century. By the time Dick joined Michael as assistant in the autumn of 1952 the string had increased to more than thirty horses and winners were flowing in a regular stream.

Two happenings wrote a postscript to Dick's time at Porlock soon after he had moved to Streatley. The first was the offer of the job of training the Australian eventing team for the 1956 Olympics, but he was committed and had to decline. In later days when he went to Australia on holiday he liked the country so much that he felt that if he had gone there, he would have wanted to stay, in which case the rest of his life would have been on totally different lines to the reality. The second was the death of Tony Collings when the Comet aircraft in which he was flying to South Africa blew up over the Mediterranean. Dick felt keenly the loss of a man with whom he had worked so closely and admired so much.

Soon after Dick's arrival Michael moved his string to Blewbury, five miles from Streatley on the north side of the Downs. The yard, Millcroft, was well equipped, most of the boxes being brick-built with a few wooden ones from an earlier era. It had come on the market because the previous owner, Gordon Johnson Houghton, had been killed at the age of only forty-two when he was thrown from his horse in front of an on-coming lorry while out with the Old Berkshire Hounds. He had made a highly respected name for himself as a trainer specialising in horses bought in France like Laurentis, Black Rock, Fast Soap and Le Lavandou. Before Johnson Houghton, Steve Donoghue, the former champion jockey who won the Derby six times, had trained there. Pope's training operation was in a lower key. Few of the horses had any class, but nearly all were owned by personal friends who were in racing for fun. Many of them liked to have a punt, and when they had a touch they would celebrate in style. His principal owner was Edwin McAlpine, whose Dobson's Stud at Henley supplied most of his horses. His Luxury Hotel provided Michael with one of his biggest successes when he won the Great Metropolitan, then an important long distance handicap, over the peculiar 2¼-mile course which wound over the Downs at Epsom. Luxury Hotel was a stayer, but Michael was equally adept at preparing sprinters like Blason. His most remarkable horse, Birdbrook, came after Dick's time but provided the most striking evidence of the skill he had always possessed. Birdbrook, who was bought cheaply by Michael for 1800 guineas because he was wrongly suspected of having a bad back, was as hard as nails, running no fewer than fifty-seven times on the flat and winning sixteen races, plus one race over hurdles. He was then given his chance as a stallion at Dobson's Stud and, remarkably for a horse who was no better than a mile handicapper, sired the brilliant Girl Friend, who was second in the 1000 Guineas and became the best sprinter in France.

Michael had a mixed stable, and regularly trained a total of twenty to twenty-five winners a year. His two best years while Dick was with him were 1955, when he had eleven winners on the flat and seventeen over jumps, and 1957, when he had twenty winners on the flat and nine over jumps. Dick had been an experienced and successful point-to-point rider, but it was from Blewbury that he was given the opportunity to ride his only two winners under National Hunt Rules on Edwin McAlpine's Sir John IV. Sir John IV was a half-brother of Sir Ken, who won the Champion Hurdle three times, is remembered as the quickest and most fluent jumper of hurdles of all champions, and would probably have been equally good as a chaser if he had not begun to jump fences when he was past his prime. Sir John IV was nowhere near that class. Dick described his quirky character: 'He was a law unto himself. He was a beautiful jumper, but would generally drop himself out in a race and then, suddenly, when he thought the time had come, take hold of his bit and away he would go.' Such characters are not easy rides and demand infinite patience, and Dick earned warm praise in the racing press for riding him to victory in the Bettisfield Handicap Chase over 3 miles at Ludlow in September 1954 and the Ermine Street Handicap Chase over the same distance at Huntingdon the following month. Dick rode him in two more races that season, but Sir John IV was not in co-operative mood on either occasion, though he did finish a bad third of four at Chepstow. The other great character among the Pope horses was Teddy Tail, of whom Dick wrote: 'He had a tube in his neck and a pair of curbs you could hang your hat on, but he always ran a good race when he was fancied and conditions were right for him.' He won six of his thirty-two races, all in the lowest class, but that did not matter in a stable that liked to have a bet.

Dick lived in The Bull at Streatley when he first joined Pope, but moved into half a large bungalow built by Steve Donoghue after the move to Blewbury, the other half being occupied by the head lad Jack Maunder and his wife. Social life centred round Wood Farm, where Alec and Tim, Michael's father and mother, lived. Alec owned the real estate firm Goddard & Smith, in which Michael's brother Peter and his twin Patrick also worked, but came down from London at weekends. The elder Popes were extremely hospitable, and treated Dick as one of the family. They had him to supper every Sunday night and kept open house on Sunday mornings when champagne corks popped, especially if the stable had had a winner. They used to give a big summer party with drinks in the garden, and a lavish party on New Year's Eve which was famous in the area. Dick's constant companion at the time was Smokey, a dog somewhere in size between a whippet and a lurcher, given to him by Michael and his wife Kay. He was fawn in colour, with a bluish tint round his muzzle. He used to sleep in a basket in Dick's room. There was a box in front of the window, and an upturned barrel outside. If Smokey wanted to go out in the night he jumped onto the box, onto the window sill, onto the barrel and away. If Dick heard any cats caterwauling he would say 'Pssst, see 'em off, Smokey', and he would be out of the window in a flash and Dick would hear him barking all the way up the road. He was very independent, and made many friends in the village. One lady told Dick that one day she was in bed, and had left the front door open. Smokey came in, ran up the stairs, jumped on the bed and spent the morning with her. Sometimes he came home with a pound of sausages in his mouth, but Dick could never discover where he got them. When the jumpers were out on winter mornings he would trot along beside Dick's horse until they turned at the bottom of the canter and would then set off as fast as his legs would carry him. He kept going flat out until the horses passed him, when he would stop and cock his leg on one of the bushes marking out the canter. He was a great character and Dick loved him dearly.

However an enormous change in Dick's life was impending. He had seen a lot of Sheilah Davis during the latter part of his time at Porlock. She, Dick and Pat Pope used to go to the cinema in Minehead about once a week and have a snack meal at Billy's Bar afterwards. They had drifted apart when Dick went to Streatley and Sheilah also left Porlock. She went for a few months to Sweden, then returned to England and worked as secretary to George Beeby, who had trained such superb chasers as the Grand National second Roimond and the Cheltenham Gold Cup winner Silver Fame for Lord Bicester. Next she went to Cyprus, where she set up a small racing stable for Pat Pope's mother Elspeth. They used to run horses at Nicosia races, and also ship them occasionally to run in Beirut. Sheilah rode in several races. In 1956 she came home for Pat Pope's marriage to Dennis Salt in Porlock, at which she was a bridesmaid, and Dick met her there. They fell in love, and quickly decided to get married. As Dick recorded: 'That was undoubtedly the best day's work I ever did, for nobody could have had a better wife than Sheilah.'

The wedding was on 9 October 1956 at the Church of Christ Church in Brick Street, Mayfair. Sheilah's father Seamus had died some years earlier, and the responsibility of giving her away devolved on her grandfather Jim Tweedie. He flunked it, taking her at first to the wrong church and causing a nail-biting delay. After the service a reception was held at 30 Pavilion Road, Knightsbridge, a popular venue for social gatherings. The honeymoon was in Paris; Dick would have preferred The Crown at Exford and a few days with the Devon and Somerset, but was overruled in favour of more cultural activities and visits to the Louvre and the palace of Versailles. One of Dick's more vivid memories of Paris was of the notices 'defense de cracher' in the Metro. They were together, racing's most devoted couple, for forty-one years until Sheilah's death in 1998.

After the honeymoon the couple moved back into The Bull for a time while Michael had a Raeburn cooker installed and various improvements done to the bungalow. They had a room over the bar, so it was somewhat noisy until the customers left after 11 p.m., but Dick remarked philosophically that you can put up with such minor inconveniences when you are first married. Sheilah had lived an exceptionally varied life before she was married at the age of twenty-seven. She was born in Assam where her father was a tea planter, but the hot and humid climate was unsuitable for children so Seamus and his wife Nora sent her back to England to live with her maternal grandparents, Jim and Alice Tweedie, at Petersfield. She spent the early years of the Second World War at school in South Africa, and returned to Assam on leaving school. When she was only sixteen she succeeded in enlisting in the Women's Auxiliary Service Burma (WASB) by craftily falsifying her age, as the minimum qualifying age was seventeen. She became the driver of a 15-cwt truck delivering comforts to the troops. A diminutive but indomitable figure, she could barely see over the steering wheel, but that did not deter her from taking her truck close to the front line.

Sheilah was tiny, fair, fresh-complexioned and very pretty; she had a well-developed sense of fun, radiated energy, and was intensely loyal, protective and hard-working. She was soon to exercise a dramatic influence on Dick's fortunes and reshape his future career in an entirely new fashion. It had been Dick's intention, after serving a reasonable apprenticeship as assistant to Michael Pope, to become a National Hunt trainer. What actually happened was beyond his wildest dreams. He became one of the foremost trainers of Classic horses in Britain.

FOUR

NEWMARKET AND HOLLIDAY

D ICK AND SHEILAH were only a very short way into their married life when she began to exert an influence on his career. In Cyprus she had made friends with a dark and beautiful girl called Pam Hirsch, who had returned to England and married Brook Holliday, the son of the leading owner-breeder Major Lionel Holliday. In the summer of 1957 Pam contacted Sheilah and told her that Major Holliday was looking for a trainer for his large private stable at Newmarket, suggesting that Dick should apply for the job. Sheilah took up the idea enthusiastically. At first Dick was reluctant. 'I've no chance. I wouldn't get it,' he told her. 'At least write to him. You've got nothing to lose,' she persisted. So Dick was persuaded, and to his surprise received a letter in return asking him to come up to Holliday's home, Copgrove Hall near Harrogate, for an interview.

It was thus that he found himself heading north by train. He was met at York by Holliday's chauffeur, Brean, who led him out to the car in the station yard and opened one of the rear doors for him. 'No, I'll sit with you,' said Dick, getting into the front. They started to talk, and Dick quickly found that Brean was a man he could get on with, and he was to become a reliable ally. Brean told him quite a lot about the Copgrove establishment on the way. The hall proved to be a large square house built of granite blocks, and before long Dick grew to realise that they were wholly in keeping with the character of the owner.

The Turf has spawned many eccentrics like George Osbaldeston, George Baird and Captain Machell, and Major Lionel Holliday was worth his place in any gallery of them. He was a hard man. Although he had left the county for his education at Uppingham and Bonn University, he was the archetypal Yorkshireman – down-to-earth, outspoken, niggardly, bloody-minded, florid and self-centred, but at the same time totally honest and straightforward in his dealings. His presence was daunting; he served for years as a magistrate, and malefactors had every reason to quake when they faced him on the bench. He had made a fortune from the manufacture of aniline dyes in Huddersfield, and used it to indulge his passion for the country sports of shooting, foxhunting and, above all, horse racing and breeding. He was a domestic tyrant, extending few favours to his children and having his second wife Marguerite, the mother of Brook, firmly under his thumb. Dick found her charming, but she was compelled to conform to the house rule of 'no smoking'. If she wanted a cigarette she had to go to her bedroom and puff the smoke up the chimney in the manner of Victorian times when the idea of women smoking was taboo. His brusque and unyielding manner meant that he had few close friends, and undoubtedly accounted for the fact that, in spite of his huge investment in racing and breeding and his unblemished rectitude, he was not elected a member of the Jockey Club, then racing's ruling body, until he was over eighty; whereas his son Brook, who gradually dissolved his bloodstock empire but served racing in many capacities, including chairman of the York Race Committee, was elected at the age of thirty-six.

Their mutual love of hunting drew Dick and Holliday together at their first meeting, and thereafter Dick found that harmony prevailed whenever hunting was discussed. Beginning immediately after the First World War, Holliday had been Master successively of the north country packs the Derwent, the Badsworth, the Grove, the Rufford and the York and Ainsty (North), carrying the horn as well as being Master of the last-named in the years immediately before the Second World War. He continued as Joint Master after the war. The kennels were at Copgrove, which is situated precisely in the middle of the country, half way between the rivers Ure and Nidd.

On that first visit Holliday took Dick round his small stud and showed him his hunters and the hounds. Afterwards he took him into the library where a shelf held a row of hunting diaries. He explained that he had always kept them with the idea that when he was old he would be able to read them again and relive the days in the hunting field that had given him so much pleasure. Then he added with the only hint of pathos that Dick ever witnessed in him: 'But, you know, now that I am over seventy-five I find they are meaningless. I have forgotten the horses and the hounds and where we went and everything.' Dick's retrospective comment was that in every other respect the old man was mentally very much on the ball.

Dick spent the rest of the day and stayed the night at Copgrove, and went home the next day. Presently he got a letter from Holliday offering him the job, but wanting him to go to Newmarket and take over the stable straight away. Dick replied that that was impossible, because he would leave Michael Pope in the lurch if he left him before the end of the season. To his surprise Holliday accepted that, saying that he respected his loyalty, which was an essential quality.

In November Dick went to Newmarket to see the horses at Holliday's private Lagrange stable, located at the junction of the Snailwell and Fordham roads. Lagrange had been built in 1883 and so called to commemorate the great French owner-breeder Count Frederic de Lagrange who won the Triple Crown with Gladiateur, immortalised as the 'Avenger of Waterloo'. Dick was taking a huge step into unknown territory, moving from a provincial stable with a mixed bag of moderate flat horses and jumpers to a large stable of high-class flat horses in the highly charged atmosphere of the headquarters of the Turf. Holliday had about fifty horses in training, nearly all home-bred, and had already won the Oaks with Neasham Belle, the Coronation Cup and the Champion Stakes with Narrator, the St James's Palace Stakes with Pirate King and the Dewhurst Stakes with Dacian – all races classified Group 1 when the Pattern race groupings were introduced in the 1970s. A combination of breeding and racing establishments on this scale was absolutely unique in post-Second World War England. For the man privileged to be its trainer there was extraordinary opportunity and extraordinary responsibility. In the circumstances most men who had never held a trainer's licence before, let alone had charge of Classic horses, would have been overawed. Dick had the self-confidence to believe from the outset that he would not fail.

On arrival in Newmarket Dick lived in a guesthouse at the top of the town for a couple of weeks until his predecessor Humphrey Cottrill and his wife moved out of Lagrange. He spent the time getting to know the horses and the staff. Humphrey was no help in giving him information about the rising three-year-olds and the older horses, but the head lad Jim Meaney and the stable jockey Stan Clayton were very co-operative and were able to tell him all he wanted to know.

On the day they were due to move into the house and Sheilah arrived with their furniture, the Cottrills would not let them into the house until 6 p.m., and then took all the electric light bulbs and turned off the heating. The Herns had little furniture because they had been living in only half a bungalow at Blewbury, and they had very little money to buy more. Fortunately they found support from a man called Dunkely, a dealer in furniture, mostly second-hand, at Liss near Petersfield. He had known the Tweedies for years, and went up to Newmarket to see what Dick and Sheilah needed. 'That's all right,' he said when he had had a look round. 'I'll get you the things, and you can pay me a bit when you can.' His generosity saw them through a difficult time.

Others were less generous. Humphrey Cottrill telephoned soon after they had moved in and said that there was a large heap of coal in the cellar. 'Rather than my having it moved and you having to get a new lot in, you might like to take it over,' he said. Dick agreed to buy it from him at an independent valuation, and the transaction was completed. Afterwards Dick discovered that there were some nice big lumps of coal on top of the pile, but underneath it was all slack. Years later Dick observed that it was probably still there.

The Newmarket training community, indeed, often seemed wanting in community spirit, or even normal neighbourliness, as was perhaps inevitable in a town where professional rivalry was intense. The first day that Dick rode out at the back of the string on a cob that Holliday kept for his own use, they were passing Phantom House, where Ryan Jarvis was standing at the gate. Ryan called out as they went by: 'Good morning, Dick. I hope you've brought your toothbrush, because that's all you'll need.' Holliday was notorious for changing his trainers at frequent intervals, and Dick had been preceded by Bob Colling, Dick Warden and Geoffrey Brooke besides Cottrill. There was a saying in currency: 'Which would you rather be: Boyd-Rochfort's hack, Jack Jarvis's jockey, or Holliday's trainer?' Cecil (later Sir Cecil) Boyd-Rochfort had a habit of beating his hack over the head with his whip when it would not stand still, and Jack (later Sir Jack) Jarvis was apt to be harshly critical of his jockeys.

There were notable exceptions to the general rule of unfriend-liness among Newmarket trainers. Jack Jarvis, although a difficult man for jockeys to work for, extended a warm welcome, and asked the Herns down for a drink one Sunday morning soon after they had arrived. He opened a bottle of pink champagne, remarking that Lord Rosebery, the principal patron of his stable for whom he had won the Derby with Blue Peter and Ocean Swell, always sent him a case for Christmas. Geoffrey Barling was another senior trainer whom Dick found outstandingly charming and helpful. He fell in with him one morning on the Heath, and Geoffrey told him: 'Now Dick, you'll find that horses need more work here than they do on the Downs.' His father had trained at Hodcott House, West Ilsley, and he was well aware of the difference between the two centres. On the Downs horses got fit with plenty of uphill work, while at Newmarket there were only the gentler slopes of Long Hill and Warren Hill.

Of the younger trainers Tom Jones was the first to extend a helping hand, lending him a hack and showing him round the Heath. Fergie and Judy Sutherland and Bruce and Betty Hobbs became close friends. At that time Bruce, later a successful trainer on his own at Palace House, was assistant to Cecil Boyd-Rochfort at Freemason Lodge.

In the racing world everybody is ready to criticise a new trainer, and Dick accounted himself lucky that he had Plaudit to give him a good start. Plaudit was the most precocious among the two-year-olds in the stable, and was a smallish bay colt, very strongly made and quick from the gate. Stan Clayton used to ride him out most mornings second lot, and he was ready to run in the Brocklesby Stakes, the first considerable two-year-old race of the season, at Lincoln in March. He started a warm favourite. Clayton jumped off in front and, pursuing his preferred tactics, made every yard of the running to win unchallenged by 3 lengths. Dick never forgot the thrill that first success with his first runner gave him. Things did not work out so happily a week later when he saddled the five-year-old Combatant in the Nottingham Spring Handicap over 1 mile 5 furlongs. Holliday liked Dick to send him a telegram when he had a runner and was not present, so after the race Dick wired: 'Combatant ran well, finished fourth, needed the race.' The next time he saw Brean the chauffeur told him: 'Excuse me telling you this, but the old Major got quite upset when he opened your wire from Nottingham, and said that you had the whole of Newmarket Heath to gallop the horse on, and still it needed the race. If I were you, I would put it a different way.' Dick thanked Brean for his advice, and developed the formula: 'So and So ran well, should improve'. That apparently was acceptable, as Dick never heard anything more about it. Incidentally, Combatant won next time out at Newbury, while Plaudit trained on well enough to win two races over 7 furlongs at Epsom the next year.

The best horse that Dick trained in his first season was None Nicer, a big and very sound filly. First time out she made all the running and won the Lingfield Oaks Trial. She tried to do the same in the Oaks, but was caught in the last quarter of a mile and finished fourth behind the brilliant French filly Bella Paola, Mother Goose and Cutter. She went on to win the Ribblesdale Stakes at Royal Ascot and the Yorkshire Oaks, finishing second to the colt Guersillus in the Gordon Stakes at Goodwood in the meantime. After that Holliday wanted her to run in the St Leger. Dick would have preferred the Park Hill Stakes, which was at her mercy, but Holliday insisted. She ran a marvellous race, but Alcide was too good for her in the last 2 furlongs and went right away to win by 8 lengths. However, she stayed on well enough to take second place, ¾ of a length in front of Nagami, who had been third in the Derby. It was certainly no disgrace to be beaten by Alcide, one of the best winners of the St Leger for many years. He should have won the Derby, but was got at before the race and could not run. At the end of the season None Nicer was rated the best British-trained three-year-old filly, though 10lbs inferior to Bella Paola.

Dick made his mark indelibly in that first season, 1958, finishing fifth in the list of winning trainers with twenty-seven winners of forty races worth £41,265, while Holliday was third in the list of winning owners and second in the list of winning breeders. The best horse in the stable that did not win a race that season was the two-year-old Galivanter. He was a typical son of the sprinting sire Golden Cloud, a big colt with plenty of speed. He ran some very good races, particularly when he was second in the New Stakes at Royal Ascot, running only in high-class races instead of taking easier options. The next year Dick started him off in a maiden race over 5 furlongs at Warwick, which he won in a canter. That gave him confidence, and he went from strength to strength, winning four more races and never finishing out of the first three in a total of eight races that season. He gave some excellent weight-carrying performances in handicaps, and was probably the second best sprinter in the country after Right Boy, who beat him by half a length in the Nunthorpe Stakes at York in August. That season Dick trained one more winner than in 1958, but winnings were down to £28,434 and he dropped two places to seventh in the list of winning trainers.

1960 was a bad year; the stable earnings were only £14,778, and Dick slumped to twenty-seventh place in the trainers' list; but there was a revival to £39,227 and ninth place in 1961. The chief agent of recovery was Galivanter, who had been pin-fired for a splint at the end of his three-year-old season and had missed the whole of 1960 after being confined to his box for three months as a result of unexplained lameness. As a five-year-old he emerged better than ever. His seasonal debut was in the Ripon City Handicap over 6 furlongs in April, when he won by 2 lengths, conceding nearly 2st to the second horse Signal Boy. Only four days later he reappeared in the Palace House Stakes, later a Group 3 race, over 5 furlongs at Newmarket and again won easily. A month later he failed by only a short head to give 24lbs to Star Combine in the misleadingly named Champion Sprint Handicap at Redcar, but could not cope with dead going at Royal Ascot and was beaten into fourth place in the Cork and Orrery Stakes. As a result of that defeat he started the outsider of three in the July Cup at Newmarket, but gave a champion's performance to win decisively from Tin Whistle and the filly Favorita, who started a long odds-on favourite. He gave an equally convincing performance to carry 9st 7 lbs to victory in the Great St Wilfrid Handicap at Ripon in August, before signing off with a relatively poor fourth place in the Nunthorpe Stakes. Other important contributors to the stable's earnings that year were Proud Chieftain, who gained big handicap victories in the

Rosebery Stakes and the Magnet Cup besides finishing third in the Coronation Cup and second in the Eclipse Stakes, and the stayer Avon's Pride, who won the Cesarewitch.

Dick spent those years at Newmarket learning and adapting to the idiosyncrasies of Major Holliday. Holliday had a house in Newmarket, Sunnyside in Park Lane close to Jack Jarvis's yard, where he stayed when he visited Newmarket. It was looked after by his mistress Mrs Jackson. He kept a pony and trap and an old horse for her use at Kremlin yard, next door to Lagrange, where the yearlings were broken. Dick and Sheilah sometimes drove the pony and trap up to the neighbouring village of Snailwell and round the lanes, and Dick used to take the horse out before she wanted to ride him to give him a bit of exercise. He was by Noble Star, about twenty-four years old, and a miserable ride, jig-jogging the whole time and never walking properly for a step. Mrs Jackson used to ride him side-saddle round the roads, and he used to settle better for her. She always wore one of the old-fashioned cloche hats that women used to wear in the 1920s, with a strand of hair wound round the brim; Dick was convinced that when the hat came off the hair came off also, but as she always wore the hat, even indoors, he never found out whether he was right.

When Holliday was staying at Sunnyside during the season, Dick used to go to see him at about five o'clock on Sunday evenings to show him the entries he proposed to make. 'What will you have, Hern, whisky and soda or fizz?' he would ask; and when they were sitting down with their drinks he would raise his glass and say: 'Well, here's damnation to the working man.' Dick always thought that that was a bit hard on the working man, whose efforts in the dye factory had made him his fortune.

Holliday had five or six terriers that were always with him and slept in his room. At Copgrove everyone was warned when he was coming down in the morning by the noise of the terriers snarling, yapping and nipping at each other. They were only partially house-trained and Mrs Holliday had pieces of polythene wrapped round all the furniture legs because the terriers lifted their legs on them. One year he took a very smart, modern house at Sunningdale for the Royal Ascot meeting. It had an open staircase and pine furniture, not at all the kind of place where he would feel at home. When Dick visited him there one day he pointed out one piece of furniture that had been well anointed by the terriers, saying: 'Look at that corner there – just asking for it.' He was very fond of the dogs. Once when he arrived at Newmarket he found that one of the terrier bitches, Gertie, was in season, so Brean had to turn straight round and drive her back to Yorkshire because there was nowhere to put her at Sunnyside.

Holliday had a grouse shoot on the moors above Grinton in Swaledale, and used to invite his trainer and several jockeys for a day's shooting on the Monday before the York August Meeting. The brothers Doug and Eph Smith were always there. Doug was champion jockey five times, and Eph lasted as first jockey to Jack Jarvis's stable for many years. They were both keen shots, and Eph was a skilled trainer of gun dogs. The first time Dick shot there he had the kennelman as his loader. It was the first time he had shot driven grouse, and he did not bag many. When they had finished the first drive Dick noticed that the kennelman was picking up the spent cartridges and stuffing them into holes in the butt. 'What are you doing that for?' Dick asked him. 'Oh,' he said, 'the Major will be in this butt for the next drive, and he is sure to count them.'

When Dick arrived at Newmarket he found that all the yearlings had nasty scabby places on their legs about the size of a 50p piece. He asked Meaney, the head lad, about them. 'Well,' said Meaney, 'we get it every year. We have a bit of plough next door in the Kremlin where we lunge the yearlings when they are broken. There's some chalk in it, and that gets down inside the boots and causes the scabs.' Dick did not believe it, and when the vet John Gray, then in practice at Lambourn, came to stay for the December Sales he asked him to come round the stables and have a look. Gray diagnosed a type of ringworm. All the tack used for breaking the yearlings was kept in the Kremlin yard, and the boots carried the ringworm spoors from year to year. Dick asked what he should do with the boots and John told him: 'Put then in the saddle-room stove.' Dick did this at once, but of course when Holliday's accountant Malcolm Pearson came down to do the annual inventory a number of pairs of boots were missing. Dick explained what had happened, and when Pearson asked how he should account for them Dick told him: 'Just put down "destroyed in the interests of hygiene".' Pearson irritated Dick because he would delve into everything like a ferret. He could never understand that horses are inclined to tear off bandages, and never stopped complaining about the numbers that went missing. Anyhow, there were no more scabs on the yearlings' legs after the old boots were burnt.

Holliday did not believe in spending money on hacks for his trainers, and sent Dick a succession of old unsound horses not good enough for the hunt servants. When the ground got hard in the summer they went lame, and as soon as Dick told him about it Holliday would say: 'You're a terrible man to lame horses, Hern. Send him home and I'll have him knocked down.' After having several of these useless horses Dick gave up and obtained an old flat-race horse called Misconception, who had formerly belonged to Peter O'Sullevan, from Bob Turnell. He was a comfortable ride, a bit dipped in his back, and carried Dick well for years, accompanying him when he moved to West Ilsley.

Nor was Holliday any more accommodating over the matter of a car. When he arrived in Newmarket Dick had a black Austin 16 which was unreliable and, in those days before the invention of power-steering, very heavy for Sheilah to drive. He asked Holliday whether he would get him a car that he could use when he went racing. 'I'll get you a car all right, but I'll take the cost out of your salary,' he answered. That arrangement did not suit Dick. Instead he got a Ford Zephyr from Bill Tarrant, who had a garage in Pershore. Bill was a professional backer and had learnt the job from Ben Warner, the bookmaker turned punter and owner, who won the Champion Hurdle with Free Fare in 1937.

With other Newmarket trainers, Dick went to many of the more distant meetings by air, flying in eight-seater Rapides from Marshall's Flying Services at Cambridge. A frequent fellow passenger was Cecil Boyd-Rochfort, who hated flying but steeled himself to do so as a matter of convenience. He used to sit at the front of the plane, and Bernard Van Cutsem, who disliked him intensely, used to get in at the back and tease him by saying: 'I've just heard the weather forecast. It's terrible. I'm afraid we're going to have a very bumpy flight.'

Boyd-Rochfort was already in his seventies when Dick went to Newmarket, and had made a big name for himself as a trainer of Classic horses. He was also training for the Queen, for whom he trained some top-class horses including the King George VI and Queen Elizabeth Stakes winner Aureole. An Etonian and former Guards officer, he was tall, good-looking and upright in his bearing. With his invariable grey Homburg, well-cut suits and highly polished brogues, he had an air of immense dignity. His pomposity was legendary, and nobody in Newmarket ever missed an opportunity to puncture it. Stan Clayton was one of the first people in Newmarket to have a telephone answering machine installed in his house. He rang up Dick one day and said: 'You must come round and listen to this before I wipe it off the tape.' Boyd-Rochfort had telephoned, and after a few rings the voice had said: 'This is Stan Clayton's house. Please leave your message after the tone.' There was a silence and then: 'This is Captain Boyd-Rochfort speaking. I wish to speak to Stan Clayton.' There was another silence, then: 'This is Captain Boyd-Rochfort speaking. I wish to speak to Stan Clayton. Is he there or is he not? I don't want to be told how to speak or when to speak. Just tell me if he is at home.' This rigmarole was repeated three or four times before Boyd-Rochfort gave up the attempt, and Stan, Dick and Sheilah were falling about laughing as they listened to the re-play.

If Holliday showed extreme reluctance to spend money on things that were necessities for his trainer, like hacks and motor-cars, he was not noticeably more generous to his own flesh and blood. His son Brook took an interest in the affairs of the stable and expressed a wish to ride in point-to-points. Holliday had a horse called Nem Con who, like most of the chesnut Nearcos, was not much good. However, he was a beautifully made horse with sound limbs, and when Holliday wanted to sell him Dick suggested that he should let Brook have him. 'In a couple of years time he will be making a point-to-point horse,' he said. 'Give him to Brook?' Holliday replied incredulously. 'Why, if I put him in the sales he'll make a thousand pounds.'

Holliday was chairman of the York Race Committee, and as the racecourse received half of the surplus over the selling price realised by the winners of selling races, he made a practice of bidding for the winner of the big two-year-old selling race at the York August meeting. Before Dick arrived on the scene, he bought Pacifico for 1450 guineas after he had won that race. He took him back to Copgrove and sent him back into training in January, by which time Dick was in charge. He was a very bad box-walker, and Dick discovered that he had had a goat as a companion when he was with his previous trainer Bob Ward. He telephoned Ward, who was away, but was told that he had given the goat to his head man as a present for his little girl. Dick asked the head man whether he would sell it, the head man put a price on it, and a bargain was struck. The goat was sent up to Newmarket by train, and Dick and Sheilah met it at the station. It was dark when they walked into the yard with it, and the horses had all been fed and let down. Dick put the light on Pacifico's box, and he turned his head and blinked. The goat went 'Maa', the horse whickered, and the goat went up and licked his nose. They loved each other. The goat acted as the most effective of tranquillisers, and Pacifico became a very useful horse who won ten races over the next six seasons. For its part the goat was a most engaging character. It was let out in the yard at stable time, and used to gallop up and down as fast as it could go. It was left in the paddock while the horses were out at exercise, and when they came in it would join Pacifico and trot in beside him. When Pacifico's racing days were over he was owned by Kit Blomfield, Sheilah's uncle by marriage, as a hunter with the Seavington, and still had his friend the goat.

The 1962 season was Dick's last, but his best, season as private trainer to Major Holliday. Hethersett, despite one devastating setback, proved himself the nearest approach to perfection that Holliday ever bred or owned, and he set Dick on the path to becoming one of the most prolific trainers of Classic winners of the twentieth century. Dick described Hethersett as 'a lovely little colt, a bare 16 hands', but unlike most small horses, he was not precocious. Dick was unable to run him as a two-year-old until the Duke of Edinburgh Stakes at Ascot in October. By then Stan Clayton had lost the job of stable jockey, and Hethersett was ridden by Harry Carr. The ground was very soft, and Hethersett revelled in it and came right away to win by 5 lengths. Afterwards Carr showed what a fine judge he was by saying as he dismounted: 'This will be your Derby horse.' The prophecy was all the more shrewd, because Hethersett was still too immature to figure prominently in his only other race that year, the Timeform Gold Cup (later the Racing Post Trophy) at Doncaster, in which he finished fifth behind Miralgo. He was given 8st 8lbs in the Free Handicap, 13lbs below the top, a clear indication that he had considerable improvement to make to reach Classic standard.

The following spring Dick mentioned to Holliday that he could do with a lead horse for Hethersett in his Classic preparation. On 21 April they were both at Kempton – they won the last race with Proper Pride – when Holliday announced: 'I've got you a lead horse.' It was the seven-year-old Badmash, whom he had bought for 1050 guineas after he had won the selling handicap. Dick was horrified. Badmash was trained by

George Todd, who loved his old platers and kept them going for years, and it was tacitly accepted that nobody bid for them. Dick hastened to see George, explained what had happened and said that he had not even known that the old man was bidding. George was unforgiving. 'Well,' he said, 'when Major Holliday dies there will be no need for them to put "no flowers by request", because he won't get any fucking flowers.'

Nevertheless Dick was able to get Hethersett fit for his first race, the Brighton Derby Trial, on 14 May. Fortunately Cecil Boyd-Rochfort, who had first claim on Harry Carr, had not got a Derby horse that year, so Carr was available for Hethersett, and Dick used to pull out two or three horses early so that Harry could ride Hethersett in his work before Boyd-Rochfort's string appeared on the Heath. There were only three runners for the Brighton Trial, which was run over the full Derby distance, namely River Chanter and Heron, but they had both been weighted within a pound of Hethersett in the Free Handicap, so they were not push-overs. Hethersett beat them both in impressive style, and as a result was made favourite for the Derby, and remained so until the start of the race in spite of a scare when he bruised a foot at exercise the previous week. The senior Newmarket vet Fred Day came to see him, and advised Dick to put a three-quarter shoe on him. This was done, and he was sound after walking for two days. Dick was able to give him a good pipe-opener on the Limekilns the day before the Derby, and he went to Epsom 100 per cent fit.

The race itself was one of the most dramatic and disastrous in the history of the Derby. The descent to Tattenham Corner is always fraught with danger as the moderate horses that have been in the van from the start begin to fall back and are involved in a concertina movement with the better horses that are beginning a forward move. Damaging collisions are usually avoided, but 1962 was the year in which the worst fears of the critics of the race were realised. They had just started to run down the hill, and Dick gave a graphic description of what ensued:

Harry Carr told me afterwards that he was just where he wanted to be, and he hadn't even picked him up. They were just at the place where, if you are on the stands, you lose the jockeys for a moment and you can just see the tops of their caps. I was watching him closely, and suddenly I lost him. I panned my glasses to the front of the field, and then to the back, and still could not find him. Then the loose horses began to appear

There were seven of them, including the Lingfield Derby Trial winner Pindaric and the 2000 Guineas second Romulus, besides Hethersett. It transpired that Romulus had run into the heels of the French horse Crossen, and had fallen to the right in front of Hethersett, who had no chance of avoiding him. The other fallers were involved in the melée that ensued. Harry Carr was badly bruised and shaken, and did not ride in public again for a month. An eye-witness standing on the far side of the course was left with an indelible mental picture of Hethersett going down and Harry standing up in his irons with the reins slipped to the buckle as if he were landing over a big drop in a steeplechase.

In the event the race was won by Larkspur, who gave Vincent O'Brien the first of his six training successes in the Derby, by 2 lengths from the French-trained Arcor, but Dick and the whole racing community were left to speculate whether Hethersett should not have won. Colour was lent to the idea that Hethersett was superior by the fact that he was given 6lbs more than Larkspur in the Free Handicap at the end of the season.

One of Holliday's best attributes was that he took unavoidable reverses very well, and he accepted the bitter disappointment of Hethersett's fall philosophically. Afterwards Brean took him back to the car and gave him a whisky and soda. They then set off to drive back to Yorkshire. Holliday sat in silence until they reached his watering hole, Punch's Hotel at Doncaster, and then he said: 'We'll win the Leger with that horse.'

Hethersett had had a heavy fall and had sustained several nasty cuts, and did not go out of a walk for a month after the Derby.

He was not fully wound up and the ground was rather too firm when he reappeared in the Gordon Stakes at Goodwood at the beginning of August, and he finished only seventh. The going was soft and he was a different horse in the Great Voltigeur Stakes at York three weeks later, and he showed that he was back in form by winning by a short head from his old rival Miralgo. He was ridden by Frank Durr, because Harry Carr was claimed by Boyd-Rochfort to ride Zagreus, who finished last, but Harry was back on him in the St Leger. There was a dry spell after York. The ground at Newmarket became very firm, and Dick went to Sandown to see whether that would be better for his winding-up gallop for the St Leger. On the way back black clouds began to build up ahead, and when he got to Six Mile Bottom the rain began to come down in earnest. The next day Dick was able to work him at Newmarket on good going, and by the time he got to Doncaster the ground was just as he liked it, on the soft side of good.

Hethersett was only fifth favourite for the St Leger, but he gave a majestic display. Carr rode a waiting race, but improved his position steadily when they had turned into the straight. With a quarter of a mile to go Carr was sitting easily, and Bruce Hobbs turned to Dick on the stand and said: 'You've won all right.' Hethersett took the lead a furlong and a half from home and strode away to win by 4 lengths. It was a performance that stamped him as a colt of the highest class. Larkspur was only sixth, but the Derby winner probably did not do himself justice on that occasion. Hethersett ran once more, in the Champion Stakes over a distance of 1¼ miles, which was too short for him, and finished second to the Irish 2000 Guineas winner Arctic Storm.

As a stallion he passed on his liking for soft ground to his best son, the 1969 Derby winner Blakeney. Sadly he did not live long enough for the notion that this was true of most of his progeny to be put to the test. He died of a tumour on the brain at the age of only seven, which left Dick wondering whether the cause may have been due to a trauma suffered in his fall in the Derby.

Holliday's entry into thoroughbred breeding had been just before the outbreak of the First World War when he bought Cleaboy Stud at Mullingar in County Westmeath. Later, when the operation had expanded, the mares were kept for most of the year at Copgrove, and the Sandwich Stud at Newmarket was bought mainly to accommodate the mares that were visiting stallions in the area. The weaned foals were sent to Cleaboy, where the big paddocks enabled them to gallop and develop their athletic ability. The stud manager during Dick's time was Desmond McKeever, a great lover of horses and utterly dedicated to his job. He had been badly wounded on active service, but that had not dimmed his marvellous sense of humour. Dick used to go over for a few days every year to see the yearlings, and became great friends with Desmond and his wife Maureen.

The decisive moment in Holliday's progress as an owner-breeder was at the Doncaster St Leger Yearling Sales in 1932, when he bought the filly by Solario out of Orlass for 1800 guineas. In relation to the low bloodstock values of the time that was a substantial but not excessive sum, because Solario was one of the most popular sires – he was third in the list of winning sires that year – and Orlass, who was then eighteen years old, had already bred six winners, including Shian Mor, a top-class colt who had been third in the Derby. Named Lost Soul, Holliday's purchase did not run as a two-year-old, but won two handicaps over 7 furlongs at Newmarket the following year. Kept in training at four years old, she did not win in ten attempts, but was placed in five races, including the City and Suburban and the Victoria Cup, two of the most competitive handicaps in the calendar.

Lost Soul was to be the foundation mare on whom Holliday's eminence as a breeder was based. She bred seven winners, including four class horses in Nearly, Goldsborough, Saved and the sprinter Dumbarnie, but it was her daughter Phase who was to prove the linchpin that kept the family fortunes rolling. Holliday was a most perspicacious breeder, but it is true that a breeder may have a profound knowledge of horses and thoroughbred pedigrees and still fail unless he has a vital dash of luck at a crucial time. Holliday's decisive slice of luck came in the summer of 1940. Fearful of the immediate prospects for racing in Britain after the fall of France, he offered all his yearlings to Joe McGrath, who had made a great name for himself in Irish business and politics, was a co-founder of the Irish Hospitals Sweep that sponsored the Irish Derby for many years, and was a leading owner-breeder. McGrath went down to Cleaboy, inspected the yearlings, and told Holliday: 'I'll take them all except the filly with the big head.' The filly with the big head was Phase.

Phase herself was a very useful performer, winning three times in the restricted wartime racing at Newmarket. At stud she proved a great broodmare, producing nine winners, including the Oaks winner Neasham Belle, Holliday's first Classic winner, and the Coronation Cup and Champion Stakes winner Narrator. Most importantly from Dick's point of view, she was the great-granddam of Hethersett.

Holliday's breeding policies were well-thought out. He made a conscious decision to use to the full the services of Nearco, the brilliant Italian-bred horse who was unbeaten in fourteen races culminating in victory in what was then the most competitive race in France, the Grand Prix de Paris, and took two shares in him when he was bought by the bookmaker Martin Benson to stand at stud at Newmarket. Nearly, a high class two-year-old bred by Holliday, was a product of his first stud season. Phase had eight foals by him, and they accounted for six of her nine winning offspring, including Neasham Belle, Narrator and Hethersett's granddam Netherton Maid, who was second in the Oaks. The dominance of Nearco and the Orlass family in Holliday's breeding is demonstrated by the fact that in 1962, the year that Hethersett won the St Leger, thirty-three of the fifty-three mares in his stud had Nearco in their pedigrees, while eighteen of them belonged to the Orlass family.

Hugh Lupus, the sire of Hethersett, was a slightly off-beat stallion for Holliday to use. By Djebel and a scion of the powerful French male line of Tourbillon, he won the Irish 2000 Guineas and the Champion Stakes but failed in such supremely testing races as the King George VI and Queen Elizabeth Stakes and the Prix de l'Arc de Triomphe. He was at stud in Ireland, was savage and had poor fertility. After Hethersett had proved his worth on the racecourse Holliday gave this explanation of the mating that had produced him:

(1) I liked Hugh Lupus and considered him a much superior animal than his form showed.
(2) His breeding was a family far from my Orlass family, which I thought might be satisfactory.
(3) I thought on conformation my Orlass mares have the substance and depth that perhaps Hugh Lupus lacked.

He added: 'There are no rules in horse breeding. Theory and practice are far apart': and then, showing a discernible, if slightly malicious, sense of humour for which he was seldom given credit: 'Do not forget the wonderful theories of Mankato (a much respected breeding correspondent), most interesting and most fascinating. But I believe in practice poor Mankato never bred a winner.'

Dick confirmed this pragmatic aspect of Holliday's selection procedures when he wrote: 'He would never keep a moderate or an unsound filly, and in consequence he had a tough and sound breed. I remember we ran a little light-framed filly called Fortune's Darling in heavy going in the Lowther Stakes at the York August Meeting, and she duly won. She wasn't really up to that class, and at the end of the season Major Holliday decided that she was not good enough to breed from and put her in the December Sales. Lord Howard de Walden bought her, and I'm afraid she never did him much good.'

When Hethersett triumphed in the St Leger Dick's time at Newmarket was running out. About the middle of the summer Dick was approached by Jack Colling to see whether he would be interested in taking over at West Ilsley when Colling retired at the end of the season. A tall, handsome man of great charm, always immaculately dressed, Jack Colling had been training at Hodcott House, West Ilsley, a mile to the west of the main Newbury to Oxford road, since 1949. West Ilsley had some of the finest downland gallops in the country, and while he was there Colling won the Oaks for Lord Astor with Ambiguity and had trained a host of other high-class horses like Hornbeam, Indian Twilight, Rosalba and Escort. The idea of taking over such an establishment was clearly attractive. Lord Astor's younger brother Jakie (later Sir John) Astor had recently bought the place from Colling, and he proposed that Dick should go there as a public trainer, but on a salary. Holliday was a very old man, he could not go on for ever, and Dick had no contract. After talking things over with Sheilah, Dick went to see Holliday, told him about the offer, and said that if he would raise his salary and give him a contract he would stay. Holliday refused, so Dick gave in his notice.

Dick always acknowledged the debt he owed to Holliday, who had boldly taken a chance by handing over his stable of high-class horses to an inexperienced trainer. The gamble had paid rich dividends for both of them. In Dick's time Holliday enjoyed a blaze of success and was leading owner twice, while Dick emerged with the reputation of one of the finest trainers in the land. However, Holliday did not have a personality that inspired affection, and he could be mean and vindictive. His lack of graciousness was epitomised by his remark that all his trainers were the same, they arrived on bicycles and left in Bentleys, which did not even have the merit of being true, and was certainly ungenerous.

Holliday's spitefulness was in evidence typically in the affair of the gardener. In the summer of 1964 the gardener at

Lagrange was very rude to Sheilah, and Dick sacked him. On hearing of the dismissal Holliday told Dick to take him back because he had worked for him for many years. Dick had no doubt that Holliday had given the order purely because he had given his notice. At first he was inclined to refuse, but the St Leger with Hethersett's live winning chance was looming up, so Dick had second thoughts and decided to bite the bullet and reinstate the man. In another matter Dick was not so amenable. An old man called Ned McCormack worked in the yard. He was too old to ride out and just did odd jobs. Holliday thought it would be a good idea if he went down to Sunnyside to bring in the coals for Mrs Jackson and help generally, and gave him one of his old suits to wear in the house. Before long Ned died and Holliday said to Dick: 'I want you to get back that suit I gave Ned.' Dick drew the line at that and refused.

There were plenty of minor recreational pleasures at Newmarket, like taking the dogs to hunt rabbits in the paddocks round Kremlin House; not many rabbits were caught, but Dick and Sheilah enjoyed it. Dick and Fergie had a bit of rough shooting at Borough Green a few miles out of Newmarket where they used to go on Saturday afternoons and shoot for the pot. Sheilah and Fergie's wife Judy used to beat the hedges and they all, including the dogs, had a good time. That was the kind of shooting that Dick enjoyed. He never had much time for shooting driven pheasants, especially if they were great fat birds that could hardly leave the ground.

The annual December Sales were always a time for socialising, and the Herns would have a house full of people staying. One guest was the well-known Irish trainer Charlie Weld, the father of the leading amateur rider and afterwards leading trainer Dermot Weld. Charlie Weld amazed the Herns the first time he came by the amount of drink he could put away and still walk straight up the stairs to bed. Owing to the number of guests Charlie was sharing a room with his compatriot George Malone, and when George followed him up to bed he found him laying out his suit on the floor. 'You would have thought that people like the Herns would have had a wardrobe,' he said. He had failed to notice that the cupboards were built in. When he left he said: 'Next year I'll bring you a goose,' and was as good as his word.

George Beeby, who had employed Sheilah as his secretary in the early 1950s, was a regular sales-time guest. A man of immense good humour, he loved a game of poker, and was just the same, win or lose. If he won a hand he would say: 'That's not so ducking fusty!' His shoes were always highly polished. Once when Dick and Sheilah were going up to bed after letting out the dogs and tidying up downstairs, they saw George's shoes outside his door. They looked at each other, picked them up, took them downstairs, cleaned them and put them back.

As a farewell to Newmarket the Herns gave a fancy-dress party at Worlington Golf Club jointly with Judy Sutherland, who had by then divorced Fergie. Everyone had to come dressed to represent the name of a racehorse. Sheilah made an extremely attractive Little Redskin, while Dick strutted the stage as Pirate King, who had won the St James's Palace Stakes. Teddy Lambton, dressed as a monk, was Langton Abbot, who had made his name and fortune when he won the Lincolnshire Handicap in 1946. Tom Jones, with a terrible false tit pinned to his dinner jacket, was Tom Tit. Ken Furbank, who farmed potatoes and sugar beet near Huntingdon and was a very keen racing man, came as PC49, and was delighted with his disguise when someone hailed him as he was walking into the club and asked where he should park his car.

Jack Jarvis, who had been the first of the old school of trainers to welcome the Herns to Newmarket, was also the last to bid them goodbye. He gave a cocktail party for them at which he presented them with a very fine visitor's book which had been signed by all the Newmarket trainers. It was a generous tribute to the way Newmarket, after giving them the mixed reception usually extended to newcomers, had taken the Herns to their hearts in the five years they had lived in the town.

On the professional side Dick's time at Newmarket concluded on the highest possible note when Dick was champion trainer for the first time. There was a pulsating finish. Dick, whose horses had earned £70,206, came to the last day of the season at Manchester a mere £922 in front of his nearest rival Harry Wragg, and victory for Harry's runner Espresso in the November Handicap would have made him an easy winner. Espresso was top-weight and the class horse of the race, but gallantly as he tried, the best he could manage was fourth place in the huge field of thirty-five. So the trainers' championship was Dick's, while his patron Major Lionel Brook Holliday was able to rejoice in the titles of leading breeder and of leading owner for the second year running.

FIVE

WEST ILSLEY – THE ASTOR ERA

THE BERKSHIRE DOWNS contain a remarkable concentration of training stables. Lambourn proclaims itself 'The Valley of the Racehorse' and it has a larger racehorse population that any other training centre in Britain apart from Newmarket. However it is by no means the only village involved in training. Hinton Parva, Kingston Lisle, Sparsholt, Childrey, the Letcombes, East Hendred, Blewbury, Compton and the Ilsleys all contain, or have contained, racing stables. Most of them are on the low-lying fringes of the Downs, with gallops on the Downs. The Ilsleys, a dozen miles east of Lambourn, are rare, though not unique, in being situated in the heart of the Downs themselves.

Racehorses have been trained at East Ilsley for at least a century and a half. James Dover trained Lord Lyon there to win the Triple Crown in 1866. There is a strip of ground beyond the Ridgeway, the prehistoric track that crosses the Downs on its route from the coast near Dover to Ilchester in Somerset, which is still known as 'the Lord Lyon gallop', though it has been under the plough for as long as anyone now alive can remember. The Ilsleys are a mile and a half apart. From East Ilsley the linking road runs under a bridge carrying the busy A34, climbs onto the southward spur of Hodcott Down, and then dips steeply into West Ilsley, which is in a bowl set in the midst of the Downs.

A private road to West Ilsley Stables leads to the south from the eastern end of the village. It passes a range of boxes called in Dick's time 'The Stud' but now 'The Keeper's Stables' and leaves a couple of well-fenced paddocks on the right before ending, after a third of a mile, at the main yard and Hodcott House. The house is a large, rambling, red brick, virginia creeper-clad building across the road from the stables. The main yard is a rectangle of solid red-brick boxes with dark-red tiled roofs, and on the south side there are flats for married lads above the boxes. Outside the main yard various ancillary ranges of boxes have been erected at various times. One, a range of a dozen boxes in similar style to the main yard, with tack room and feed barn, was put up by Dick as a fall-back in case his principal training operation should fail. Beyond the main yard a track runs up the hill to cross the road half a mile east of the village and give access to Hodcott Down and the winter gallops. The summer gallops can be reached either via Hodcott Down and the south side of the Ridgeway, or by walking the horses through the village and turning right up a track at the western end.

High-class horses were trained at West Ilsley throughout the twentieth century. Frank Barling was there for most of the first two decades before moving to Newmarket. Dick Gooch followed from 1919 to 1938. Eric Stedall was next. Dick's immediate predecessor Jack Colling moved there from Newmarket in 1949. Colling was very good looking, soft spoken, charming and a brilliant shot. He specialised in exploiting the merits of geldings, whose durability and reliability he valued highly. Among the best of them were Portobello, who was unbeaten as a two-year-old and won the championship sprints, the July Cup and the Nunthorpe Stakes, in 1939; and, at the opposite end of the distance scale, the dour stayer Grey of Falloden with whom he won five races, including the Ripon St Leger Trial in 1962, before handing him over to Dick. Another of Jack Colling's characteristics as a trainer was his shrewdness in placing moderate horses to win races at meetings all over the country, especially in his native Yorkshire. He was equally adept at preparing good class horses like Bellacose, Portobello, Ambiguity and Hornbeam when they came his way. In his youthful days as a jockey he had ridden Blink to finish second in the substitute Derby of 1918 for Major Waldorf Astor, later the second Viscount Astor. For most of his life Astor had his horses with Alec Taylor and Joe Lawson at Manton, but he renewed his association with Colling by sending him horses during the Second World War. Appropriately the best horse he trained for Waldorf was the supremely tough gelding High Stakes, who won a total of thirty-four races and, in spite of his habit of carrying his head in the air, was as game as they come.

The Astors were fabulously rich. They made their fortune in the first half of the nineteenth century from the fur trade, importing tea and coffee, trading with China and heavy investment in real estate in New York. At one time it was estimated that one-fifteenth of all the wealth in private hands in the United States was owned by the Astors. Waldorf's father, later the first Viscount, settled in England, and Waldorf completed his education at Oxford. While at the university he became fascinated by the thoroughbred, and purchased for a small investment the mares that were to be the foundation of his hugely successful Cliveden Stud. The first was Conjure, purchased for £100 with the original intention of breeding jumpers, and he also bought Popinjay for a bargain price. The sixth Earl of Rosebery described the transaction to a correspondent half a century later:

> Astor was at Oxford with my brother, and asked him whether he thought my father would sell him Popinjay. My father said he could have her for £1000, but Astor said he only had £800. This amused my father so much, as the Astors were the richest family in the world at the time, that he let him have her for £800. He only sold her because she made a bad noise, even as a two-year-old.

Whether she transmitted her wind infirmity to some of her descendants or not, Popinjay was certainly a very influential mare, and her descendants in the direct female line included the Oaks winners Pogrom and Saucy Sue and the St Leger winners Book Law and Provoke. For her part, Conjure was the dam of Winkipop, who gave Waldorf his first Classic victory when she won the 1000 Guineas in 1910, and was the ancestress in the direct female line of the 2000 Guineas winner Court Martial and the three Oaks winners Pennycomequick, Short Story and Ambiguity. Success in bloodstock breeding depends on a mixture of luck, good judgement and sound stud practice in varying proportions. Luck obviously played an important part in Waldorf's selection of foundation mares.

The number five figured largely in Waldorf's life. His wife Nancy was one of five beautiful Langhorne sisters from Virginia; he had five winners of the Oaks and five seconds, though never a winner, in the Derby; and he had five children, of whom William (Bill, the third Viscount) was the eldest and John Jacob (Jakie) was the youngest. Nancy was articulate, formidable and often impossible, and she was an unsympathetic mother. She was the first woman Member of Parliament and, as the chatelaine of Cliveden, their seat on the Thames near Maidenhead, entertained the rich and the famous and presided over the 'Cliveden Set' that was supposed, in the main erroneously it now seems, to be a hotbed of political intrigue.

Two years before his death in 1952 Waldorf gave up all his racing and breeding interests and divided his bloodstock between his eldest and youngest sons. Bill and Jakie tossed for first pick, and after that made alternate choices. As the heir, Bill retained the Cliveden Stud, while Jakie moved his share of the bloodstock to a new stud which he had created at Hatley Park, his home at Sandy in Bedfordshire. Although Bill continued the racing and breeding operation, of the two brothers Jakie was the more dedicated to the thoroughbred, and kept up to twenty-five mares at Hatley Park. When the Cliveden Stud was sold to Louis

Freedman after Bill's death in 1966, it was in a sadly run-down condition.

Jakie rode as an amateur both on the flat and over jumps. The Second World War had interrupted his racing activities. He served in 'Phantom', the GHQ reconnaissance regiment, rising to the rank of major, and was at one time the squadron-leader of John Hislop, the future owner-breeder of the 'Horse of the Century' Brigadier Gerard, trained by Dick. After the war he went into politics, and for eight years represented his mother's former constituency, Plymouth Sutton, in Parliament. His attachment to politics seemed to be somewhat lukewarm, and in the end the call of racing became too strong. He was elected to the Jockey Club, then the ruling body of racing, and was one of its most active and progressive members. He also served racing as a member of the short-lived Turf Board, as a member of the Racecourse Betting Control Board and as a member of the Totalisator Board. His prominence in the world of breeding was demonstrated by the fact that he was President of the Thorough-bred Breeders Association, holding that post for a five-year term. In view of his family connection with the place and his own dedication to racing, it was only natural that he should purchase the West Ilsley stables when Jack Colling decided to retire at the end of the 1962 season.

Once, when she was trying to console a friend who was complaining that her son was chinless, Nancy Astor remarked that she should not worry; Jakie was chinless too, but he was very intelligent. Her description of his appearance was both unmotherly and inaccurate, but she was right about his intelligence. He was also a man of vision and compassion. He realised that to attract and keep first-class staff in a remote place like West Ilsley it was essential to provide them with good housing. Accordingly he embarked on an ambitious building programme which resulted in twenty-five new cottages in the village. Dick played his part by employing on a permanent basis a foreman, a decorator and a plumber with the responsibility of ensuring that everything was in order. Sheilah made a point of visiting all the families at regular intervals and acting on any complaints. It was Dick's dictum that if the wives are happy, then the men are content too.

Dick was fortunate in inheriting first-class staff from Colling. Frank Haslam, the Head Man, retired at the same time, but continued to come into the yard at stable time. He was very good on legs, and would feel any leg that was doubtful. His son Buster was travelling head man. He was by far the senior man in the yard, but he wanted to continue to travel. As a result Dick promoted Geordie Campbell, the second travelling man, to be head man, and these appointments proved entirely satisfactory. Geordie remained in the job for thirty-three years, until Dick's final year as trainer, and Dick said of him: 'Nobody could have had a more hardworking, conscientious or loyal man. The yard was his life.' He did not believe that Buster would have been so successful, because he lacked Geordie's man-management skills. On the other hand Buster was above reproach as travelling head man. Always smartly turned out himself, he turned out his horses in equally immaculate condition, and never missed a thing if a horse was slightly off colour or unsound. He slipped up only once, when he forgot to declare blinkers for a horse. His oversight upset him so much that he did not speak for a week. When the time came to leave West Ilsley in 1990 he could not bear the thought of starting afresh at a new place, and hanged himself down at the boxes known as The Stud. His death came as a grievous shock to the Herns and everyone in the yard.

Another first-rate man who had been with Jack Colling was Vic Chitty. He stayed with Dick throughout his time at West Ilsley and moved with the horses when they were transferred to Kingwood at the end of 1990. He became Dick's head man for one season when Geordie retired, and carried on as head man to Dick's successor Marcus Tregoning. Dick himself engaged Reg Cartwright as a stableman soon after he arrived at West

Ilsley. Reg had been leading apprentice in Ireland, but had been working for several years at the nearby Atomic Energy Research Establishment at Harwell before coming to Dick. He was a first-rate work rider, and Dick took out a licence for him to ride in public, giving him a number of mounts.

Sheilah had no responsibility for hiring and firing staff, but she did once exercise a power of veto. A very attractive girl with long blonde hair had applied for a job in the yard. Dick was interviewing her in his office, and she was standing in front of his desk with her back to the window. Dick was about to tell her that she was engaged, when he noticed Sheilah passing outside, and as she passed the window she gave a barely perceptible shake of her head. The blonde did not get the job.

Another legacy from the Jack Colling days was the retention of Joe Mercer as first jockey. Joe had been with Colling since 1953, when he won the Oaks for Bill Astor on Ambiguity, and he remained with Dick for a further fifteen years. Dick paid him this warm tribute many years later:

> Joe was absolutely first class and a great stylist. I never knew him to hit a horse unnecessarily and very often, if he knew a horse was doing his best, he didn't even pick up his stick. In any case, he would never pick up his stick until he had really pushed the horse for some way. Many of the jockeys riding today should be made to watch films of Joe riding a finish.

A final asset which Dick received from Colling was the owners, who all stayed on. In addition to the Astor brothers they included Lord Durham, Lady Ashcombe, Lord Hambledon and Lord Rotherwick. Dick summed them up: 'They were all non-betting owners, many breeding their own horses. They were a delightful lot to train for.' There were sixty-two horses in the stable for the start of the 1963 season, but in the course of years the size of the string increased to over a hundred.

One of the first problems that the Herns had to face at West Ilsley was their own accommodation. One of the conditions of the sale to Jakie was that Jack Colling had the right to stay in Hodcott House for the rest of his life. Various options were considered, including building a new house in the paddock adjoining the yard. Plans were drawn up and approved, and work was about to begin when The Old Rectory, immediately beyond All Saints Church in the middle of the village, came on the market. It was a substantial house and suitable in every respect. Jakie bought it, together with two adjoining paddocks, and it became the Herns permanent home.

The weather gave the Herns a chilly welcome to West Ilsley. One morning just after Christmas 1962 Dick looked up at the sky and saw skein after skein of geese, all very high and flying south. 'They knew what was coming,' said Dick. Snow began to fall before the New Year, and for weeks lay 9 inches deep on the Downs. It is in such circumstances that good neighbourliness really counts, and Dick was lucky to have two such good neighbours as the local farmers Norman Hinds and Jimmy Gore. Norman used to collect the milk and the papers for the whole village every morning from East Ilsley, going across the fields on a tractor. He was a keen racing man and for years had a horse or two in training with John Beary at East Hendred, including Loppylugs, who won the Cambridgeshire in 1956. The old horse was in retirement at Rowles Farm when Dick arrived, and Norman offered him to Dick as a hack. Dick tried him, but soon decided that it would take too long to turn him into a useful hack.

A straw bed was laid out on the green in front of Hodcott House for the horses to walk round during the winter of 1962–63, and Jimmy Gore used to take a rotovator up on the Downs and rotovate a piece of ground 6 furlongs long. The horses would trot up the incline, walk down, take a turn at the bottom and then trot up again. It got their backs down and kept them pretty fit. They did not have a canter until the first week in March, but after so much trotting uphill in deep snow it did not take long to get them ready to race. Easter was late that year, in mid-April, and Dick saddled Grey of Falloden to win the important long-distance handicap, the Queen's Prize, at Kempton on Easter Monday. Darling Boy, the best horse in the stable, was also soon in action. He won a handicap at Newmarket two days after the Queen's Prize, and returned to Newmarket two weeks later to gain a much more significant victory in the Jockey Club Stakes. Hethersett, whom Dick had trained to win the St Leger for Major Holliday the previous September, was an odds-on favourite. He had been provided with a pacemaker, High Flown, and when he took the lead 3 furlongs from home the race looked all over. However, Joe Mercer was biding his time, and when he asked Darling Boy for his effort with a furlong to go he outpaced Hethersett to win cleverly by a length. These victories were eminently satisfying, because Darling Boy was owned by Jakie Astor, the proprietor of the West Ilsley stables, and Grey of Falloden was owned by his brother Bill. Without any spectacular achievements, the results of the 1963 season could be regarded as a quietly pleasing start to Dick's occupation of West Ilsley. The sixty-two successes represented the extremely high average of a win for every horse in the stable, while the stakes earnings of £39,719 gave him a respectable thirteenth place in the list of winning trainers.

Dick was learning to appreciate the excellence of the West Ilsley gallops. The summer gallop was on the Downs north-west of the village, while the winter gallop was east of the village on Hodcott Down and much closer to the yard. Jack Colling gave Dick one valuable piece of advice: 'Never roll the summer gallops.' If they were not rolled, they never lost the resilience of the old turf that had taken centuries to build up. They have to be repaired by hand and must not be used when the weather is too wet. The winter gallops were of a completely different texture. They could be cut up in the spring and autumn, chain harrowed and rolled, and they would recover well. If there was a rainy spell in summer, Dick would switch back to the winter gallops for a few days. Dick compared the training facilities very favourably to the gallops he had become accustomed to at Newmarket:

> Having come from Newmarket with all the strings passing each other and having to queue at the bottom of Warren Hill in the spring of the year, I found it was lovely to be able to do exactly as I liked on the Hodcott Downs. If you had a horse just recovering from a bruised foot, you could canter him on the best going. You can't do that sort of thing at Newmarket. Of course they have a number of all-weather gallops there now, made of every sort of material, but I don't think the grass gallops are anything like as good as they were forty years ago because there are so many horses in training there.

The results in 1964 indicated that the fortunes of the stable were moving in the right direction as, although the number of wins dropped to forty-three, the stakes winnings rose to £49,161 and lifted Dick to ninth place in the list of winning trainers. The main strength of the stable was in stayers. Tree Leopard gained a hard-earned victory in the Goodwood Stakes, but the real hero was Grey of Falloden, who won four races and emerged as a top-class stayer through his last two victories in the Doncaster Cup and the Cesarewitch. At Doncaster Joe Mercer brought him very late to beat Raise You Ten, who had recently won the Goodwood Cup, by ¾ of a length. His winning margin in the Cesarewitch was again ¾ of a length, and the magnitude of his achievement is indicated by the fact that a 3lb penalty had increased his weight to 9st 6lbs, 1lb more than the previous record-winning weight carried by Willonyx in 1911 in the most testing long-distance handicap in the Calendar. It was a most gallant performance, as he was giving 16lbs to the second horse Magic Court, who had won the Champion Hurdle the previous March.

Typically, as he had been trained by Jack Colling, Grey of Falloden was a gelding; and typically, as he was a product of Cliveden Stud, he was on the small side. Dick found that the horses bred at Cliveden tended to be small but sound, whereas the horses bred by Jakie on the clay land at Hatley Park tended to be big but much less sound. Dick suggested that Jakie should transfer all his young stock to Warren Stud at Newmarket, which he also owned; but after having had the soil and the water at Hatley tested, Jakie turned down the suggestion. Years later, when he cut down his breeding interests drastically, Jakie did concentrate his bloodstock at Warren Stud, and Dick found that they had fewer leg problems as a consequence.

Although his image in the public eye was tarnished by association with the Cliveden sex scandals in which Stephen Ward and the two young temptresses Christine Keeler and Mandy Rice-Davies were among the principals, Bill Astor was an exceptionally kind man of whom Dick was very fond. He was so delighted by the Cesarewitch victory that he wanted to have a painting of the finish, and asked Dick whether he could recommend an artist. Dick said that he thought Peter Biegel would do a good job, and he was commissioned to paint the picture. He went to West Ilsley and made a sketch of Grey of Falloden, and then asked Dick whether he could get him some photographs of the finish. These had all been taken from the stands, looking out across the heath. 'That won't make a very good background,' said Biegel. So he turned the picture round so that the stands were in the background. He went to Newmarket to paint the stands, and then to Kempton on a busy day to paint in the crowd.

When the picture was finished Biegel and the Herns were invited to lunch at Cliveden. Biegel came up to West Ilsley, and they went on to Cliveden together. While they were having drinks in the hall before lunch, Bill said to Biegel: 'Now then, bring in the picture.' Biegel went out to his car and fetched the picture, which he propped on a chair. They all admired it. 'Right,' said Bill, 'bring in the other picture.' Biegel went out again and returned with another, almost identical, picture, which he also propped on a chair. 'Now,' Bill said to Dick, 'which do you like? Which do you think is the better picture?' Dick pointed to one of them, and said that he slightly preferred it because it had one more horse in it, Herbert Blagrave's Chinese Lacquer, who was fourth. 'Right,' said Bill, 'then that one is yours.' It was the first inkling that Dick had had that he was to be given a picture, and he was very touched by the gesture. The picture was hung in an honoured position in Dick's dining-room, where it is to this day.

Tree Leopard was owned and bred by Lord Durham, another owner whom Dick held in high regard. He asked Dick to go down to the Ashley Heath Stud at Newmarket and see his year-lings. He went on a Saturday afternoon, but when he arrived he found that the stud groom Adamson was drunk – so drunk that he could not remember the names of the mares or anything about the yearlings. Dick pondered a long time what he should do, and decided finally that it was his duty to tell Durham. To his surprise, Durham took the information very calmly. 'Oh yes,' he said, 'Adamson does like to take a drink on a Saturday, but he has worked for me for a long time, so I know his little ways.'

If the results of the 1964 season indicated that the fortunes of the West Ilsley stable were on the upgrade, the 1965 season showed further improvement and Dick ended up in third place in the list of winning trainers with thirty-eight races won of a value of £66,416. It was the year of Provoke and Craighouse. They had both been backward as two-year-olds, Provoke run-ning only once and Craighouse not at all. Provoke had a lot of trouble with tiny splints about the size of a pea, and it was not until the middle of his three-year-old season that he toughened up. He was beaten in his first two races before gaining his first success in a maiden race over 13 furlongs at Newbury in late June, and he was succcessful again in another minor race over 1½ miles at Ascot a month later. He next went to the York August Meeting, where he won the Melrose Handicap over 1¾ miles in a desperate finish. He prevailed by a head over Santa Vimy, who had been considered unbeatable by her trainer, the big handicap specialist Sam Hall, with the rest of the field a long way behind. It was after that race that the decision was made to let Provoke take his chance in the St Leger.

It was a bold decision, because the final Classic race seemed to be at the mercy of Meadow Court, who had proved himself a top-class colt by winning the Irish Derby and the King George VI and Queen Elizabeth Stakes, performances far superior to anything that Provoke had yet accomplished. Naturally he was a very hot favourite, starting at 11–4 on. The night before the St Leger the Herns were staying at Punches Hotel with Joe and Ann Mercer. After dinner they sat down to play cards, and could hear the rain teeming down and drumming on the window panes. This was music to their ears, because Provoke loved soft ground. The rain continued all night, the next morning, and during the afternoon, and by the time the St Leger was off at 3.18 the ground was absolutely saturated. The jockeys' colours were so covered in mud that they were almost indistinguishable; when the runners loomed out of the murk 2 furlongs from home one horse was far in front, and the commentator assumed that it was Meadow Court and called him; but Dick knew his own horse and was not fooled, and with growing excitement watched Provoke gallop strongly all the way to the line to beat Meadow Court by 10 lengths.

The race threw up several statistical oddities. Provoke's winning time of 3 minutes 18.2 seconds was the slowest of the century, which was hardly suprising in view of the conditions and did not detract from the merit of his performance. His starting price of 28–1 was the longest of any St Leger winner since Royal Lancer, who started at 33–1 in 1922; and Meadow Court's starting price was the shortest of any St Leger favourite since Bahram started at the same price, and won, in 1935. The result gave Dick a great thrill, because Provoke was owned and bred by Jakie Astor, who had engaged him as trainer at West Ilsley in the first place. It was a triumph for one of the original Astor stud families, because Provoke was by Aureole out of

Tantalizer, who traced her pedigree back to Popinjay in the female line.

Counting chickens before they are hatched is a dangerous game in racing. Paddy Prendergast, the trainer of Meadow Court, and Frankie More-O'Ferrall, who managed the colt for the Canadians Max Bell and Frank McMahon and 'the old groaner' Bing Crosby, had been so sure that victory was in their grasp that they had arranged a celebratory party at Punches Hotel on the night after the race. In spite of the defeat the party was still on, and they showed their good sportsmanship by inviting the Herns to join them.

Ten days later it was the turn of Bill Astor to win a Classic race when Dick saddled Craighouse for the Irish St Leger at the Curragh, where he was Dick's first runner in Ireland. Craighouse had had even less racing than Provoke, as he did not run at all as a two-year-old and this was only the fourth race of his career. He had begun by winning the Wood Ditton Stakes, for horses that had never run, at the Newmarket Craven Meeting. He had been successful again in the Hackwood Stakes over 1¼ miles at Newbury in July, and then finished third in the Great Voltigeur Stakes, the principal St Leger trial, at York in August. Despite his lack of experience, he was a convincing winner of the Irish St Leger, beating another British-trained runner, Alcalde, by 2 lengths.

P. G. Wodehouse remarked that it is just when things seem to be going splendidly that Fate creeps up behind you with the piece of lead piping. The year 1966 opened with bright prospects at West Ilsley, and the expectation that Provoke and Craighouse wouild carry all before them in the important long-distance races. As matters turned out, Craighouse ran only once, unplaced in the Paradise Stakes at Ascot in April, and Provoke never got to the racecourse at all. The whole season was calamitous. The reason was the onset of the dreaded virus. In those days very little was known about equine viruses. No vaccine was available to give protection against equine 'flu. There was no blood testing, and the endoscope was unknown. However, it was not 'flu that laid the West Ilsley horses low. Equine 'flu produces easily observable symptoms – fever, watery nasal discharge, persistent coughing, shivering and loss of appetite. The condition known simply as 'the virus' is insidious and far more sinister, leaving horses apparently healthy but incapable of sustained physical effort. An affected horse could run well in a race up to the point when he was asked to quicken, but he would then become lifeless and fade away to nothing. Others had more definite symptoms: they lacked energy, became dull in their coats and had slightly drippy noses. Worst of all, in 1966 it was not understood that the only effective remedial action was to shut up, give the horses complete rest and wait for the disease to burn itself out. Any attempt to keep an infected horse in work could result in permanent damage to its health.

All sorts of things were done to try and find out the cause, but to no avail. Many fanciful theories were put forward. One was that the pigs which Dick kept on the muck heap to fatten and sell for the benefit of the lads' Christmas boxes were to blame. He got rid of the pigs, but the virus persisted. Fumigation and other methods of disinfection were tried; but still the effects of the virus persisted. It was a very frustrating time for the owners, the lads and everyone connected with the yard. Although 1966 saw the impact of the virus at its height, with only £9945 in winning stakes earned and a drop to fifty-sixth place in the trainers list for Dick, three years were to pass before the yard was clear of infection. It was lucky that the owners were a very patient collection of people, who understood horses and their problems and gave full support and sympathy to the trainer.

Provoke and Craighouse were left with their potential only half fulfilled. They were both sold to Russia as stallions. They were flown to Moscow, but there was no unloading ramp for horses at the airport. Some wire netting covered in straw was placed on top of the passenger ramp, and both horses walked down safely. Neither lasted long. Provoke slipped on an icy road, broke a hind leg and had to be destroyed, and Craighouse also died young.

The only factor mitigating the gloom of 1966 was an approach from the Queen's stud manager Richard Shelley, who said that the Queen would like to send him six yearlings that autumn. Sir Cecil Boyd-Rochfort, who had been her principal trainer, was retiring at the end of the season, and fresh arrangements for her horses had to be made. Ian Balding already trained some, and Dick was to be added to the team. It was a lovely surprise, and Dick accepted the new responsibility as a great honour. The Queen had no racing manager as such until the appointment of Lord Porchester (the seventh Earl of Carnarvon on the death of his father eighteen years later) in 1969, and for the time being the line of communication was either through Richard Shelley or directly to the Queen herself.

Although the stable was not free of the virus in 1967, the effects were less catastrophic and Dick recovered to sixth place in the trainers list with sixty wins worth £47,161. The star performer was Remand, a chesnut colt bred and owned by Jakie Astor, by Alcide out of Admonish by Chanteur II. He did not come from one of the old Clivedon families, but from a mainly French family which had produced such good horses as the French Derby and Prix de l'Arc de Triomphe winner Le Pacha. Admonish was a full sister of Escort, who had won the Royal Lodge Stakes in 1961 and finished fourth in the Derby the following year. Thus Remand had all the pedigree credentials to be top class and Dick described him as 'a really good one, a proper horse.' He was unbeaten as a two-year-old that season. Joe Mercer rode him when he made his debut in a race over 6 furlongs at Salisbury on 9 August, but broke two vertebrae in his neck when Native Copper slipped up and fell in a race at Folkestone five days later. The fall put Joe out of action for the rest of the season and may have deprived him of the jockeys' championship, because he was in front with seventy-eight wins at the time of the accident. Lester Piggott rode Remand in his two subsequent races that year. He rode a typically cheeky race on him in the Solario Stakes, never letting him off the bridle before winning by ¾ of a length. Remand was equally impressive when winning the Royal Lodge Stakes over a mile at Ascot in September, coming from behind to beat Riboccare by 4 lengths in effortless fashion. His excellence was reflected in his Free Handicap mark of 9st 5lbs, only 2lbs below the leader Petingo. He was obviously a leading candidate for the Derby in 1968.

Remand did very well over the winter, and Joe Mercer, fully recovered from his neck injury, was fit to ride him when he reappeared in the Chester Vase. The race is always regarded as a good test for Epsom, and Remand showed that he was well in line for a bid for the Derby when he outpaced the enormous Connaught in the last furlong to win by ½ a length. That performance was eminently satisfactory, but Dick gave a graphic account of the disappointing sequel:

> Shortly afterwards a number of the horses were sick, and it was obvious that we had a recurrence of the virus problem. We isolated Remand down at the Stud, but he must have caught the virus just before going to Epsom. In the paddock he seemed to have suddenly lost a lot of weight, his coat was standing up like a hedgehog and he looked terrible. In that condition how he managed to run such a good race and finish fourth only 4 lengths behind Sir Ivor and Connaught I shall never know. The race took so much out of him that he was barely recognisable the next day, and had lost stones. It was quite impossible to train him again as a three-year-old and, having put up such a marvellous performance when under the weather, he was never the same again.

Although of course Sir Ivor was a very high-class horse who had won the 2000 Guineas and produced a brilliant burst of speed in the last furlong to win at Epsom, Remand had beaten Connaught at Chester and must have gone very close to winning if

116

he had been at his best. It was a great shame, as he represented Jakie's best chance of winning the Derby.

———————

By the autumn of 1968 Remand's feet had become so shelly that it was impossible to keep any shoes in him. It was before the days of stick-on shoes. Jakie had him sent up to Hatley, and he used to go out to exercise on the beautiful turf in the park. Ted Fitzsimmons, who had come from Newmarket with Dick and did the horse, went up to Hatley Park with his wife Marie to look after him, and spent the winter there. By the spring Remand's feet had grown again and it was possible to shoe him properly. He ran three times as a four-year-old, winning the Westbury Stakes at Sandown in May and the Cumberland Lodge Stakes, in which he beat a good field, at Ascot in September, but he was only fourth in the Coronation Cup over the Derby course in between times, and was certainly not the horse he had been before the virus hit him.

In the autumn of 1968 Brook Holliday, who had inherited the bloodstock on the death of his father, Dick's former patron Major Lionel Holliday, sent some yearlings to be trained at West Ilsley. They included the beautiful bay filly Highest Hopes, who turned out to be the best horse sired by Hethersett in his short stud career. She ran only once as a two-year-old, and was then the easy winner of a maiden race from a big field at Newbury in September. She was clearly very promising.

Joe Mercer was absent at the beginning of 1970. He had been riding in India during the winter, but found that exchange regulations prevented him taking his earnings out of the country when it was time to return home. He invested in diamonds to circumvent the regulations, but unfortunately he was caught and sentenced to three months in prison. His incarceration passed relatively pleasantly, as he was employed as the prison governor's gardener, but it was not the same thing as riding high-class horses in England. His great friend Jimmy Lindley deputised on

117

Dick's horses as often as his commitments to Jeremy Tree, who had first claim on him, permitted and went down to West Ilsley twice a week to ride work. Jimmy was on Highest Hopes in her first three races that year.

Her reappearance was in the Ascot 1000 Guineas Trial on 11 April, in which she outclassed her opponents to win by 8 lengths. The race took so little out of her that she ran again in the Fred Darling Stakes at Newbury six days later. The race proved a farce, as the first two, Highest Hopes and Humble Duty, passed the post with their jockeys sitting stock still. Jimmy Lindley on Highest Hopes was perfectly justified, as there was no point in giving the filly a harder race than was necessary to win. Lester Piggott on Humble Duty, who had been the champion two-year-old filly of 1969, had the pretext that she was not fully wound up and hated the prevailing heavy ground. When Lester decided to ride a horse with forbearance there were no half measures. If the race had been run thirty years later, there is no doubt that the Stewards would have asked some searching questions, and the spectators who witnessed the unedifying spectacle were surely entitled to an explanation.

The two fillies met again in the 1000 Guineas, in which they started joint favourites at 3–1. This time the result was very different. Humble Duty won comfortably, but Highest Hopes, after being prominent in the early stages, dropped right out and finished tailed off. Tests revealed nothing the matter with her, but her running was too bad to be true, and both Dick and Jimmy were profoundly suspicious that she had been got at. Dick gave her a rest and time to recover, and did not run her again until the French Oaks in the middle of June, by which time Joe Mercer was back in action. The ground had dried up considerably by then, and Dick wanted to work her somewhere on a watered gallop to complete her preparation. He suggested that he should take her to Newbury racecourse, only 9 miles away, but Brook replied: 'Why don't you bring her to Newmarket? They've got a watered gallop there.' Dick agreed reluctantly.

It meant sending her overnight, with a lead horse, two lads and a travelling man, and going up to Newmarket himself. Brook came down from Yorkshire. She worked well, and the gallop put her just right for her visit to Chantilly, where she ran a terrific race, finishing strongly to be second 2 lengths behind the Irish filly Sweet Mimosa.

Highest Hopes returned to France a month later for the Prix Eugène Adam at Saint Cloud, a race usually contested exclusively by colts, and won decisively from the top-class four-year-old Caro. She ran next in the Yorkshire Oaks at the York August meeting, in which she was beaten by the Oaks winner Lupe, but was back in France for the Prix Vermeille, a race classified Group 1 when the international Pattern race system was introduced the next year, and gave the finest performance of her career to win by 2 lengths from Miss Dan. The value of the form was enhanced when next time out Miss Dan was third in the heady company of the Prix de l'Arc de Triomphe, and the win of Highest Hopes was rendered all the more satisfactory by the fact that her two previous conquerors Sweet Mimosa and Lupe were unplaced.

The Prix Vermeille was the most important race that Brook Holliday ever won, but the sequel was sour. When Dick sent in the bill for the trip to work at Newmarket – it amounted to no more than £60 – Brook refused to pay it, saying: 'You are charging training fees, and if your gallops are so firm that you have to send her to work on the watered gallop at Newmarket, that's your affair.' There was a kind of logic in his argument, but the flaw in it was that it was at Brook's suggestion that she was sent to Newmarket, and that if Dick had been allowed to have his way she would have gone much more cheaply to Newbury. Dick explained what had happened to Jakie Astor, who advised him: 'I should tell him that he either pays the bill or he takes his horses away at the end of the season.' Brook still refused to pay, so his association with West Ilsley was terminated.

Brook Holliday did much good for racing. He served on the York Race Committee for many years and ended up as its chairman. During his time tremendous improvements were made both to the amenities and the standard of racing at the most illustrious racecourse in the north of England, but Brook could never be accused of not having a mind of his own. His association with West Ilsley lasted two years. By contrast Lord Rotherwick had horses with Dick for more than thirty years. A member of the ship-owning Cayser family, Bunny Rotherwick was a mild-mannered man and a delight to deal with. Besides training for him, Dick helped with the matings of his mares at his Cornbury Stud. He owned a number of useful horses. One of them, Colum, was an exact contemporary of Brigadier Gerard. Without aspiring to the greatness of his stable companion, Colum was on the fringe of the top class, and the eight races he won during three seasons in training included the Dee Stakes at Chester and the Prix Ridgeway at Deauville. Bunny had to wait for a long time for his solitary success in a Classic race. At the Newmarket December Sales in 1978 Dick bought for him the eleven-year-old mare Whitefoot for 30,000 guineas. She was by the Derby winner Relko and came from the same family as the 1000 Guineas winner Full Dress II and the perennial champion National Hunt stallion Deep Run. She was in foal to Run The Gantlet, and the resulting filly, named Swiftfoot, turned out to be a top-class stayer and won the Irish Oaks.

Another charming and mild-mannered man who was a long-term patron of the stable was Tom Egerton, who served the interests of racing well for many years as chairman of Tattersalls Committee that adjudicated on betting disputes. He lived at Chaddleworth, only a few miles from West Ilsley, and he and his wife Anne became good friends of the Herns. Dick was very pleased that their son Charles made a good start to his training career. When Anne was pregnant with him Dick took them up on the gallops in the Land-Rover one day, and was convinced that the prenatal experience must have helped him on his way to becoming a trainer!

By the time Swiftfoot won the Irish Oaks a great many things had happened and there had been far-reaching changes at West Ilsley. Jakie Astor had sold the place. There was a new regime and many new owners and, as a result of training the British 'Horse of the Century' Brigadier Gerard, Dick was established as a leading member of his profession more firmly than ever.

SIX

BRIGADIER GERARD AND THE HISLOPS

B RIGADIER GERARD was beyond dispute one of the greatest
horses of the twentieth century. Dick reckoned that Brigadier Gerard and Nashwan were the best horses he trained, but gave the palm to the Brigadier because he was supreme at a mile and was durable enough to keep his brilliant form over three seasons. He was beaten once in his eighteen races, but any horse must be allowed one defeat, a single occasion when he has an off-day or his luck runs out. Those American super-horses of earlier days, Man o' War and Native Dancer, each suffered one defeat in twenty-one starts without their claims to greatness being questioned. Any attempt to detract from Brigadier Gerard's reputation runs headlong into the buffers of his eleven victories in races now classified Group 1, the championship grade of the British racing calendar. Time and again he took on the best of his contemporaries and beat them. Physically he was a perfect model of the thoroughbred; temperamentally he was less than perfect, because he had inherited an excitable streak and needed careful handling. Nevertheless he was a phenomenal racehorse, and his ability to win races when conditions were not to his liking was a sign of true excellence.

Great racehorses have graced the British Turf at intervals since the earliest times, from Flying Childers to Eclipse, to St Simon, to Ormonde, to Sceptre, to Pretty Polly to Bahram. Brigadier

Gerard was unique not through his athleticism, which he shared with those giants of the past, but because his career on the racecourse and at stud was interwoven as tightly as the webbing of a rifle thong with the lives of his trainer and his owner-breeders John and Jean Hislop. His deeds and his fame prompted catastrophic character changes in the Hislops and destroyed the relationship between the Herns and the Hislops beyond hope of repair. The lives of none of his predecessors had similar overtones.

Born in Quetta on 12 December 1911, John Hislop was the son of an officer in the Indian cavalry and, like Dick, was taught to ride from a very early age. By the time he was six he had a dun pony, which he rode in jodhpurs with a puggaree wound above a cherubic face, like a proper young sahib. However, an idyllic childhood on the sub-continent came to an abrupt end three months after his seventh birthday when his father died of pneumonia at the age of only forty-two, and he and his mother had to return to England. It had been his father's wish that he should follow him in a military career, and accordingly he was sent to Wellington College, the national memorial to the 'Iron Duke' and then primarily an army school, with sixty per cent of its pupils going into the forces. Although John found the cricket and rugger playing ethos of Wellington alien and his sporting tastes were confined to horses, he got through his time there without much trouble and passed into the Royal Military College at Sandhurst. The RMC gave him opportunities to ride and hunt, but after a year a health problem again caused a sudden change in his life; he became ill, had to undergo an operation for the removal of a kidney, and was invalided out of the army. The loss of a kidney may have disqualified him from a career as a regular officer, but it did not prevent him from serving first in the Field Artillery, then the Anti-Tank Artillery and finally in Phantom, the unit responsible for transmitting information direct from the front line to GHQ, during the Second World War; and ultimately it proved fortunate, because it diverted his attention to the much more profitable and fulfilling world of the thoroughbred.

Having been discharged from the army in 1930, he decided on a career in racing and went as pupil-assistant trainer to Victor Gilpin, first at Newmarket and later at Michel Grove on the Duke of Norfolk's estate on the South Downs. He soon began to get rides both on the flat and over jumps, and achieved a high degree of competence as a race rider in the years immediately preceding the war. Competition was fierce in those days, as the ranks of amateurs included many extremely capable army officers like Fulke Walwyn, who later turned professional, Peter Payne-Gallwey and Perry Harding. John was equal to the best of them. He twice dead-heated for the title of leading amateur on the flat, and was third on the list of amateurs under National Hunt Rules in 1938–39, the last season before the war. By the time he was demobbed from the army at the end of the war he was almost past his prime as a rider over jumps, but still managed eighteen more winners and third place on Kami in the 1947 Grand National. He was pre-eminent as an amateur on the flat and was champion for eleven consecutive seasons. Between 1946 and his retirement from the saddle in 1956 he had 177 mounts and won on eighty-seven of them, an astonishingly high strike rate of forty-nine per cent. Several trainers, particularly Sam Armstrong, made a practice of putting him up on high-class horses to obtain easy pickings in amateur riders' races. Crouching low in the saddle with perfect balance, he seldom drew his whip and gained the reputation of a great stylist – though some of his contemporaries used to remark, somewhat cynically and a little unkindly, that it is not too difficult to be stylish when you have a stone in hand.

By then John was well into his second marriage. His first was a short-lived wartime affair to Barbara Jameson, who afterwards distinguished herself, under her second married name of

Harcourt-Wood, in many forms of equine and canine sport and was joint breeder of the Cheltenham Gold Cup winner Captain Christy. His second was to a war widow, Jean Thackeray, the daughter of the National Hunt trainer Bertie Bankier. Jean was black-haired, attractive in a lush way, opinionated, assertive and shrill. She was taller than John, and her personality became ever more forceful.

Although the Second World War caused a gap in John's race riding, its effects on his career were not entirely baneful. It brought him into contact with John Jacob (Jakie, later Sir John) Astor, who was for a time his squadron leader in Phantom and afterwards became a leading owner and breeder, and the sculptor John Skeaping. More importantly, a lengthy spell in hospital after a bad fall in a novices chase at Cheltenham gave him the opportunity to take his first steps in racing journalism, having articles accepted by *Men Only* and *Horse and Hound*, and to make a systematic study of thoroughbred breeding. He collected every book on the subject he could find and, as he wrote in his memoirs *Anything But A Soldier*, emerged with one basic conviction:

> In the breeding of thoroughbreds, or any other species as far as that goes, there is no substitute for a clear understanding of the basic principles of genetics, a thorough knowledge of conformation and of the background and characteristics of the sires and mares, and their immediate ancestors, with which the breeder is dealing.

He was able to put the fruits of his studies into practice when he bought the mare Orama for £370 in 1941 when bloodstock prices had touched rock bottom. Orama had already bred the Classic filly Beausite, who was second in the 1000 Guineas and fourth in the Oaks, and had a filly foal at foot by Flag Of Truce when John bought her. He sold the filly, who was named Respite, as a yearling and in due course she became the dam of the 2000 Guineas winner Nearula. Later Orama bred Oceana, who was exported to Australia where she became the dam of Todman, one of the most brilliant horses ever bred in that country, and Noholme, another top-class racehorse and a successful sire in the United States. John got rid of both Respite and Oceana, and was left with nothing to carry on the family line; obviously he had yet to learn the lesson that it is essential to retain some of the daughters of a foundation mare in order to ensure future success.

John developed further strands to his career as a journalist and a breeder while he was still riding. He became racing correspondent of *The Observer*, wrote articles on breeding at different times for the two racing dailies, *The Sporting Life* and *The Sporting Chronicle*, and was general manager of the glossy racing and breeding periodical *The British Racehorse*. His journalistic style was as polished as his riding style, and owed much to the tuition of an eccentric but inspiring Wellington master, Rollo St Clair Talboys. Incongruous in the military atmosphere of the college, Talboys dressed invariably in a dark blue suit, light blue shirt and flowing blue silk tie. He would float through the quadrangles, his leonine head tilted slightly to one side and crowned by a grey homburg, with an air of aloof distaste for his surroundings, like Cardinal Wolsey treading the foetid streets of Tudor London with an orange pressed to his nose. John was one of many Wellingtonians who owed much to his civilising influence.

With the experience of Orama behind him, as a breeder John drew inspiration from the 'peerless' Pretty Polly, the brilliant winner of three Classic races in 1904, whose praises had been regularly sung by Miss Clay, the riding mistress at his prep school. His regard for Pretty Polly was strengthened when he found many of her descendants in Victor Gilpin's stable in the 1930s. Gilpin was training for Colonel Giles Loder, who had inherited the stud of his uncle Eustace Loder, the owner-breeder of Pretty Polly, and in John's time there the family was represented by such good horses as Colorado Kid, winner of the Doncaster Cup, and Fairbairn, winner of the Princess of Wales's

Stakes. He was determined to acquire one of her descendants as soon as possible as the foundation mare for a fresh venture in breeding. The opportunity came when Pretty Polly's five-year-old great granddaughter Brazen Molly was submitted at the Newmarket December Sales in 1945 and, as she was barren that year, John was able to buy her for 400 guineas – only 30 guineas more than he had paid for Orama in the darkest days of the war. It was a fateful purchase, because Brazen Molly was destined to be the granddam of Brigadier Gerard.

The breeding value of Brazen Molly was proved when her son Stokes, who had been sold as a yearling, finished second in the 2000 Guineas. It was later, in 1956, when John had established a small stud at his home, East Woodhay House 4 miles south of Newbury, that the defining moment came with the birth of Brazen Molly's daughter La Paiva. Although she was by the French Derby winner Prince Chevalier and showed good form on the home gallops, La Paiva was a failure on the racecourse, and even George Todd, the Manton trainer whose ability to place bad horses successfully was legendary, could not conjure a win out of her. The best she could do was to finish second in a moderate maiden race over a mile at Salisbury as a three-year-old and Jimmy Lindley, who rode her in five of her seven races, described her as a 'right cow'. Eventually she went blind, and her eyesight may have been defective even when she was in training. In spite of her shortcomings, at the age of twelve and on 5 March 1968, La Paiva became, as a result of a mating with the local stallion Queen's Hussar, the dam of Brigadier Gerard, the bay colt who was to be hailed as one of the greatest racehorses of the twentieth century.

Good horses deserve good names, and Brigadier Gerard, who was named after a dashing hussar officer in a Conan Doyle story, was singularly blessed in this respect. He looked something out of the ordinary from his earliest days. Dick saw him as a yearling at East Woodhay and was impressed by him as 'a fine, beautiful horse'. West Ilsley was little more than a dozen miles from East

Woodhay and was the nearest large stable with excellent training facilities. Dick had already trained a few horses for the Hislops, including Brigadier Gerard's half-brother Town Major, who won his first race as a two-year-old at Sandown but afterwards was disappointing. He was an excitable horse, and it took some lengthy sessions on the lunge to cure him of a habit of giving a buck every three strides when at exercise. Dick needed no second invitation to train Brigadier Gerard. John decided to break him at home as a yearling, and he moved to West Ilsley in the middle of November. John wrote in his book *The Brigadier* that he was already making running plans, proposing a first race for him in early June, with a main objective of the Middle Park Stakes in October. As Dick remarked, there was a little trainer inside John, struggling to get out, but these premature running plans were ridiculous. 'At that stage we didn't even know whether he had an engine or the right attitude to racing.' Dick added: 'You can never tell. One of the best horses I ever trained, judged on his work at home, was Admirals Launch. He won the Craven Stakes first time out as a three-year-old, but then began to funk and sweat up before his races, and never won again. Incidentally, he was a son of Brigadier Gerard.'

Brigadier Gerard was a medium-sized colt with black points and a small white star when he went into training, but grew rapidly over the ensuing winter, and ended up as a big horse standing 16 hands 2 inches. Part-grown or fully grown, he was a magnificent individual, and when the sculptor John Skeaping came down to the stables to take measurements for the statue that now stands in the preliminary parade ring at the Newmarket Rowley Mile course, he described his proportions as 'absolutely perfect'. Like many good horses he had character. When he first arrived at West Ilsley he used to weave and was difficult to catch in his box, so that for the first month he had to wear a headcollar with a shank which restricted his movement but enabled him to reach his manger and his water. That taught him manners. He was coltish, and always became excited if a pony came close to him He continually jig-jogged if he was behind other horses, but settled well at the head of the string, so that was where he was always placed. As a four-year-old he grew lazy and tended to pull himself up whenever he saw Dick on the gallops. Dick had to park his Land-Rover out of sight and conceal himself in a ditch, peering through the grass, and then Brigadier Gerard would work up to the end of the gallop. One of his most admirable characteristics was his soundness. As Dick remarked: 'I never remember being unable to do what I wanted with him on the day I wanted to do it. I don't remember him ever being lame for any reason.'

Dick made a practice of getting on with his two-year-olds early in the year so that they were three-quarters fit before the ground became firm. He used to send fifteen to twenty of them, even the big backward ones, as fast as they could go up a 3-furlongs gallop called the Monkey Run on Hodcott Down in late March or early April, and that would tell him those that had the vital resource of speed. Jimmy Lindley rode Brigadier Gerard when it was his turn to take part in the Monkey Run gallop. As he mounted, Dick said to him: 'You want to watch this horse, he drops everyone the first time they ride him.' Brigadier Gerard whipped round, and Jimmy duly took a tumble. In the gallop he jumped off, went full tilt, and was soon in a clear lead. At the finish Jimmy glanced over his shoulder, and saw that the closest of the others was 50 yards behind. The evidence that Brigadier Gerard was something out of the ordinary was unmistakable.

He would have been ready to fulfil John's plan of a race in late May or early June if a slight temperature and a spell of firm going had not forced a postponement until the Berkshire Stakes over 5 furlongs at Newbury on 24 June. Dick expected him to run very well, but did not strongly fancy him to win. Sheilah loved to do the Tote Jackpot, and when they got to Newbury she asked Dick: 'Shall I put him in?' Dick advised her not to, telling her to put in something else instead. Starting at 100–7 in a field of five, Brigadier Gerard proceeded to carry Joe Mercer to an easy 5-lengths victory. As Sheilah got the other five Jackpot winners, she took a long time to forgive Dick for putting her off. Brigadier Gerard's work companion Colum, also running for the first time, paid him a marked compliment by winning a race by 3 lengths in a field of twenty at Newbury the next day, and the form looked good.

The Brigadier's remaining three races that season were over 6 furlongs, and the initial favourable impression of his prowess was confirmed when he won the Champagne Stakes at Salisbury in July by 4 lengths and the Washington Singer Stakes at Newbury in August by 2 lengths, starting at odds-on on each occasion. His final appearance as a two-year-old was, as John had hoped, in the Middle Park Stakes at Newmarket in October. That involved a sharp upgrade in class, because the race was one of the most important for two-year-olds and was made Group 1 when the Pattern race classifications were introduced two years later. Two others, Mummy's Pet and Swing Easy, were preferred to him in the betting, but the result was no different from his three previous races. Fireside Chat led to halfway, but then Joe Mercer sent Brigadier Gerard on and he raced ahead to win comfortably from Mummy's Pet and Swing Easy.

By that time Brigadier Gerard was accepted as a high-class colt and was allotted 9st 5lbs in the Free Handicap, but My Swallow, on 9st 7lbs, and Mill Reef, on 9st 6lbs, were both rated marginally superior. My Swallow, like Brigadier Gerard, was unbeaten, and got the better of the otherwise unbeaten Mill Reef by a short head in the Prix Robert Papin at Maisons Laffitte in July. Although there were some other very fast two-year-olds around in 1970, it was clear that these three were colts of exceptional merit. At the end of the year the Hislops received an offer of £250,000 for Brigadier Gerard, a huge sum at the time, but they rejected it out of hand.

Anyone with an appetite for a clash of Titans looked forward with eager anticipation to the 2000 Guineas of 1971. 'I decided to send the Brigadier to run for the 2000 without racing him beforehand,' John wrote loftily in *The Brigadier*. In fact it was an agreed decision made after consultation. 'I was convinced that I could get him fit without a race,' said Dick. 'He was a very clean-winded horse and did not need a great deal of work. There was no point in risking a hard preliminary race against Mill Reef or My Swallow.' As he was not to have a race before the Guineas, he was sent for a gallop on Newbury racecourse just to give him a change of scenery, and readily disposed of a useful horse called Grey Sky over 7 furlongs, which provided satisfactory proof of his well-being.

His final gallop took place on Saturday 24 April, a week before the Guineas. It was over 7 furlongs on the Trial Ground, parallel to the ancient track of the Ridgeway which runs along the spine of the Downs from Kennett to Goring, and the horses galloped the reverse way to give him a change and because horses always work better going towards home. It was a foul morning. A gale was blowing, and while the horses were exercising heavy rain began to fall. The other horses in the gallop were the four-year-old Duration, who had won a mile handicap at Warwick the previous week, and the three-year-old Magnate. The apprentice Lindsay Davies, who afterwards became one of the stable's main work riders, was on Duration, and Joe Mercer was on Brigadier Gerard. Joe had been instructed to give Duration 3 lengths start, and they finished upsides, with Duration going flat out and Brigadier Gerard still on the bit. Dick thought that the gallop had done the job of sharpening up the Brigadier. His task that morning had been demanding. He had been set to carry a lot more weight than Duration, and when they got back to The Old Rectory for breakfast it was discovered that the suede jacket that Mercer had been wearing was so sodden with rainwater that it weighed 8lbs. In consequence Brigadier Gerard had been taking on a useful older handicapper on no less than 34lbs worse terms than weight for age, which was a very positive indication that he had made good progress over the winter.

Brigadier Gerard was sent to Newmarket on the afternoon before the 2000 Guineas, and when John, Dick and Sheilah went to inspect him at evening stables they found him on excellent terms with himself and in perfect physical condition. John graciously told Dick that he had never seen a horse better trained in his life. Guineas day dawned fine, and the fast going on Newmarket Heath was exactly as Brigadier Gerard liked it. The feeling of optimism in his camp increased when his gallops companion Duration, carrying a 7lb penalty for his Warwick victory, won the race before the Guineas, an apprentice handicap in which he was ridden by Lindsay Davies, easily by 5 lengths. Nevertheless My Swallow and Mill Reef had both won their preliminary races easily, and Brigadier Gerard started only third in the betting at 11–2, with Mill Reef favourite at 6–4 and My Swallow at 2–1 in a field reduced to no more than six by the reputation of the three principals. In the race there was only one horse in it at the finish. Fast as My Swallow ran for the first 6 furlongs, and hard as Mill Reef struggled in the later stages, Brigadier Gerard swept past them more than a furlong from home and, a thrilling sight in the bright spring sunshine, outpaced them in the last furlong of rising ground to beat Mill Reef by 3 lengths, with My Swallow ¾ of a length further back in third place. Although the time of the winner was no better than average, there is no doubt that this was one of the best races for the 2000 Guineas ever run. The received wisdom had been that the 2000 Guineas of 1886 had been the best ever, when Ormonde beat Minting by 2 lengths with the third horse a distance behind. Ormonde went on to clinch the Triple Crown, while Minting, whose connections realised that further tilting against Ormonde was pointless, was sent to France to win the Grand Prix de Paris easily. Brigadier Gerard and Mill Reef were certainly no worse than Ormonde and Minting, and at the time My Swallow was not far behind them. His exertions in the Guineas took the edge off My Swallow and he was beaten in his two subsequent races, but he had proved himself an exceptionally fast colt. Mill Reef went from strength to strength, winning in succession the Derby, the Eclipse Stakes, the King George VI and Queen Elizabeth Stakes and the Prix de l'Arc de Triomphe and breaking the course records in the second and last of those races. But he had been no match for Brigadier Gerard over a mile.

The Brigadier had a real struggle in his next race, the St James's Palace Stakes at Royal Ascot. The going was very soft, which he hated, but he got there in the end to beat Sparkler by a head. The story was similar in the Champion Stakes four months later, when the going again was soft, and Brigadier Gerard had another long, hard grind to beat Rarity by a short head. In the meantime he had routine tasks to win the Sussex Stakes, the Goodwood Mile and the Queen Elizabeth II Stakes. At the end of the 1971 season Brigadier Gerard was recognised not only as a brilliant horse over the right distance and on the right ground, but also as a horse with the extra dimension of ability that enabled him still to win when conditions were unfavourable.

There was never any question of the Brigadier being retired at that stage of his career. Neither Dick nor the Hislops gave that option a thought. Three imperatives were to govern his third season in training. Firstly, he was to be asked for proof that he was the complete Classic horse by winning over 1½ miles; secondly, he was to be called on to demonstrate that in maturity he was at least as good as ever; and thirdly, he was to meet Mill Reef again and show that his superiority over that talented contemporary was not confined to races over a mile. The third imperative could not be fulfilled because Mill Reef, having won the Coronation Cup, broke a leg on Ian Balding's gallops at Kingsclere and was barely saved for stud. The second imperative was triumphantly achieved; the first imperative also was achieved, though some doubt about whether he was a genuine mile-and-a-half horse remained.

His first three races – the Westbury Stakes, the Prince of Wales Stakes and the Eclipse Stakes, all over 1¼ miles – presented few difficulties. He started at long odds-on and won convincingly each time. Then came the King George VI and Queen Elizabeth Stakes at Ascot on 22 July and the moment for decision whether his stamina could be stretched to 1½ miles in good company. He was a little fortunate in that the field, in the absence of the last two Derby winners Mill Reef and Roberto, was hardly up to the highest standards of the race. The other four Classic winners were either not of the first international calibre or, like Riverman, a doubtful stayer. However, the challenge was a real one, and when the previous year's Irish St Leger winner Parnell took up the running 5 furlongs out and went all out for home it was obvious that Brigadier Gerard was going to be well tested. However, Brigadier Gerard had moved within a length of the leader, going easily, as they turned into the straight and, as Parnell was a stayer without powers of acceleration in the closing stages, Dick felt that victory was assured. Brigadier Gerard moved inexorably into the lead with more than a furlong to go and, although Parnell struggled bravely, went on to win by 1½ lengths. That was not quite the end of the matter. The cheering that had broken out when the Brigadier took the lead was silenced abruptly with the announcement of a Stewards Inquiry. Brigadier Gerard had veered to the right towards the inside rail after taking the lead, and Willie Carson had snatched up Parnell momentarily and switched him to the left behind Brigadier Gerard. There were agonising minutes before a further announcement that the placings remained unaltered was made, to the intense relief of the connections of Brigadier Gerard and his innumerable admirers in the crowd. Recalling the race in 1999, Dick commented: 'I think we were lucky. As the rules stand now and are generally interpreted by the Stewards, we should probably have lost the race. Brigadier Gerard was at the end of his tether in the last furlong, because he did not really stay the trip. After all he was by Queen's Hussar, who was a miler, and his grandsire Fair Trial was an influence for speed. You could not really expect him to stay a mile and a half, but

ck and Sheilah after their wedding at Christ Church, Brick Street on October 9th, 1956.

Above: Dick with Michael Pope at the Newmarket Sales, *c*1956.

Left: Sheilah and Dick in the garden of Lagrange, with four friends, *c*1960.

Below: Dick in conversation with Mrs Jackson on Waterhall, *c*1960.

ivanter, the first good sprinter trained by Dick, on Waterhall. March 1961.

hersett (*left*) on his way to the gallops during his preparation for the Derby, 1962.

Harry Carr on Hethersett.

Provoke winning the St Le
on a very wet day, 1965.

Hethersett winning the St Leger, 1962.

Dick with Jack Colling, his predecessor at West Ilsley, at the Newmarket Sales, c1970.

k with Brigadier Gerard, 1971.

Opposite above: Dick in 1977, with twelve horses belonging to the Queen. Dunfermline, winner of the Oaks and St Leger, is at the left end of the rear rank. Stan Clayton (*front right*) in light jersey and hunting cap.

Opposite below: Troy in the winner's enclosure after the Derby in 1979. Dick (*right*) is about to shake hands with Peter Reynolds, manager of Ballymacoll stud.

Left: Dick and Sheilah at the 'Horse of the Year' dinner for Brigadier Gerard in 1971.

Below: Dick on Kilcoran, out with the Quorn, the day after his fifty-third birthday in 1974.

Henbit, ridden by Willie Carson, led in by Mrs Plesch after winning the Derby in 1980. His lad is Bonzo Wilder.

Bespoke, ridden by Hywel Davies, jumps the last hur before winning at Kempton. October 19th, 1985.

Nashwan, ridden by Willie Carson, entering the winner's enclosure after winning the 2000 Guineas in 1989. Dick (*right*) doffs his panama.

his class and courage saw him through. Fortunately the field for the race that year was sub-standard.'

Brigadier Gerard had passed that test, albeit by the skin of his teeth, but in his next race, the Benson and Hedges Gold Cup over 1 mile 2½ furlongs at York in August, his 'aura of invincibility was mercilessly stripped from him', as the *Bloodstock Breeders Review* expressed it. It was the first running of a race which was later to have the permanent title of the International Stakes, and the prospect of Brigadier Gerard in opposition to the Derby winner Roberto aroused enormous public interest. Dick and Sheilah flew up to York and landed on the old disused aerodrome from which the course is approached past the coach parks, and they found them full to overflowing with coaches not only from Yorkshire but all over the country, bringing many thousands of enthusiasts in the expectation of seeing the Brigadier's sixteenth victory. Roberto was a very high-class horse, but he was inconsistent and had run badly in the Irish Derby since winning at Epsom. Roberto's owner-breeder John Galbreath had sent over Braulio Baeza, one of the leading jockeys in the United States, to ride him, and Baeza proceeded to ride the race of his life. In a typical American tactical move, he sent Roberto ahead from the start and set a blistering pace. Most of the spectators, who had made Brigadier Gerard a 3–1 on favourite, expected Roberto to fold up in the straight, but Joe Mercer was not fooled for a moment. He was pushing Brigadier Gerard hard 3 furlongs from home, and the Brigadier responded to close to within a length of the leader. Cheering broke out from the crowds thronging the stands, but quickly died away when it became evident that their hero had no more to give. Roberto began to increase the gap again and finally passed the winning post with 3 lengths to spare.

The sense of anti-climax was palpable. Few were ready to admit that the horse hailed as a world champion could have been fairly and squarely beaten. Many critics argued that Mercer had given Roberto too much rope, but that was clearly untrue.

Desperate to find an excuse, Jean Hislop contended that the Brigadier had discharged a large clot of mucus from his nostrils in the racecourse stables after the race, and that this must have interfered with his breathing. Dick would have none of this. 'He had a thin trickle from one nostril, but that was insignificant. He never coughed, had a temperature or was in any way a sick horse afterwards,' he asserted.

In fact, there was very little wrong with the Brigadier's performance. Both he and Roberto had broken the course record, while Gold Rod, who had finished only a length behind him in the Eclipse Stakes, was 10 lengths behind this time. Moreover Rheingold, beaten by a short head in the Derby, finished 15 lengths behind Roberto. If there were an explanation for the defeat other than meeting a potentially brilliant colt who excelled himself on the day, it was probably that he had not quite fully recovered from his hard race over a distance in excess of his best in the King George VI and Queen Elizabeth Stakes less than four weeks earlier. The Ascot race is a tough affair that can take a lot out of a horse, especially if he does not get the trip. Grundy was a badly beaten fourth in the York race three years later after his epic duel with the Hern-trained Bustino at Ascot. Grundy never ran again, but Brigadier Gerard showed his exceptional combination of class and resilience by coming back to win his last two races, the Queen Elizabeth II Stakes and the Champion Stakes, confirming his superiority over Riverman in the latter race.

Brigadier Gerard retired to stud at the end of his four-year-old season with his reputation almost fully restored. The faith of the betting public was never shaken, and they sent him off at long odds-on for his last two races. So many aspects of his career testified to his great class and his marvellous soundness and constitution, not least the facts that he was the only English Classic winner of the twentieth century to have been unbeaten in ten or more races at two and three years old, and the only English Classic winner of the twentieth century to have won seven or more races at four years old. His record of consistent achievement in a long series of the most important races in the calendar is likely to stand for a very long time. He never ventured abroad, but in the early 1970s participation in foreign races was not the regular feature of the programme of a top-class horse that it became in later years, and races like the Japan Cup and the Dubai World Cup did not exist – not that the cautious Hislops, jealous of his record, would have risked him if they had existed. The Hislops never wanted to run abroad, arguing that there were plenty of suitable races in England.

At the time of his retirement the standing of the Hislops in the eyes of the racing public was at a peak seldom attained by any owners or breeders in the history of the Turf. They were universally admired as small owner-breeders with a minimal investment in bloodstock who had seen off the big battalions, submitted their champion to the fullest exigencies of the racecourse test in England and rejected a tempting offer which, if accepted, might have caused his career to unfold in a very different and less exacting manner. The encomium written by John would have been echoed by many not blessed with his literary powers: 'Bred in England in the face of competition against all the wealth and resources of the foremost studs in America and Europe, he embodied that fusion of the best qualities of a racehorse only found in a champion of champions. Though in law he belonged to Jean and me, in spirit he belonged to England, to all who stood in admiration around him, to the thousands who followed his career and had never seen him, even to those ignorant of his name. In him every Englishman could justly take an equal pride, for he was part of our heritage . . .' Looking to his future at stud, he expressed the pious hope that 'he will do much to maintain the English thoroughbred in that position of supremacy which has made him the envy of all nations from the time of his evolution.' If these comments seemed a little over the top, in essence they were justified.

If he had added that they were the luckiest people alive to have bred such a horse, a champion of champions, by sending a non-winning, jady mare to a second-class stallion just because he was cheap and stood at Lord Carnarvon's Highclere Stud 3 miles away from East Woodhay as the crow flies, everyone would have praised their candour, rejoiced with them in their good fortune and regarded them with affectionate respect for ever. That was what John and Jean signally failed to do. With hindsight it is possible to discern the seeds of character decline before Brigadier Gerard ever ran, because John had long boasted a very good conceit of himself as a breeding pundit and Jean been scornful of anyone she considered less successful or less well accepted in racing society than herself. This hubris fed steadily on the glory of their horse's deeds until, by the autumn of 1972, they were wholly corrupted. Had John been the Roman emperor Caligula, he would have made Brigadier Gerard a senior minister; lacking the necessary prerogative of appointment he, and Jean too, allowed the horse to usurp their judgment and distort their sense of proportion.

To do John justice, it must be said that he never tried to interfere with the training of Brigadier Gerard and left that side of his development strictly to Dick. He liked to think that he kept a tight rein on running plans and, in his book *The Brigadier*, made out that he dictated them. In fact, all decisions were made jointly with Dick. After the end of Brigadier Gerard's racing career John became increasingly offhand and arrogant, and the relationship of the Hislops and the Herns, from being that of friends and equals, deteriorated into that of masters and servants from the viewpoint of the Hislops. Brigadier Gerard's three-years younger sister Lady Dacre was sent to West Ilsley. She was black, very excitable, and an insoluble problem to train. As a two-year-old she ran second in a race at the Doncaster St Leger meeting, but at the end of the season John informed Dick that he thought that she would be better off in a smaller stable and that he had decided to transfer her to Henry Candy. She stayed in training until she was four years old, but never won a race. She was the last horse that Dick trained for the Hislops.

The departure of Lady Dacre from the stable foreshadowed ever more rancorous, if inexplicable, attitudes of the Hislops towards the Herns. These attitudes were exemplified years later when the wealthy biscuit manufacturer Garfield Weston telephoned Dick, told him he had bred a good-looking colt by Brigadier Gerard and invited him to go over and see him. Dick did so, and liked him. John too had heard of the colt's promise and invited himself to see him. After inspecting him, John asked Weston if he had decided to whom he would send him to be trained. 'I was thinking of Dick Hern,' replied Weston. 'I must try to persuade you not to do that,' said John. Hearing of that comment made Dick determined to take the colt, but unfortunately, like many of the sons of Brigadier Gerard, he had little ability and failed to win a race.

Jean became increasingly rude and aggressive. One day Dick met her mother, Chris Bankier, at Newbury races. 'Well,' she said to Dick, 'Johnny's bred a good horse, but I'm afraid I bred a hairy-heeled 'un.' Newbury, her local course, inspired Jean to some of her worst excesses, and her behaviour became increasingly violent. On one occasion there she attacked a lady destined for high rank in the racing hierarchy with her umbrella in the members' enclosure, and received a formal warning from the Senior Steward of the Jockey Club as to her future conduct. Much of her intolerable behaviour could be attributed to drink. After Brigadier Gerard had won the Sussex Stakes at Goodwood as a three-year-old, the Hislops called on the Herns at their house at West Wittering, where Jean, by way of celebration, consumed three-quarters of a bottle of gin. Afterwards she took the wheel to drive home with John, whose one wonky eye prevented him from driving, slumped in the passenger's seat. In the 1970s the police were not as much on the look-out for drink-driving as they were twenty years later, and they got back to East Woodhay without misadventure. Trainers in the

Lambourn area suffered from frequent abusive telephone calls from her, and when the Hislops moved from East Woodhay to Exning near Newmarket in the 1980s 'Colonel Mad', the pen-name of Jeffrey Bernard in *Private Eye*, wrote: 'Unwelcome in the Royal County for many years, Jean Hislop hopefully will no longer be bothering Berkshire trainers with her endless flow of distasteful insults.'

John could not bring himself to admit that luck had played the biggest part in the breeding of a horse as great as Brigadier Gerard. Instead he wrote his biography, *The Brigadier*, which proved to be a massive exercise in jobbing backwards in which he attempted to show that Brigadier Gerard had been the product of careful planning and selection. From the point of view of bloodlines, he argued, what La Paiva needed was strong reintroduction of the influence of the great sire Phalaris through the three crosses of his best son, Fairway, which were present in the fourth remove of the pedigree of Queen's Hussar. In addition, Queen's Hussar was inbred in the third remove to Fair Trial, whom he described as a 'thoroughly desirable in-fluence'. If this was so clearly what La Paiva needed, it should have applied to all her matings, but in practice there was no consistency in the choice of her mates. Of the nine other stallions besides Queen's Hussar that were used, five did not have a single cross of Fairway and two, Rockefella and Midsummer Night II, were rarities in the second half of the twentieth century in that they had pedigrees devoid of Phalaris altogether. Nor did the stallions fit into any kind of aptitudinal pattern, as they ranged from the pure sprinter Gratitude through the miler Queen's Hussar and the Derby winner Royal Palace to the extreme stayer Pandofell. The conclusion that the choice of mates for La Paiva was dictated by a spirit of hopeful experimentation, not to men-tion questions of cost, rather than profound reasoning, is ines-capable.

The impression that the breeding of Brigadier Gerard was a matter of luck, not judgement, is confirmed by the fact that the only time the mating of Queen's Hussar with La Paiva was repeated the product was Lady Dacre, who was highly strung, lacked constitution and failed to train on; as far as the essential ingredients that go to make up a good racehorse are concerned, she was the direct opposite of Brigadier Gerard.

In the end Brigadier Gerard, from being the pride of the Hislops, became their nemesis. In the early 1980s the finances of British racing were at a low ebb, with a sharp reduction of the Levy Board funding on which it was dependent. The Thoroughbred Breeders Association (TBA) devised a scheme, based on the American model of the Breeders Cup, by which a contribution equal to the average price of nominations sold to it in the year in question would be drawn from each stallion into a central fund and distributed in the form of prize money, breeders'prizes and support for veterinary research. The scheme, entitled the European Breeders Fund – it was gradually enlarged to include Ireland, France, Germany, Italy and Switzerland – gained the immediate blessing of the Jockey Club and the Racecourse Association and was hailed by the Home Secretary Willie Whitelaw, the guest of honour at the TBA awards luncheon in January 1983, as 'an admirable example of self-help'.

The incentive for stallion owners to join the scheme was that fifty per cent of all two-year-old races were to be restricted to the progeny of stallions that had paid a due contribution. Support from stallion owners was almost universal, but the Hislops proclaimed their uncompromising opposition from the outset. John resigned immediately from the TBA, and castigated the scheme as 'illogical, unethical and dangerous in principle', while Jean added her opinion that the announcement of the scheme by the TBA had been ill-mannered. 'I don't believe that enough stallions will subscribe,' she said.

As to the number of contributors, Jean was quickly proved wrong. There was a strong consensus in favour of the EBF in the Jockey Club, where John attacked the scheme fruitlessly, and Captain John Macdonald-Buchanan, a former Senior Steward, remarked: 'As far as I know, there is practically universal support for the scheme. Mr Hislop speaks as though there is a groundswell of opposition. I have never heard of any opposition to it.' By 31 December 1983, the latest date for the payment of contributions so that the much needed sponsorship of racing could begin in 1984, no fewer than 213 British-based stallions had contributed, and the only noteworthy exception was Brigadier Gerard.

The Hislops maintained a two-pronged offensive against the EBF. John chipped away relentlessly at meetings of the Jockey Club. He argued that the restriction of races to EBF-qualified horses was detrimental to breeding because it introduced an element of the closed shop, that the Jockey Club, the EBF and the racecourses would find themselves liable to action in the civil courts, that the manner in which the EBF had been promoted was 'devious and misleading'; that coercion had been used against stallion owners; and that the scheme had been inefficiently administered and was in need of close supervision. All these points were answered categorically at meetings of the Club. After two years of pointless repetition of these objections, the patience of the Senior Steward Lord Manton snapped, and he informed John that he had wasted a great deal of the Club's time, and a great deal of its money through legal costs, and that no further objections would be heard.

Jean took upon herself the responsibility of the main critic of the EBF outside the Jockey Club, and declared her intention to go on fighting even after John had been officially silenced. She disparaged the scheme at length to anyone she could persuade to listen, and carried on a lengthy correspondence with the Jockey Club in which she demanded a committee of inquiry into the activities of the EBF and the actions of the Jockey Club in support of it. She made a habit of telephoning the EBF office in The Avenue, Newmarket, at three o'clock in the afternoon and bombarding either the chief executive Sam Sheppard or one of his staff with her endlessly repeated criticisms for periods of up to three-quarters of an hour. It took not a bomb, but a strimmer starting up deafeningly in the garden below the EBF office windows, to halt her malicious flow. Her contention was that the scheme was bound to fall down because the contribution from each stallion was the average price paid for nominations in the relevant year, and it was impossible for the EBF Trustees to have the figures for all the prices on which a correct average must be based. What she ignored was the goodwill of stallion owners towards the scheme and their willingness to supply all the necessary figures. She believed that the EBF would be forced to reveal the figures for each stallion and that these would be challenged by mare owners who had negotiated prices above or below the average. This never happened because confidentiality between stallion owners and the EBF was a cardinal point of EBF policy and an essential condition of acceptance of the scheme. The terms of the EBF Trust Deed gave the Trustees the definitive power to determine the contribution for each stallion, and this power was exercised by expert Trustees appointed for the purpose. In the end the evidence that the EBF was an established fact welcomed by the racing and breeding community at large took the sting out of Jean's incessant sniping, but it was a long time before the line between Regal Lodge, the Hislops' residence at Exning, and the EBF office fell silent.

All that sound and fury from the Hislops availed nothing. The EBF was an incomparable boon to British racing, boosting its finances by more than £10.5 million in the first fourteen years of operation. There was much speculation as to the motives for the Hislops' opposition, and ultimately it became clear that Brigadier Gerard himself was at the root of the matter. Their violent reaction to the announcement of the scheme was a reflex inspired by a sense that it would diminish the Brigadier. By 1983 his reputation was in steep decline, and they were afraid that they would be compelled to expose the extent of that decline by revealing the sharply reduced price for which his nominations were being sold. Ironically they would have been protected by the confidentiality clause, but by the time they realised this fact they had become entrenched and it was impossible for them to back down without losing face.

EBF or no EBF, Brigadier Gerard was indeed diminished. The years 1970 to 1972 were vintage years in British racing, perhaps the best of the century, highlighted by the presence of two incontestably great horses, Brigadier Gerard and Mill Reef, who combined to a rare degree the virtues of blinding precocious speed, top-class ability over middle distances and retention of form into a third season. Brigadier Gerard came out decisively the better the only time they met, in the 2000 Guineas, and was supreme at a mile; but Mill Reef gave performances of unsurpassed quality in the Derby and the Prix de l'Arc de Triomphe. They both raced successfully at four years old, but there again Brigadier Gerard had the edge, because he retired still as sound as the day he was born, whereas Mill Reef shattered a leg in training.

It was a different story at stud. By a strange coincidence they stood only half a mile apart, Mill Reef at the National Stud and Brigadier Gerard at Egerton Stud, just off the Cambridge road from Newmarket. Proximity was not matched by comparable achievement. Mill Reef was champion sire in the British Isles twice, siring the Derby winners Shirley Heights and Reference Point and twelve other individual winners of Group 1 races. Brigadier Gerard was never champion, and sired only two Group 1 winners, one of them the St Leger winner Light Cavalry. By Jean's admission, at the time of the foundation of the EBF the price of a nomination to Brigadier Gerard was 'probably about £5000'; at the peak of his stud career Mill Reef commanded a fee of £100,000. The Hislops, who had retained sixteen of the forty shares in Brigadier Gerard, certainly did not improve his chances of success as a stallion by barring access to commercial breeders and attempting to control the mares that were accepted to him, but the truth is that like most horses that are flukes of breeding, he was a thoroughly indifferent sire. His genetic legacy was in no way equivalent to his athletic prowess.

In practice the absence of Brigadier Gerard from the list of contributors made a negligible difference. In 1984, the year that racing began to feel the benefits of the EBF, he occupied the lowly place of eighty-eighth in the list of sires of winners, and had only four two-year-old winners. He covered only fifteen mares that year, and seven in 1985 for the production of three live foals, and was then retired from stud duties. John's prediction, so eloquently expressed in *The Brigadier*, that he would do much to maintain the supremacy of the British thoroughbred, fell a long way short of fulfilment. He was a paragon of athletic excellence, brought to and kept at a pinnacle of physical and mental fitness by Dick Hern throughout his years in training, but he was a fluke that no amount of jobbing backwards could convert into a product of a studiously planned mating.

As old age approached John shrank physically while retaining some of the cherubic appearance, if somewhat clouded by an air of petulance, of his youth in Quetta. Jean, by contrast, swelled and her colour heightened so that she might have stepped straight from a Rubens painting in modern dress. Her tone and manner became increasingly aggressive and violent. Once the darlings of the racing world, they were in the end disliked, scorned and the butt of irreverent humour. It was sad, for all lovers of the thoroughbred but for none as much as Dick Hern, that so great a racehorse as Brigadier Gerard should have ended his days inevitably tarred with the brush of his owner-breeders' excessive pride and self-delusion.

Jean died on 28 July 1997, having outlived John by three years. She was not condemned universally. Tony Morris, writing in *The Racing Post*, found that she was 'never outrageous: cheekily mischievous, perhaps, a woman with a tremendous sense of fun'. The many who had suffered from her rudeness and arrogance were less generous. Dick Hern was much closer to the consensus of the racing community when he summed her up: 'She was the most unpleasant woman I ever met.'

SEVEN

WEST ILSLEY – THE SOBELL ERA

T HE RACING CAREER of Brigadier Gerard coincided with a change of ownership of West Ilsley stables. Sir Gordon Richards had been leasing the racing stables at Whitsbury Manor in Hampshire, but had decided to give up training at the end of 1969. Consequently his patrons, including Michael Sobell, Arnold Weinstock and Lady Beaverbrook, had to make new arrangements for their horses. Sobell and Weinstock had been eying Manton, the famous Wiltshire training establishment which had reached a pinnacle of success under Alec Taylor and Joe Lawson in the first half of the twentieth century, but Manton was not for sale. Instead they turned to West Ilsley. The financial circumstances of Jakie Astor had deteriorated as a result of new tax regulations, which disadvantaged income derived from the United States, and he was prepared to sell. The transaction was completed and the horses owned by Sobell, Weinstock and Lady Beaverbrook moved in.

Sobell, who was knighted for his work for charity in 1972, and Weinstock had both immigrated into Britain from Europe as children. They grew up to be brilliant businessmen. Sobell became chairman of GEC (Radio and Television) in 1968. He was exceptionally long-lived and had passed his hundredth birthday when he died in 1993. Weinstock, who married Sobell's daughter Netta when he was twenty-five, began his working life in the Administrative Office of the Admiralty, but moved to more lucrative employment in industry. In 1954 he joined Radio and Allied (Holdings) Ltd, and later became managing director. Seven years later Radio and Allied merged with GEC, and in due course he became managing director of that too. In 1970 he was made a Life Peer, and sat as an independent in the House of Lords.

It would be difficult to exaggerate the benefits which businessmen like Sobell and Weinstock have brought to the economy of Britain in the form of direct employment, exports and the prosperity of satellite firms, and in many other ways. It would be equally difficult to overestimate the benefits they have brought to the bloodstock industry through their constant endeavours to breed and race horses of the highest class. Sobell went into quality breeding in 1960 when he bought the Ballyma-coll Stud in County Meath and the best of the bloodstock of the late Dorothy Paget. 'DP', as she was called, had earned the respect, if not the love, of the racing public, who always appreciate nonconformity. The eccentric DP had invested heavily in every kind of racehorse from ponies to hefty chasers, and liked to have a punt on her own horses whenever she had the chance. She was a familiar sight on the racecourse, round and pale of face and shapeless of figure, dressed in her invariable uniform of blue felt hat with upturned brim, long grey overcoat and fleece-lined suede boots. Although her returns from her horses were in no way commensurate with her huge investment, she did have the satisfaction of winning the most coveted races on the flat and over jumps. She bred and owned the Derby winner Straight Deal, and owned Golden Miller, who won the Grand National and the Cheltenham Gold Cup (five times) and was the second greatest steeplechaser of all time after Arkle. Thanks in large measure to the expertise of her manager Charlie Rogers, she built up a core of choice bloodlines at Ballymacoll which were the foundation of the success of Sobell and Weinstock as owner-breeders. It may be mentioned parenthetically that they have been equally well served by their stud manager Peter Reynolds, who has ensured a flow of quality winners.

In 1960, the year of the purchase of the Paget bloodstock, there was a happy omen for the future when the filly Sunny Cove won the Park Hill Stakes over the St Leger course. At Ballymacoll she made a telling impact as the granddam of the top-class miler Sun Prince, while her family provided Sun Princess, the best filly Dick ever trained.

In 1972 Dick had probably the best three milers ever gathered in the same stable at the same time in Brigadier Gerard, then four years old, and the three-year-olds Sun Prince and Sallust. In later years Dick used to wonder how he had been able to devise racing programmes for all three without them ever clashing. It is true that Brigadier Gerard was concentrating on longer distance races at that stage of his career, but he still ran in two important mile races, the Lockinge Stakes and the Queen Elizabeth Stakes, so it was a remarkable achievement.

Sallust and Sun Prince were both among the best of their generation as two-year-olds. At the end of the season the compiler of the Free Handicap could barely separate them, giving Sallust the edge with 8st 11lbs, 1lb more than Sun Prince. Of the pair, Sun Prince was the more straightforward character. He was third on his debut at Newbury, and then went to Royal Ascot and won the Coventry Stakes. In July he went to Maisons-Laffitte and won the Prix Robert Papin, beating another very speedy British-trained colt, Deep Diver. He did not do so well in his last two races, finishing unplaced at Longchamp in September and finishing third in the Middle Park Stakes the following month. Sallust took much longer to learn what racing was all about. He sweated up badly when he finished in the middle of the field in his first race at Newbury in April, and sweated up again when he ran fourth in the Windsor Castle Stakes at Royal Ascot. Dick was not sure that he really got down to his work at Ascot, so he fitted him with blinkers in his next race, a maiden race at Salisbury, which he won easily. He next ran second to the extremely fast filly Stilvi in the National Stakes at Sandown, and wound up his activities for the season by gaining a clear-cut victory in the Richmond Stakes at Goodwood.

The next year both horses fully confirmed the excellence they had shown as two-year-olds. Sallust continued to improve throughout the season, and no longer needed blinkers to make him concentrate. He was only fifth in his first race, the Ladbroke 2000 Guineas Trial at Kempton, but was unbeaten after that, winning five times off the reel – the Diomed Stakes over 8½ furlongs at Epsom, the Prix de la Porte Maillot over 7 furlongs at Longchamp, then the big Goodwood double of the Sussex Stakes and the Goodwood Mile, and finally back to the Longchamp 7 furlongs for the Prix de la Forêt. His last was probably his best performance, as he beat the top-class French-trained miler Lyphard. He was then sold to the Irish National Stud.

Sun Prince would have had a better record that season if the going had not been soft, which he hated, for his first two races. He was fifth in the Greenham Stakes and finished third to High Top and Roberto in the 2000 Guineas on a pouring wet day. On the stand before the race Dick was standing next to Sir Jules Thorn, the owner of High Top, with High Top's trainer Bernard Van Cutsem beyond him. Thorn turned to Dick and asked: 'Tell me, what distance is this race?' Dick could hardly believe his ears. Here was the owner of the favourite for the 2000 Guineas, and he did not even know the distance of the race. It was an exceptionally good 2000 Guineas. Roberto went on to win the Derby, and was of course the conqueror of Brigadier Gerard in the Benson and Hedges Gold Cup. Sun Prince got the fast ground he needed at Royal Ascot and won the St James's Palace Stakes, but did not run again that season as he took a long time to recover from a pulled muscle. Sun Prince stayed in training as a four-year-old. He did not recover his form completely, but won the Queen Anne Stakes at Royal Ascot and was third in the Eclipse Stakes and the Sussex Stakes.

Three years later there was a major change at West Ilsley, when Joe Mercer's retainer was not renewed for the 1977 season and he was replaced as first jockey by Willie Carson. Joe had been at West Ilsley for twenty-four years, first with Jack Colling and then with Dick, and the news of his dismissal was badly received by the racing press and community. It was ironic that Dick, who placed such a high value on loyalty in relations between employers and employees, should be accused of disloyalty, but there is no doubt that the termination of Joe's employment was a prime cause of a certain coolness that marked Dick's relationship with some sections of the press for a further dozen years. The truth was that Arnold Weinstock did not appreciate Joe's jockeyship and had been complaining about him to Dick for several years, and thought that he was too severe on two-year-olds. Here was another irony, because one of the salient features of Joe's style was his forbearance and reluctance to use the whip; but he did believe in using a two-year-old's speed and letting him run, whereas Arnold liked to see his horse brought from behind at the finish. Another factor was that Arnold saw Joe on account of his age – he was forty-two in 1976 – as a waning asset, and wanted a younger man. He became insistent when Willie Carson, who had already been champion jockey twice and was Joe's junior by eight years, became available as a result of the death of Bernard Van Cutsem, who had had first claim on his services. Dick resisted and argued Joe's case for as long as he could, pointing out strongly his virtues as a stable jockey and his long record of faithful service. In the end he realised that either Joe or he had to go, and he was forced to yield to Arnold's wishes.

As Joe had to leave West Ilsley, he could not have had a better or a more sympathetic replacement than Willie, who matched Dick in the value he placed on loyalty. Indeed, his loyalty to Dick was to make trouble for him at the time of the West Ilsley lease crisis of 1988–1989. He and his wife Elaine became staunch friends of the Herns, just as Joe and Anne Mercer had been before them. Happily the friendship between the Herns and the Mercers remained unbroken.

It was gratifying for Dick that Joe's career did not suffer; he got the very good job of first jockey to Henry Cecil's stable, and in 1977 rode 102 winners, his first century for twelve years. After the parting Dick felt that he had made a mistake in not telling Joe that Arnold was complaining about his riding. He had not wanted to upset him. He believed that Joe was a great stylist and was doing everything right, and hoped that reason would prevail and that Arnold would drop his campaign to get rid of him. That did not happen.

The first really top-class horse that Willie Carson rode for Sobell and Weinstock was the filly Cistus. A brown filly foaled in 1975, she was, appropriately enough, a daughter of Sun Prince, and was wonderfully game and consistent, winning five of her twelve races and finishing second twice and third once. Moreover, she had a very good temperament and was an excellent traveller. Her two victories as a two-year-old included the Listed Waterford Candelabra Stakes over 7 furlongs at Goodwood, and she was second in a big field for the Group 1 Criterium des Pouliches over a mile at Longchamp on 'Arc' day. The next spring she returned to Goodwood to win the Lupe Stakes over 1¼ miles, and next time out ran the race of her life to finish second to the exceptional filly Reine de Saba in the French Oaks. Further victories followed in the Group 3 Child Stakes over a mile, the Group 2 Nassau Stakes over 1¼ miles back at Goodwood, and the Group 2 Prix de l'Opéra over 9½ furlongs run, like the Criterium des Pouliches, at Longchamp on 'Arc' day. Her admirable record of achievement was marred only by one setback, and that was not due to any fault of her own. She had been ante-post favourite at the beginning of the week in which the 1000 Guineas was run, but Dick's then secretary forgot to declare her and she was unable to run. It was an oversight of which the impeccable Brian Holmes, Dick's secretary for the last nineteen years of his training career, would never have been guilty. Perhaps surprisingly, Arnold Weinstock took it graciously, recognising the fact that racing secretaries are fallible human beings.

The racing careers of Cistus and Troy overlapped, Troy being the younger of the pair by one year. A bay colt by Petingo out of La Milo, Troy came from one of the old Ballymacoll families, as his granddam Pin Prick was bred by Dorothy Paget. Sadly both sire and dam died the year Troy was foaled, Petingo being eleven and La Milo thirteen years old. Troy was a horse who always had a special place in Dick's affections as his first Derby winner. He looked a high-class horse from the time he came into training, and his two-year-old form was full of promise. His best performance that season was in the Group 3 Lanson Champagne Vintage Stakes at the Goodwood July Meeting, which he won from another high-class colt in Ela-Mana-Mou. Although Ela-Mana-Mou turned the tables when they met again in the Group 2 Royal Lodge Stakes over a mile at Ascot in September, Troy was obviously a potential Classic colt. He showed that he had made the right progress when he won the Group 3 Classic Trial over 1¼ miles at Sandown the next April. Dick wanted to give him another race before the Derby, and chose the Listed Predominate Stakes at the Goodwood May Meeting. The plan ran into difficulties when Willie had a fall at Chester and broke his collarbone, and it was touch and go whether he would be fit to ride at Goodwood. He just made it. Troy was only his second ride after resuming, but all was well as he outclassed his opponents.

The Derby was run on a Wednesday, which was just as well because a deluge waterlogged the course and forced the abandonment of the next day's card. In the race Dick's second runner, the Queen's colt Milford ridden by Lester Piggott, was sharing the lead with Lyphard's Wish as they rounded Tattenham Corner, with Troy more than halfway down the field tucked away on the inside rail. Dickens Hill burst clear with 3 furlongs to go and went all out for home. At almost the same moment

Willie found an opening and switched Troy to the outside. The speed which Troy then showed was sensational, and he swept past Dickens Hill well over a furlong from the finish and went right away to win by 7 lengths, the longest winning margin of any Derby winner since Manna won by 8 lengths in 1925. Years later Dick had this pertinent comment on the way Troy had finished: 'When you look at films of the race you can see that when he was accelerating throughout the last 2 furlongs he was turning over the turf behind him as he galloped, and he was the only one doing so.'

Troy and Dickens Hill, who had held on to second place at Epsom, met again in the Irish Derby, and again finished first and second. This time Dickens Hill was held up for a late challenge, but he could not get on terms with Troy, who had another decisive win by 4 lengths. After the race Tony Murray, the rider of Dickens Hill, said with resignation: 'Now we have tried it both ways, and I don't see why the result should ever be different.' At the same time Dick paid this tribute to Troy: 'He has a marvellous temperament, is no problem to train and has great speed.' Troy met older horses for the first time in the King George VI and Queen Elizabeth Stakes and struck a telling blow for his age group when he beat the French-trained four-year-old Gay Mecene by 1½ lengths. He was a big horse, a good doer and needed a lot of work. Dick felt that the interval of more than two months between the Ascot race and the Prix de l'Arc de Triomphe was too long for him to be without a race, and was anxious to run him in the Benson and Hedges Gold Cup at the York August Meeting, but had an awful job to persuade the Weinstocks to let him run there. In the end he had practically to give them a written guarantee that he would win before they gave permission. In the event Troy, despite having a lot of ground to make up in the straight, won easing up by ¾ of a length from Crimson Beau. Despite being a big, heavy horse, he had such a good action that he wanted fast ground, and was much less effective in the soft. Heavy rain had made the ground unsuitable when he ran in the 'Arc', but he still ran a good race to finish third behind the top-class filly Three Troikas. That was his last race. He retired to the Highclere Stud sound; indeed he never had a day's lameness in his life. It was a bitter blow when his stud career proved even briefer than that of his sire. He was only seven when he was found dead in his box one morning as a result of a twisted gut. Dick afterwards expressed surprise that there had not been a night watchman to look after such a valuable horse, the winner of two Derbys. If he had been more closely supervised, his condition might have been observed in time for remedial surgery.

Troy ran twice at Goodwood, which was one of Dick's favourite courses. He was always happy to run high-class horses on the undulating track set in beautiful countryside high on the Sussex Downs. Sallust, Cistus, Prince Bee and Morcon won at Goodwood three times each, and altogether he saddled the winners of no fewer than forty-two Pattern and Listed races there. For many years he first rented and then purchased a house at West Wittering, where Chichester Harbour opens to the sea and only 10 miles from Goodwood, which provided short periods of relaxation from the exacting routine of training a large string of horses during the May and July meetings. The Herns always hired a cook and used the opportunity to entertain some of their friends in congenial surroundings. In later years their most regular guests were the witty Sarah (Lady) Allendale, Desmond and Molly Baring and Mikey and Pat Seely. The Barings were Berkshire neighbours of the Herns, living at Ardington on the north side of the Downs only 3 miles from West Ilsley as the crow flies. The front of their house was embellished by two pillars surmounted by cannon balls recovered from the battlefield of Inkerman, and it was supposed to be lucky to touch them. Molly, like Dick, loved a sing-song, and knew most of his favourite songs like *Won't You Come Home Bill Bailey, It Happened In Monterey* and *Baby Doll.* Usually they settled down to play cards, bridge or poker with variations, after dinner. The mornings, to borrow a phrase from the travel brochures, were 'at leisure'. Mikey would certainly be out at sea, indulging his passion for windsurfing; while Sheilah, in the manner of the Lewis Carroll character who hunted for haddock's eyes among the heather bright and worked them into waistcoat buttons, would sometimes go onto the beach to exercise her gift of serendipity in respect of rare cowries which she put to use as counters for their games of poker.

Although Troy was absent, he had a worthy successor as a four-year-old in training at West Ilsley in his old rival Ela-Mana-Mou who, apart from their two encounters as two-year-olds, had finished behind him in fourth place in the Derby and in third in the King George VI and Queen Elizabeth Stakes. The Weinstocks bought Ela-Mana-Mou from Mrs Audrey Muinos at the end of 1979. The Muinos were rich Greek restaurant owners, and Dick thought it odd that they should want to sell the horse. He soon found out the reason. He was a charming little horse, good in every way. His first race was the Earl of Sefton Stakes at the Newmarket Craven Meeting, and he duly won, but was slightly jarred up afterwards. The next day Greville Starkey, who had ridden him when he was trained by Guy Harwood at Pulborough, asked Willie Carson how he was. 'All right, as far as I know,' said Willie. The significance of Greville's question was revealed when the bloodstock agent Peter Wragg, who had negotiated the deal, was talking to a stud hand who had looked after Ela-Mana-Mou when he was trained by Guy Harwood. 'You know there was a lady physio who used to come over from Guildford to treat him every week,' he said. When he heard that, Dick realised that the horse must have been jarred up when he was with Harwood, and that he would have to be very careful not to run him on firm ground. Dick asked his secretary Brian Holmes whether he could find out about a lady physio who lived in Guildford and treated human beings and racehorses. Besides being a very efficient secretary, Holmes had a happy knack of knowing the right person in the right place at the right time. He had a pal who had been in the army with him and lived in Guildford, and he found her. Her name was Pam Leadham, and she was engaged to come down to West Ilsley each week and work on the horse's back and shoulders. It was extremely lucky that a chance remark to Peter Wragg had alerted Dick to Ela-Mana-Mou's chronic problem. Carefully handled, Ela-Mana-Mou had a triumphant campaign, gaining three more victories in the Group 2 Prince of Wales's Stakes at Royal Ascot and two Group 1 races, the Coral Eclipse Stakes and the King George VI and Queen Elizabeth Stakes. The going was good on all three occasions, but it only came right just in time for the big Ascot race. The going had been firm and Dick had been prepared to pull him out, but rain that morning softened the ground. The luck deserted him in the 'Arc', when the going at Longchamp was unseasonably firm. He was fitted with rubber undershoes to remove some of the jar, but he still could not stride out freely and was beaten into third place behind Detroit and Argument. It was still a fine performance, as he had the previous year's first and second, Three Troikas and Le Marmot, behind him. Murphy's Law was in full swing; in 1979 Troy, who wanted fast ground, found it too soft; and in 1980 Ela-Mana-Mou, who wanted it soft, found it too firm. These vagaries of the weather may have deprived Dick of two 'Arc' victories.

Simon Weinstock, in whose name Ela-Mana-Mou ran, was Arnold's only son. He was still at school when he first visited West Ilsley in 1970, and then pleased Dick by asking to see Highest Hopes, which showed that he already appreciated a good horse. Dick thought that his understanding of horses would be enhanced if he learnt to ride, and suggested that he should go down to Devon and do a course with the former Olympic rider Bertie Hill. It was all arranged, but the whole idea was scrapped at the last moment. Probably Arnold thought that as he had been able to get by as an owner-breeder without being able to ride, his son could do likewise.

There was a contrast between the educational backgrounds of

Arnold and his son. Arnold had been educated at Albion Road Central School and the LSE, where he took a degree in statistics; Simon went to Winchester and Magdalen College, Oxford, which might be considered a better preparation for socialising with the English upper classes than for a career in business. In practice he appeared to take little trouble to cultivate the social graces, but he had inherited a flair for business. Having started with the merchant bankers Warburgs, he joined GEC, becoming first commercial manager and then commercial director. He took a steadily increasing interest in the stud and racing stables, paying particular attention to the matings of the mares. His death at the age of only forty-four was a tragedy not only for his family but for racing and breeding, as he would certainly have wished to continue the bloodstock empire whose foundations had been so securely laid by his father and grandfather.

The Sobell and Weinstock partnership bred and owned Sun Princess, who was acclaimed by Dick as the best filly he trained. A bay foaled in 1980, she had close connections with horses that had already represented her owners with distinction. She was a daughter of English Prince by Petingo, the sire of Troy, while her dam Sunny Valley came from the same old Ballymacoll family as Sun Prince. She was backward as a two-year-old and ran only once, finishing second in the Blue Seal Stakes at Ascot, but Dick was already aware that she had terrific ability. She was a difficult filly to settle, but that problem was coped with in her canters at home by putting her immediately behind Geordie Campbell's hack, with her nose touching his tail. As a three-year-old she won the Oaks by 12 lengths and, after finishing third to another outstanding filly, the year older Time Charter, in the King George VI and Queen Elizabeth Stakes, she returned to winning form with a comfortable victory in the Yorkshire Oaks. After that Dick was very keen to run her in the St Leger, but the Weinstocks were against the idea because they thought it might take the edge off her for the 'Arc'. Their attitude was understandable as, having been third with Troy and Ela-Mana-

Mou, they wanted desperately to win the race. Dick was opposed to giving too high a priority to the 'Arc' because there were so many imponderables involved – the draw, which could have a big effect on a horse's chance, the pace set by the leaders, and the unpredictability of the going in Paris in October, which had militated against the chances of Troy and Ela-Mana-Mou. In the end he persuaded the Weinstocks to let her take her chance at Doncaster, but he knew that they would use any excuse to make him take her out. The Herns were staying with Bobby and Maria Chaworth-Musters at Felley Priory near Nottingham for the meeting. It rained heavily during the night before the race, and it was still raining when they woke up in the morning. Dick decided that he must go over and walk the course at once and, having done so, found that the going was on the soft side but not too bad for Sun Princess. As the time for racing approached Dick went to the weighing room to await the arrival of the Weinstocks. Presently Peter Scott came running in and told him: 'Arnold and Simon are in the car park, and they don't look like running.' That was all the warning Dick needed. As the Weinstocks came in he greeted them brightly: 'Hello, I hope you had a good run. I've had a walk round and the going is not too bad at all.' That took the wind out of their sails momentarily, and they agreed to Dick's suggestion to wait and see how the early races were run before making a decision. The first race was a ladies' race, and the runners finished legless. 'Don't pay any attention to that. The ladies can't hold their horses together and they always finish tired. Willie is riding in the next race, and he will be able to tell us what the ground is like,' Dick told them. The race concerned was the Group 2 Flying Childers Stakes for two-year-olds over 5 furlongs and Willie's mount was Chapel Cottage. They went up on to the weighing roof to watch the race, and to his dismay Dick noticed that Chapel Cottage stumbled and came down on her head about the 2-furlong marker, though Willie managed to stay in the saddle and she recovered to finish third. When he came in Willie said: 'It's not bad at all – just a bit on the easy side.' Fortunately the Weinstocks had not seen that Chapel Cross had nearly fallen, and they agreed to run. In the event Sun Princess came through to take the lead more than a furlong from home, and ran on strongly to beat the French colt Esprit Du Nord by ¾ of a length. The race did not take too much out of her and she was at the top of her form again for the 'Arc' three weeks later, when she ran a fine race to be second to the year-older filly All Along. It was not running in the St Leger that had cost the Weinstocks another chance of winning the 'Arc'; Time Charter and Diamond Shoal, who had beaten her at Ascot in July, both finished behind her on this occasion.

The move of the horses owned by Sobell, Weinstock and Lady Beaverbrook from Whitsbury Manor meant a big influx at West Ilsley, and some of the former owners, including John Pearce, Lady Rothermere and Lord Ranfurly, had to be disappointed. As a result the increase in the number of horses was kept to manageable proportions, rising from seventy-eight in 1970 to eighty-five the next year. Lady Beaverbrook (Lady B as she was called) had several similarities with Dorothy Paget, the founder of Ballymacoll. They were both eccentric, they were both super-stitious, they were both vastly rich, and they were both lavish spenders on bloodstock. However it would not do to over-emphasise the resemblances, because there were equally con-spicuous differences; for example DP was excessively fat, and Lady B was excessively thin. Degrees of corpulence are some-times determined by the caprices of metabolism, but in the case of these two ladies they were related directly to calorie intake. Whereas DP was prone to consume huge meals at any hour of the day or night, Lady B's feeding habits were inhibited by an obsessive fear of food poisoning, and she ate very little. On one occasion she was invited to a luncheon as 'Lady Racehorse Owner Of The Year'. 'Of course I shan't eat anything,' she told Dick. 'Surely you could have a little smoked salmon,' he suggested, but she objected. 'Someone will have handled it, and you never know where those fingers have been.'

Once when Dick wanted to run one of her horses at Salisbury she demurred. 'But the food there is horrible,' she said. 'Lady Beaverbrook,' Dick replied, 'if we go on like this, we shall run out of racecourses.' She laughed. In any case, it was extremely unlikely that she would have tasted the racecourse food. She preferred to take her own lunch, sandwiches wrapped in a white linen napkin, and eat it in her beaver-brown Rolls in the car park.

Born Marcia Anastasia Christoforides, she was the daughter of John Christophorides, a tobacco merchant of Cypriot extraction. She grew up in Sutton, Surrey, and by the time she was twenty she had become interested in politics and Lord Beaverbrook's Empire Free Trade crusade. She wrote to the editor of *The Sunday Express*, then owned by Beaverbrook, with some suggestions for the campaign. This led to the advice that she should apply for a job to Beaverbrook's fellow Canadian businessman, Sir James Dunn, who took her on as his secretary. Dunn was chairman of the Algoma Steel Corporation, and was so impressed by her efficiency that in due course she was promoted to the position of assistant secretary of the corporation. She became his constant aide and companion, nursed him through a near-fatal illness, and in 1942 became his third wife.

Dunn died four years later, but in 1963 she became the second wife of Dunn's old friend Lord Beaverbrook, who died a year later. She thus had the rare distinction of being married to two Canadian multi-millionaires, and easily outlived them both. This marital policy was only half successful as, although Dunn left her a large fortune, Beaverbrook left her nothing except a portrait of himself, which she kept well out of sight on an upper wall. Beaverbrook's miserly legacy had a negligible effect on her spending power; apart from her Dunn fortune, she was a shrewd businesswoman in her own right, and when she sold her personal holding of Algoma Steel shares she realised £7.2 million. Beaverbrook had a brief flirtation with racing in the 1930s, but soon gave up when he discovered that the expenditure of large sums

of money did not necessarily bring success. In contrast to her
late husband, Lady B took up racing with much greater determination.

Seven was her lucky number. The large majority of her horses,
with the exception of the Coronation Cup winner Easter Sun,
who was born on Easter day, and the St Leger winner Minster
Son, who was named after his breeder Willie Carson's stud, had
seven-letter names. If one of her horses was number seven on
the card it was regarded as practically a guarantee of success.
She was introduced to racing by the sixth Earl of Rosebery, the
owner-breeder of the Derby winners Blue Peter and Ocean
Swell, and became a determined buyer at the yearling sales with
the will and the cash to challenge the wealthy foreign buyers
and retain some of the best horses in Britain. She loved to attend
Tattersalls yearling sales at Newmarket and do her own bidding,
seeing off rival bidders with relish. She attached so much importance to names that sometimes she would ring up Weatherbys
and book a name before she had even bought the horse.

One day when she was buying yearlings at Newmarket she
told Dick that it was all Dunn money she was spending, and
that she was going to call the first horse she bought All Dunn.
'Then you ought to call the next two Over Dunn and Under
Dunn,' he remarked, and she saw the joke, although a sense of
humour was not her strongest point. She loved her horses and
when Rampage, thought to be an even better two-year-old than
his contemporaries in the stable Sallust and Sun Prince, staggered
and fell after 2 furlongs of the New Stakes at Royal Ascot, she
insisted on walking down the course to see him, leaning on
Dick's arm and in floods of tears. The post-mortem revealed
that his lungs were full of fluid, but the exact cause of death was
never established.

The greatest character among the horses owned by Lady B
was Boldboy, who won fourteen of his forty-five races and was
placed on twenty-seven occasions. He was equally good from 6
furlongs to a mile, and his eight Pattern race victories included

the Challenge Stakes twice, the Clerical Medical Greenham Stakes, the Diadem Stakes, the Lockinge Stakes, the Duke of York Stakes, the Vernons Sprint Cup and the Prix de la Porte Maillot; he also won the Listed Abernant Stakes three times. Sir Gordon Richards bought him for Lady B as a yearling in Ireland. He was very good looking but rather temperamental, like many of the progeny of Bold Lad. He was a rig, and suffered from claustrophobia. It was very difficult to get him into the stalls, and when he did go in he used to put his legs right through to the next door stall and lean on the side. Dick had a special mock-up stall made for him with inch-and-a-quarter thick boards at the sides let right into the ground so he couldn't get his legs through. It was necessary to be very hard on him to make him tractable in the stalls. Dick explained: 'I used to have to put him on the ground and let him get up and try again. If he still wouldn't go in I would put him on the ground again. Eventually we got him reasonable, but it was always tricky getting him into the stalls on the racecourse.'

Dick had great difficulty in persuading Lady B to have him gelded at the end of his two-year-old season, but the operation was the making of him as a racehorse. He was top class, and could go on any ground. He never lost his claustrophobic tendencies, and hated being in his box. He would race round and round it, and had to be tied up. When he had finished racing Lady B made an arrangement with Jakie Astor for him to live in retirement at the Warren Stud at Newmarket. Two boxes were built, one for him and one for his gelding companion, with an adjoining paddock. A board was placed at the back of his box with the names of all the races he had won painted on it, just as if he had been a stallion. He lived happily to a ripe old age.

The top-class horses that Dick trained for Lady B included Relkino, Bustino, Niniski and his son Petoski. Niniski was by the Triple Crown winner Nijinsky, but was a staying horse who followed up a third place in the St Leger by gaining Group 1 victories in the Irish St Leger and the Prix Royal Oak at Long-champ. For a horse of his type he was a remarkably successful stallion at Kirsten Rausing's Lanwades Stud at Newmarket, siring a number of high-class horses besides Petoski. Bustino and Relkino were both Classic horses. Bustino was bought for the relatively small sum of 21,000 guineas at the Newmarket Houghton yearling sales in 1972. He ran only once as a two-year-old, finishing third in the Acomb Stakes at the York August Meeting. After that he got a slightly dirty nose, so he was put away for the rest of the season. He began the next season well by beating the subsequent Derby winner Snow Knight in the Classic Trial Stakes at Sandown, and had Snow Knight behind him again, this time in third place, when he won the Lingfield Derby Trial. Therefore it came as a shock when he could finish only fourth in the Derby, which Snow Knight won by 2 lengths at the forlorn price of 50–1. Bustino got a shockingly bad run, losing a lot of ground in some scrimmaging at the top of the hill. He was running on strongly at the finish, and Dick thought that with better luck in running he could have won. He liked the top of the ground, and it was too soft when he was second to the great stayer Sagaro, who was to win the Ascot Gold Cup three times, in the Grand Prix de Paris, then run over a distance only half a furlong less than 2 miles. He returned to winning form in the Great Voltigeur Stakes at the York August Meeting, when he beat the Irish Derby winner English Prince by 4 lengths. He was also a convincing winner of the St Leger, in which Lady B's other good three-year-old, Riboson, served him well as pacemaker and kept going gallantly to take third place.

Dick's plans for Bustino as a four-year-old were frustrated by Lady B's insistence that he should run only in Group 1 races. Apparently she feared that running in any lower category of race would depreciate him. For that reason Dick had to take him out of the Group 2 Yorkshire Cup at the last minute. Instead he ran Riboson, who proceeded to win, which showed how far Bustino would have won. Bustino went straight to the Coronation Cup over the Derby course, which he won in the new record time of 2 minutes 33.31 seconds, while Riboson was last after making the running until 2 furlongs from home. That cleared the decks for the clash of Bustino and the year younger Grundy, who had won the Derby and the Irish Derby, in the King George VI and Queen Elizabeth Stakes. The race was to prove one of the epic encounters in the history of the British Turf, though this was not foreseen by the market, as Grundy started at 5–4 on.

Knowing that Bustino would stay every inch of the 1½ miles and that the only way to beat Grundy was to stretch him all the way, Dick took the precaution of entering three pacemakers. Unfortunately the best of them, Riboson, went wrong, and he had to rely on the other two. Highest, ridden by Frank Durr, made the running for 4½ furlongs. Kinglet, ridden by Eric Eldin, then took it up, but he was done for 3 furlongs from home and Bustino had to take up the running. He led into the straight, but by then Grundy had moved into second place. For some time Bustino was holding the Derby winner, but then Pat Eddery drew his whip and Grundy began to make relentless inroads into Bustino's lead. Grundy drew level a furlong from home, and in the final stages both horses and jockeys were giving everything they had got. It was only in the last hundred yards that Grundy wore down his rival and gained a ½ length victory in a race which lived for ever in the memories of all those privileged to witness it.

Joe Mercer never drew his whip on Bustino because, he said, he knew that he was trying his heart out. His forbearance showed what a great and sympathetic jockey he was. Dick felt that the absence of Riboson made the vital difference between winning and losing, because he would have been able to lead into the straight and Bustino would not have had to go on so soon. The superb quality of the first two horses is amply demonstrated by the facts that they lowered the course record by as much as two and a half seconds and that the great mare Dahlia, who had won the race in each of the previous two years, was beaten into third place by 5 lengths. All the circumstances of the race and the enthusiastic reactions of the crowd were so exhilarating that Dick remarked to Sheilah when they were on their way home in the car: 'You know, I don't feel deflated at all. Our horse ran such a marvellous race that I am just as excited as if he had won.'

Neither of the principals was unmarked by the experience. Grundy, though outwardly still in good form, ran a lifeless race in the Benson and Hedges Gold Cup three weeks later and finished in fourth place more than 10 lengths behind Dahlia. That was his last race. Bustino had a slight leg and Dick, mindful of the saying of the distinguished National Hunt trainer Tim Forster, who trained three Grand National winners, that 'there is no such thing as a slight leg – it's like being slightly pregnant', decided that he should be retired. He was syndicated and stationed at the Queen's Wolferton Stud, where he was respectably successful, siring the Derby second Terimon and Easter Sun for Lady B and other good horses like Paean and Height Of Fashion besides a number of good jumpers like the top-class hurdler Mysilv.

The King George VI and Queen Elizabeth Stakes of 1975 had a unique sequel, because it was the only instance of a single race bringing about a change in the official weight-for-age scale. The authorities, notably the Senior Handicapper David Swannell, judged that Grundy and Bustino were identical in ability, and for that reason the difference between a three-year-old and a four-year-old over 1½ miles at the end of July was reduced from 14 to 13 lbs.

After Bustino had won the St Leger in 1974 Lady B had instructed Dick to go to the Houghton Sales and buy her the best colt he could see. It was a tall order because, however comely a horse may be, it is impossible to see inside him and inspect the engine. However, he decided to apply the principles of selecting a yearling which he enunciated later in life:

If you had to buy a horse by one point alone, I think you would choose his head. He must have a good eye, room between the jaws and good big ears. He must have quality and soundness, and a flat horse should not be too big. He should have width in his quarters, sloping shoulders and plenty of girth.

He recalled that Sir Gordon Richards hated a horse that was light of his middle. When he used to go round looking at yearlings with him, Gordon would write diagonally across the catalogue page 'Drainpipe', and the horse was eliminated from further consideration.

At the Houghton Sales in 1974 Dick soon latched on to a colt by the Derby winner Relko out of the fast and appropriately named mare Pugnacity from Holliday's Cleaboy Stud, whose colts were being sold that year. He conformed to Dick's principles of selection, and was a glorious rich bay in colour. He looked at a great many other colts, but kept coming back to him, and finally decided that he was the one. When he came up for sale, the bidding was keen, but he was knocked down to Dick for 58,000 guineas, the top price for any yearling in England or Ireland that year. Lady B named him Relkino.

Dick always loved Relkino, but he was not the easiest horse to train. As a two-year-old he was a very hard puller, and either Stan Clayton, who was assistant trainer at the time, or Harry Grant, known as 'The Whisperer' on account of his soft voice, rode him in all his work. They both had beautiful hands and could hold him. The racing careers of Bustino and Relkino overlapped for one season, and Relkino made a successful debut in the Ecchinswell Maiden Stakes over 6 furlongs at Newbury a month before Bustino ran in the big race at Ascot, but ran badly in his only subsequent race in his first season, the Washington Singer Stakes on the same course. The next year he opened his campaign by winning the 2000 Guineas Trial at Ascot at the beginning of April, and ran his best race in the Derby. He was in second place at Tattenham Corner and took the lead a furlong and a half from home, but was no match in the final stages for Empery, who drew away to beat him by 3 lengths

Dick decided that he had not quite stayed the Derby distance, and he never ran over a longer distance than 1¼ miles again. His ability to stay was inhibited by the fact that he became very difficult to settle as a three-year-old. The solution was to fit him with a double-mouthed snaffle – a snaffle with two mouthpieces on the one ring and the joints offset. A horse finds it difficult to set himself against it, and Relkino settled well for Willie Carson in it. As a four-year-old he won the Lockinge Stakes at Newbury in May, but he wore the double-mouthed snaffle for the first time in the Sussex Stakes at the Goodwood July Meeting when he was third to Artaius. The next time out in the Benson and Hedges Gold Cup he started at 33–1 but turned the tables on Artaius, the odds-on favourite, to win by 4 lengths. His only subsequent race was the Champion Stakes, in which he again ran well to be second to the brilliant French-trained filly Flying Water.

As the years went by Lady B's eccentricity and unpredictability made her increasingly difficult to deal with. On Dick's advice she moved some of her horses to Clive Brittain at Newmarket, and eventually sent all her horses there, explaining to Dick: 'You used to telephone only once a week, but Clive Brittain rings up every day.' By then she was a lonely old woman, and the daily calls gave her an interest and helped to pass the time, though often Clive could have little new information about her horses to impart. One of the horses Clive trained for her was Terimon, who was second to the Hern-trained Nashwan in the Derby in 1989. Another was Mystiko, who won the 2000 Guineas in 1991. She died three years later. She had no children, and there was nobody to carry on her racing empire.

Sobell, Weinstock and Lady B brought another great asset with them from Whitsbury Manor besides their horses. That was their former trainer Sir Gordon Richards, who became their racing manager. Dick and Gordon got on extremely well from the start. Dick had the most sincere admiration for Gordon. Like many other people, he was convinced that his strong personality, intelligence and forthright nature would have enabled him to succeed in any walk of life that he had chosen to adopt. Strangely, he did not do as well as a trainer as had been expected, but Dick believed that the reason for his comparative failure was that the tremendous expenditure of energy involved in riding 4870 winners and being champion jockey twenty-six times had left him ill-prepared for the demands of another but equally exacting profession. His big head, short legs and rolling gait made him an unforgettable figure. For many years he had been undisputed cock of the walk in the jockeys changing-room, and set a shining example to all his professional rivals except in one respect – his riding style. Like Lester Piggott after him, he was a genius, and any attempt to copy their highly individual and unorthodox methods would have been fatal.

When he became racing manager Gordon was worried what to do with his old hack, a chestnut pony called Pip. Dick solved the problem by offering to keep Pip at West Ilsley. This proved a good arrangement, as Gordon was able to drive over from his home at Kintbury near Newbury and ride out on work mornings. As racing manager he was an ideal colleague. Ninety-nine times out of a hundred he accepted Dick's suggestions for the horses, and when he did make a comment it was always pertinent. Dick sometimes consulted him about matters entirely divorced from racing, and found invariably that his advice was absolutely sound. His sense of humour and his fund of reminiscences made him a delightful companion.

On one occasion when the two Weinstocks were there they went up onto the Summer Downs in the Land-Rover. After watching the canter they got back into the vehicle. Gordon and Simon were in the back, and as they began to move the back door swung open. Gordon leant out to pull it shut just as Dick accelerated, and Gordon lost his balance and fell out. Fortunately he was unhurt, and as he ran to catch up he shouted: 'That would have looked well as a headline in the papers: "Dick Hern kills Gordon Richards"'. On another occasion mats of the kind in use at Epsom and Ascot had been put down on crossings. Dick suggested that they should go up and try them before any racehorses were put over them. Dick gave the lead, but when he reached the crossing Pip ducked and Gordon fell off. He was wearing a big mackintosh, and as he descended it billowed out like a parachute. Again Gordon was unhurt, and they had a good laugh.

One of Gordon's reminiscences concerned the 1929 Cesarewitch, in which he was riding West Wicklow and one of the leading lightweight jockeys, Johnny Dines, was on Friendship. In the Dip the great stayer Brown Jack, who was conceding lumps of weight to the others, was beaten, and West Wicklow and Friendship began to draw away. It looked as if Friendship was going at least as well as West Wicklow and, as they came close together locked in combat, Gordon leaned across and grabbed Johnny Dines by the balls. Johnny yelled out and stopped riding for a couple of strides, and by the time he got down to work again West Wicklow and Gordon were a length ahead with the race won. There had obviously been an incident of some sort, and a Stewards Enquiry was called. 'What happened, Richards?' asked the chairman Lord D'Abernon. 'Well, m'Lord,' said Gordon, 'they were two tired horses, and as they rolled together our whips got entangled.' The explanation was accepted. Some time later Gordon and Lord D'Abernon met out shooting. Referring to the enquiry, D'Abernon said: 'I knew you were telling the truth, Richards. You looked me straight in the eye.'

At the beginning of the first week of November 1986 Jakie Astor was going over to see his horses at West Ilsley and stay to lunch. Dick thought it would be fun to have Gordon too, and invited him to join them. He opened a bottle of champagne before lunch, and the little man was soon in fine form and in reminiscing mode. He told the story of how one Derby day as he walked into the weighing room at Epsom Captain Allison, who was the senior Jockey Club starter for many years, came up to him and said: 'Gordon, my wife is coming today. She doesn't often go racing these days. Is there anything she can have a pound on?' Gordon told him that he thought he would win the first race, a 5-furlong sprint. The story continued: 'We lined up, and I knew I could take every chance, so I came into the tapes as fast as I could go, because he would have to let me go. I got an absolute flyer.' 'Did you win, Gordon?' Dick asked. 'No,' he said. 'I was beaten by a short head.'

That was Gordon's last visit to West Ilsley. A week later he collapsed and died of a heart attack when shaving, but that visit left very happy memories of him.

The Sobell-Weinstock era brought other Classic successes to both the present owners of the West Ilsley stables and their predecessor. In 1974 Sobell and Weinstock won the Irish 1000 Guineas with Gaily, a top-class filly over a mile who also stayed 1½ miles and went on to be second in the Irish Oaks and third in the Prix Vermeille, and fifteen years later Helen Street went one better for them in the Irish Oaks. Jakie Astor won the Irish 2000 Guineas with Sharp Edge in 1973 and the St Leger with Cut Above in 1981. Sharp Edge was bred as a result of a mare swap with another patron of the stable, the eternal pessimist Dick Hollingsworth, and Hollingsworth seemed almost to derive a perverse satisfaction from the fact that the exchange had benefited Jakie much more than it benefited himself.

However, it was not only these 'old patrons' who were projected into the Classic picture by Dick. One day in the autumn of 1978 he met Mrs Arpad (Etty) Plesch at the Newmarket Sales, and she told him: 'I have two yearlings at the Hadrian Stud. You can have whichever you like, and I will send the other to France.' Dick thanked her and went up to the Hadrian Stud, on the Woodditton road just outside Newmarket, and had a look at the two colts. Luckily he chose Henbit, because the other colt, though good-looking, turned out to be no good. Henbit was a little bit on the leg, but full of quality. He was slightly weak as a two-year-old, but showed plenty of promise by winning one of his three races, the Kris Plate over a mile at Newbury in September, and finishing fourth in the Dewhurst Stakes over a furlong less at Newmarket. He was unbeaten as a three-year-old, winning in succession the Classic Trial Stakes at Sandown and the Chester Vase, two of Dick's most favoured races for getting a horse ready for Epsom, and finally the Derby itself.

His performance in the Derby proved that he was a very brave as well as a top-class colt. From fifth place entering the straight he made steady progress to take the lead more than a furlong from home, and at that point looked like winning comfortably. Well inside the last furlong he suddenly changed legs and faltered, but kept going well enough to hold the late challenge of Master Willie by ¾ of a length. He was Etty Plesch's second Derby winner, as the unconsidered Psidium had won for her in 1961.

The aftermath was not so happy. He was very lame when he returned to the winner's enclosure, and X-rays taken when he got home revealed that he had cracked his cannon bone badly. He had to stand in his box for three months, and there was no question of running him again that season. He was kept in training as a four-year-old, but never recovered his form. He worked well at home, but he would not let himself down in a race, probably because he remembered his injury. He had made a vital contribution to a triumphant season for the West Ilsley stable in which Dick Hollingsworth's filly Bireme had completed the Epsom Classic double by winning the Oaks and Ela-Mana-Mou had gained his Group 1 victories in the Coral-Eclipse Stakes and the King George VI and Queen Elizabeth Stakes. They were mainly instrumental in propelling Dick to the top the trainers table with sixty-five wins of a value of £831,964, his highest seasonal total up to that time. It was his third trainers' championship, and each had been in a different decade; he had headed the list previously in 1962 and 1972.

The injury that Henbit suffered in the Derby prompted Dick to some reflections on the advisability of committing horses to running in it:

There is no doubt that the Derby is the race that every trainer, owner and jockey wants to win, but it's run over a very difficult course, where the ground is generally firm. There is no depth of soil at Epsom, and a lot of horses come back badly jarred. There is no point in running a horse that has no chance, or only a very outside chance. A lot of owners insist on running because they want to have a runner in the Derby, but it's a great mistake. The bad horses go on as hard as they can to make a show up to the top of the hill and then, when they start to drop back, it is just when the fancied ones want to be improving their position. That is why the Derby is such a rough race, and why there is such a great chance of a horse being struck into. It requires a jockey with a cool head; so many leave their brains behind because it is such a prestigious race.

Besides the perennials like Geordie Campbell and Buster Haslam, Dick had some excellent staff to work for him at West Ilsley. One was Reg Cartwright, who became his main work rider. He had been leading apprentice in Ireland until he had a bad fall, and had some amusing stories about racing in Ireland during the war when there was no petrol. He was attached to the Kildangan stable, where they had an old sprinter called Dead Level. He was broken to harness and the head man drove him to the Curragh, a distance of 7 miles. He was then taken out of the gig and washed down. Later in the afternoon he ran and won, and was then put back in the gig and driven home to Kildangan. After his accident Reg came to England and worked at the Atomic Research Establishment at Harwell, a few miles down the road from West Ilsley, before coming to work for Dick.

Another key member of the West Ilsley staff was Stan Clayton, who was assistant trainer at the time he was riding Relkino in much of his work. Dick had an association with him dating from his earliest days in Newmarket, when Stan had been first jockey to Major Holliday. He had been invaluable to Dick, showing him round the gallops and all the intricacies of Newmarket Heath. When he retired from race-riding he went as assistant trainer to Bruce Hobbs at Palace House in Newmarket. Bruce had a very high opinion of him, describing him as 'the best work rider he had ever come across and a delightful little man'. Stan also possessed a lively sense of humour. When he left Bruce he had spells as a trainer in Italy and Sweden before returning to England and taking up the post at West Ilsley.

Stan's latter years were dogged by ill health. He had a stroke and then suffered from kidney failure. For a long time he had to make regular visits to Oxford for dialysis treatment, and then had a dialysis machine installed in his home at The Malthouse in West Ilsley, but his condition deteriorated steadily.

There was also a health problem with Gorytus, who as a two-year-old was one of the best horses Dick ever trained, but in his case the problem was not due to natural causes. The name is pronounced GOR-ETUS, which was a quiver for arrows used by the ancient Greeks. He was classically bred, by the Triple Crown winner Nijinsky out of the 1000 Guineas winner Glad Rags. Dick was asked to train him by Mimi Abel-Smith, who had married Billy Abel-Smith after the death of Bernard Van Cutsem. Mimi was American by birth and lived in Virginia where her mother Mrs Jimmy Mills, who bred and owned Gorytus, had Hickory Tree Farm.

Mimi told Dick that he was a beautiful colt, and when he came to West Ilsley in the autumn of 1981 Dick was not disappointed as he was perfectly proportioned, if rather big. Owing to his size he was not hurried, and did not run until the Acomb Stakes at the York August Meeting, though he was fit to run a good deal earlier. His debut could not have been more impressive, as he beat the odds-on favouriite Salieri, who had won his two previous races easily, by 7 lengths in a time which beat the existing course record by more than a second. He was equally impressive in his next race, the Group 2 Laurent Perrier Stakes at Doncaster, and won by 5 lengths. Mr and Mrs Mills had come over for the race and were delighted, and so was Dick because, apart from his performance, he did not turn a hair when the press were milling round him and flash bulbs were going in the winner's enclosure. The press were ecstatic; Richard Baerlein, one of the shrewdest judges, hailed him as the best two-year-old he had ever seen – better even than his sire Nijinsky.

The next week Dick was standing on the bank beside the paddock at Ayr when Phil Bull, the founder of Timeform and a man in close touch with the betting market, came up to him and said: 'Well done at Doncaster.' Dick thanked him very much. 'You know what your main trouble is going to be now, don't you?' said Phil. 'No, what's that?' said Dick. 'Security,' said Phil. 'Some bookmakers have laid him to lose so much money in the 2000 Guineas that if he wins they could not pay.' The next outing of Gorytus was in the Dewhurst Stakes. There were only four runners because he had frightened off most of his potential opponents, and he started at 2–1 on. He jumped off, but was not going even for a furlong. His situation soon became so hopeless that Willie Carson virtually pulled him up, and he trailed in last by 30 lengths. 'There is something very wrong with this horse, he never went at all,' said Willie as he dismounted. The horse was reeling about like a drunken sailor.

Of course he was taken to the dope box, and hardly seemed to know where to put his feet as he walked round the yard. John Grey, the vet who looked after the West Ilsley horses, was there, having a day out at the races. The Jockey Club vet allowed him to go into the dope box, and he found that the horse's heart was all over the place. They waited for an hour to see whether he was fit to be taken home, and at the end of that time his heart had returned to normal. Blood tests were done in England, Ireland and America, but no trace of anything that could have stopped him was discovered. Obviously he had been given something, but it was impossible to find out what it was. He did well over the winter, but he was never the same horse again on the racecourse. He was fifth in the 2000 Guineas, fourth in the Benson and Hedges Gold Cup and a close fifth in the Waterford Crystal Mile – respectable performances, but nothing like his brilliant two-year-old form. He was nervous on his visits to the racecourse, whereas he had shown no signs of nerves before. Mr and Mrs Mills took him back to the United States, where he ran several times and won one moderate race before being sold to Japan as a stallion. It is impossible to avoid the conclusion that Phil Bull's warning was well founded.

Prince Of Dance was another West Ilsley horse whose racing career ended tragically, though not in the same sinister circumstances. A contemporary of Nashwan, he finished first in all his four races as a two-year-old, though he was disqualified after the Washington Singer Stakes. He followed in the footsteps of Gorytus by winning the Laurent Perrier Champagne Stakes, and on his last appearance dead-heated with Scenic in the Group 1 Dewhurst Stakes. Although he was overshadowed by Nashwan at home, he was clearly Classic material. His three-year-old campaign began satisfactorily with a victory in the Newmarket Stakes. A week before the Derby Steve Cauthen went down to West Ilsley, rode him in a half-speed gallop over 6 furlongs and accepted the mount at Epsom. Willie Carson was to ride Nashwan. In the race Prince of Dance began to lose his action coming down the hill and finished in the ruck. After the Derby he gradually lost control of his hindquarters like a wobbler, and a fortnight later John Grey had no alternative but to put him down. The cause of the rapid deterioration of his condition was cancer of the spine. He had been a high-class horse and certainly a very well-bred one, as he was the first foal of Sun Princess by the great sire Sadler's Wells.

By that time – 1989 – Sobell and Weinstock were no longer the owners of West Ilsley. In 1982 it had been made known that the Queen would like to acquire the place, which was not too far from Windsor and within easy reach of Highclere and her stud Polhampton Lodge at Kingsclere, and the current owners were prepared to sell. Sobell was nearly ninety and had taken little part in the running of West Ilsley, leaving that side of things to the Weinstocks, while his increasing deafness made communication difficult. His interest in many charitable enterprises was as keen as ever. He built homes (hospices) for people terminally ill with cancer and retirement homes for nurses. One day Dick and Sheilah went over to his house at Englefield Green to tell him about his horses, as the impediment to his hearing made it impossible to have a proper conversation on the telephone. Face to face, he could hear adequately if his interlocutor spoke slowly and distinctly. Sheilah remarked that little had been done for retired stable lads in the area. Sobell reacted without hesitation, saying that he would give £100,000 to create the necessary homes in the village. The building was quickly arranged through the Stable Lads Welfare Trust.

The homes are contained in a close almost opposite The Old Rectory. A plaque on the wall of one of the cottages bears the brief inscription:

Fir Tree Cottages
Donated By
Sir Michael Sobell
To
The Stable Lads Welfare Trust
1982

The cottages, with their plaque, are a memorial to a man whose impact on racing and breeding as a whole, and on West Ilsley in particular, was wholly benign. He will be remembered as much for his benevolence as for the vision that led him to invest in Ballymacoll and its bloodstock or the brilliance of the British Classic winners – Troy and Sun Princess – that carried his light blue and yellow colours.

A luncheon party which the Herns gave at The Old Rectory to celebrate the Classic victories of Sun Princess marked the closing stages of the Sobell era. A marquee erected on the lawn, with access from the French window via an awning, accommodated the guests for the meal. It was a great success. The guests included the Queen, who obviously enjoyed herself. The same could not be said of another of the guests, Lady B, whose eating inhibitions again were paramount. She refused all the luscious dishes (smoked salmon and prawn cornets, chicken coronation, and fruit tartlets) provided by Willie Carson's wife Elaine, a professional caterer. Instead she demanded, and was duly served, a cheddar-cheese sandwich.

EIGHT

THE QUEEN AND WEST ILSLEY

FOR DICK THE QUEEN'S PURCHASE of West Ilsley Stables brought one fundamental change. Throughout his training career up to that point he had been a salaried employee, not only under the Astor and Sobell-Weinstock ownership of West Ilsley but before that when he was private trainer to Major Holliday at Newmarket. He now became a tenant, with a rent on a sliding scale geared to the success of the stable in any particular year: it was to be fifty per cent of the trainer's percentage of the sums earned by the stable's horses in prize money. If the stable had a bad or moderate year, the rent burden would be light; but in a good year, as in 1983 when he was champion trainer or in 1989 when the horses won more than £1 million, the rent would account for a high proportion of the overheads. The lease was to run for seven years from November 1982, when the Queen's purchase was completed, to November 1989. Fortuitously the change in status from employee to tenant had a happy outcome, as at a time of crisis it gave his occupation of the stables a vital measure of protection which an employee would not have enjoyed.

The change, of course, greatly increased Dick's responsibilities and worries in the financial sphere. For the first time, he was on his own. Under the Weinstock regime – Michael Sobell, though nominally a partner, took little interest in the running of the place and seldom visited it – Dick had been absolved from the problems of profit and loss. Arnold Weinstock is a deeply civilised man. His taste is demonstrated by the sumptuous appointments, immaculate gardens and superb views of his country house at Lacock, while his chief recreational interest, apart from thoroughbreds, is classical music; he is a Trustee of the Royal Philharmonic Society Foundation Fund. He is also one of the most successful British businessmen of the last half century, and he applied business methods to West Ilsley Stables. His accountants spent a week at West Ilsley at the end of every year checking minutely every item of income and expenditure. Weinstock himself authorised major items, like the ordering of a new horsebox specially designed to meet the stable's requirements. Once convinced of the need, he did not spare the expense. With his training in accountancy, Dick's secretary Brian Holmes gave his full approval to Weinstock's methods of supervision. Most importantly, Dick's salary was paid regularly into his private bank account each month. This comfortable patriarchal system came to an end in November 1982.

Dick had been training for the Queen for many years before she bought West Ilsley stables – to be precise from the autumn of 1966 when she sent him the first batch of yearlings. None of that batch was precocious, and his first success for her was gained by Forestry, a chesnut colt by Hornbeam, who won the Bristol Maiden stakes over 1¼ miles at Bath as a three-year-old on July 17 1968. He was moderate, and that was the only time he won. He was followed by St Patrick's Blue, a chesnut colt by St Paddy, who won the Cranbourn Chase Maiden Stakes over the same distance at Ascot nine days later. He then started odds-on favourite for the Ripon St Leger Trial, but was beaten by 8 lengths by Deep Sapphire, who turned the tables in dramatic fashion, as he had been third 10 lengths behind St Patrick's Blue at Ascot. He was gelded and trained on to become a reputable stayer, winning the Rufford Abbey Handicap over 2¼ miles at the St Leger meeting the next year, and the Clevedon Handicap over 2 miles at Bath and the Timeform Gold Trophy over 1 mile 6 furlongs and 132 yards at Redcar as a five-year-old.

The successes of St Patrick's Blue were no more than a prelude to the achievements of a much better stayer, the two years younger Charlton. Charlton ran only once as a two-year-old, when he showed promise by running on strongly at the finish of a race over 6 furlongs at Lingfield, a distance much too short for him. He did very well during the winter, and when he reappeared over the more suitable distance of 11 furlongs in the Spring Maiden Plate at Newbury he won easily. He had enough class to finish third in the King Edward VII Stakes at Royal Ascot and fourth behind the Triple Crown winner Nijinsky in the St Leger, and won his other two races that season, the Predominate Stakes at Goodwood and the Eglinton Stakes at York. He did well again during the following winter, and began his four-year-old campaign by winning the Group 3 Henry II stakes over 2 miles at Sandown. He ran next in the Ascot Gold Cup, in which he finished fourth but was promoted to third on the disqualification of the luckless Rock Roi, who failed a dope test after finishing first. He returned to winning form in the William Hill Gold Trophy over the St Leger course in July, beating the odds-on favourite Prince Consort. Charlton was third to the top-class French filly Miss Dan in the Group 2 Prix Kergorlay at Deauville, and ran the race of his life under the big weight of 9st 7lbs in the Ebor Handicap, beaten by 2 necks and a short head by horses to whom he was conceding a stone or more.

Charlton was a bay colt by Charlottesville, who had completed the elusive double of the French Derby and the Grand Prix de Paris in 1960, when the latter race enjoyed far greater prestige than it did in later times after its distance had been reduced from 15 to 10 furlongs. This double before the end of June called for an exceptional combination of courage, class and stamina, and Charlton inherited enough of those qualities from his sire to be a stayer of genuine merit. However, it was as a golden age of fillies, not colts, from the Royal Studs that the 1970s were to be most notable. Several of these high-class fillies were trained by Ian Balding, but the first of them to be trained by Dick was Albany, by the Queen's 2000 Guineas winner Pall Mall out of Almeria, an outstanding racemare whose five victories included the Group 1 Yorkshire Oaks, while she also finished second in the King George VI and Queen Elizabeth Stakes. Albany had shown promise by being placed in two of her three races as a two-year-old in 1970, but her temperament had become so unruly by the following spring that it seemed impossible for her to realise her potential. As a desperate expedient it was decided to put her in foal. The Queen's old friend Lord Porchester had been appointed as her racing manager in 1969, and in mid-April Albany was boxed 15 miles down the road to his father Lord Carnarvon's Highclere Stud on the far side of Newbury to be covered by the resident stallion Queen's Hussar. She got in foal to the first cover, and in no time she was back at West Ilsley and in full training. Pregnancy transformed her temperament; she behaved with perfect decorum when she ran in, and won, the Sandleford Priory Stakes at Newbury on 21 May, and a fortnight later she ran a creditable race to finish fifth behind Altesse Royale in the Oaks. She had every chance 2 furlongs from home, but failed to stay, which was not entirely surprising since her sire was no more than a miler. On 24 July she was at Chantilly for the Prix de Minerve over 1¼ miles, in which she was beaten by a neck by Cambrizzia, which was no disgrace at all because Cambrizzia was a top-class filly who afterwards was placed in two of the most competitive races in France, the Prix Vermeille and the Prix de l'Arc de Triomphe. Three weeks later she again travelled to France, where she rounded off her racing career in style by gaining a 2½ lengths victory in the Prix de Psyche over the same distance, at Deauville.

Allegiance, the product of the early mating of Albany with Queen's Hussar, did not win a race, but Albany later proved her worth as a broodmare by breeding three colts of much above average ability in English Harbour, winner of the Listed Predominate Stakes, Buttress, winner of the Group 3 Queen's Vase, and Dukedom, winner of the Group 3 White Rose Stakes.

Albany was only the beginning. She initiated the golden age, but she was soon surpassed by Highclere. Having done the Queen one good turn by getting in foal and exercising a calming influence on Albany, Queen's Hussar did even better by siring Highclere, the Queen's first dual Classic winner, who was foaled in Albany's three-year-old season. Highclere came from the family that was the cornerstone of the Royal Studs at Sandringham during the twentieth century; it sprang from Feola, who was purchased for King George V as a yearling in 1934 and finished second in the 1000 Guineas and third in the Oaks. Highclere's granddam was Feola's best daughter, the temperamental Hypericum, who won the Dewhurst Stakes and the 1000 Guineas for King George VI. It is a remarkable fact that Dick had the privilege of training the only two top-class horses ever sired by Queen's Hussar – Brigadier Gerard and Highclere.

Highclere, described by her trainer as 'a lovely bay filly with plenty of scope and a good stride', ran three times as a two-year-old. She made her debut in the Princess Maiden Stakes at the Newmarket July meeting, finishing second 3 lengths behind Polygamy. She was second again, this time only a neck behind Celestial Dawn, in the Princess Margaret Stakes at Ascot later in July; and on her third and last appearance that season she beat an eighteen-runner field for the Donnington Maiden Stakes over 7 furlongs at Newbury in September, though her margin of a neck over the second horse Reigning Grace hardly justified her starting price of 5–2 on. These performances brought her a mark of 7st 11lbs in the two-year-old Free Handicap, 11lbs less than the joint top-weighted fillies Bitty Girl, Melchbourne and Gentle Thoughts and 5lbs less than Polygamy. It was a respectable mark, but not high enough to presage Classic victory the following season.

Events were to prove that both Highclere and the tiny Polygamy, also Berkshire-trained by Peter Walwyn at Lambourn, made exceptional improvement during the winter, and in the 1000 Guineas they provided a race so thrilling and memorable that it could be accounted the female equivalent of the epic duel between Grundy and Bustino in the King George VI and Queen Elizabeth Stakes a year later. Dick had sent out Brigadier Gerard to win the 2000 Guineas without a preliminary race as a three-year-old, and decided to pursue the same policy with Highclere. However, he also decided to equip her with blinkers because she tended to look about her in a race and he hoped they would help her to concentrate. Bitty Girl set a fast pace for 5 furlongs before her stamina limitations were exposed, and Gentle Thoughts then led for another furlong before she too ran out of steam. Going down into the Dip, Joe Mercer sent Highclere ahead, partly to escape the attentions of Mrs Tiggywinkle, and went all out for the finishing line. Meanwhile Polygamy was improving her position, but in the Dip she ran into severe traffic problems which culminated in a hefty bump from the swerving Mrs Tiggywinkle. Despite her small stature, Polygamy was knocked out of her stride only for a moment, and she went in furious pursuit of the leader up the final hill. Urged on to the utmost by Pat Eddery, Polygamy clawed back Highclere's lead stride by stride. Polygamy was determination personified, but Highclere responded to Joe Mercer's calls with equal courage. They flashed past the winning post with nothing between them, and the difficulty in separating them was accentuated by the fact that Polygamy was travelling the faster and was definitely in front a stride past the post. Sitting with the Queen in the Stewards Box, Dick thought that Highclere had been beaten. 'Never mind, Ma'am, she's run a great race,' he told her. On the way down to the unsaddling enclosure Dick saw Bob McCreery, who said: 'I was standing on the line, and I think you just won.' This cheered Dick up a lot, because Bob is the soundest of judges. The camera showed that he was right: Highclere had won by a short head that was really only a whisker. As the authoritative *Bloodstock Breeders Review* observed:

> A dead heat might have done more justice to the epic struggle, but nothing could detract from Highclere's superbly rugged performance, from Mercer's immaculate jockeyship, or from Dick Hern's magnificent training technique.

There is a saying that the luck tends to even itself out in racing, though there are plenty of racing men and women, apparently dogged by perpetual misfortune, who would deny its truth. It certainly rang true in the case of Polygamy, who had been clearly out of luck in the 1000 Guineas but had luck on her side just as clearly in the Oaks. She came from a long way back to take the lead inside the last furlong and show her habitual tenacity to beat Furioso by a length, but the result would surely have been different if Dibidale had not been the victim of outrageous misfortune. She cruised up to the leaders at Tattenham Corner looking as if defeat was out of the question, but then disaster struck. Early in the straight the spectators saw a black object, her weight cloth, plunge to the ground, followed by a white object as her number cloth fluttered away in the wind. Finally her saddle slipped round right under her belly. By an amazing display of riding virtuosity Willie Carson stayed on her back and kept her going to finish in third place, though of course he was disqualified. Just how unlucky Dibidale had been was indicated when she beat Polygamy easily in the Irish Oaks, though Polygamy was probably over the top by that time.

One satisfactory feature of these Classic results was that British-owned and bred fillies came out top of the pile. Highclere was missing from the Oaks field at Dick's suggestion for two reasons: first, it was considered that she might not act well on the Epsom course, and second, there was some doubt of her stamina in view of her pedigree, so the 10½ furlongs of the Prix de Diane (the French Oaks) at Chantilly should suit her better than the 12 furlongs of the Oaks. In view of the blank record of British-trained horses in the Prix de Diane and the Prix du Jockey Club (the French Derby), it was a shrewd, imaginative and extremely bold decision, though Dick's mind was attuned to the idea by the fact that he had saddled Highest Hopes ('Ighest 'Ops according to the French racereader) to be second in the race four years earlier.

All the necessary arrangements were made for the Queen to fly over and see the race. Chantilly, which is also the chief training centre of France, with about 3000 horses stabled there, is 25 miles north of Paris. The course is beautifully situated, with a backdrop of broad-leaved woods and dominated by the imposing classical facade and Mansard roof of the Grandes Ecuries, the palatial stables built for the Prince de Condé which now houses a museum dedicated to the horse. Prix de Diane day is a smart occasion, with many of the gentlemen in the principal enclosure wearing top hats and the ladies decked out in Royal Ascot style finery. On the morning of the race Dick and Sheilah, with Joe and Anne Mercer, flew over from Newbury to Charles de Gaulle airport in a small aircraft and took a taxi to the course. As they approached Chantilly the traffic got thicker and thicker and they started to worry about getting there on time. They explained that Dick was the trainer and Joe the rider of Highclere, where-upon the driver cried out 'A l'exterieur,' pulled to the outside and proceeded to take every sort of chance. When asked why there were so many people he replied: 'Pour la Reine.' He got them to the course on time and they found that in addition to the smart people, a huge crowd of ordinary racegoers had gathered to see Highclere and the Queen, who was immensely popular with the French racing public.

The Queen flew to the military airfield at Creil, where she was met by a representative of President Giscard d'Estaing and the British ambassador and whisked straight to the main Chantilly training ground, Les Aigles. She was given a good idea of the facilities when her car was driven round the circuit following three horses at full gallop. She was then taken to the Villa Pharis,

the Chantilly residence of the President of the Société d'Encouragement Marcel Boussac for a lunch of melon, lobster cocktail,
saddle of lamb and ice cream, with Château Haut Brion to drink.
After lunch she was driven up the racecourse in the Presidential
open Citroën-Maserati to tumultuous cheering from the crowd.
It was a sweltering hot and humid midsummer day, and eye
witnesses remarked that she was the only person in the place
looking cool in her outfit of green, blue and yellow silk and
turban-style green hat.

At saddling time the Queen went down to the boxes under
the trees at the far end of the paddock to see Highclere got
ready. When she was led from the boxes to the parade ring the
Queen walked behind her with Henry Porchester on one side
and Dick on the other. Gendarmes had formed a line with arms
linked to hold the crowds back, but so great was the pressure
of people wanting to see the Queen that the line was swaying
to and fro. Dick thought that it was going to break at any
moment and they would be submerged by a wave of onlookers,
but it held and they got safely to the parade ring. The local
Steward Comte Edouard Decazes, who was following them,
found himself being swept along helplessly on a tide of humanity
and was heard to mutter: 'Disgraceful'; and Peter (later Sir Peter)
O'Sullevan, the Voice of British Racing, was so badly jostled in
the throng that he lost a shoe – a telling argument, surely, for
the use of lace-ups.

Highclere won the race much more easily than anyone could
have expected. Tropical Cream and Hippodamia set a fast pace,
but by the time they reached the last turn in front of the Grandes
Ecuries Highclere was poised on their heels. As they entered the
straight a gap opened on the inside, and Joe Mercer seized his
opportunity and shot her through. From that point she was
always in command, except for a moment when she faltered and
changed legs, and she ran on strongly to win by 2 lengths from
Comtesse de Loir. It was a true Classic performance. The time
was only fractionally outside the record set by Allez France in

the race the previous year, and Comtesse de Loir was a very good filly who had already won the Group 1 Prix Saint Alary and went on to be second, beaten by no more than a head, to Allez France in the Prix de l'Arc de Triomphe.

The occasion was historic. Highclere was the first Classic winner for a reigning British monarch in France, the first British-trained winner of the Prix de Diane in the twentieth century and the first British-owned winner of the Prix de Diane since the sisters Fairy Legend and Mary Legend won for Sir Mortimer and Lady Davis in 1927 and 1928. The crowds were delirious with joy, and such was the crush round the winner's enclosure that Dick had a job to get to the filly before Joe had unsaddled and gone to weigh in. Their delight was shared not only by the royal party and the Herns but by at least one other British spectator, namely Henry Porchester's father the sixth Earl of Carnarvon. He had always been touched by the delicate compliment the Queen had paid him by naming Highclere after his stud where her sire Queen's Hussar was stationed. He wrote in his memoirs: 'I was present at Chantilly on the day the filly won and Her Majesty got a reception such as you could not believe unless you saw it yourself. She was cheered, mobbed and looked very pleased. I burst into tears !'.

Afterwards the Queen, again the recipient of rapturous applause, was driven round the course in the Presidential car, before being taken back to Creil for the flight home. On their way back to the airport by taxi the Herns and the Mercers stopped in the first village they came to and bought two bottles of champagne, which they drank on the plane. After such a hot day they were all a bit sweat stained as they came into Shoreham to clear customs. The pilot turned and told them: 'There's a message waiting for you here from Lord Porchester.' It said that they were to clear customs and go straight on to Heathrow as the Queen had asked them all to dinner at Windsor Castle. At first Dick thought it was a leg-pull, but was quickly persuaded that the message was genuine.

When they reached Heathrow the main runway had been closed for them and they flew straight in. A big car was waiting to take them to Windsor Castle, where they were met by the Queen, Prince Philip and Lord Mountbatten at the front door of the Private Apartments. Although she had obviously been back some time, the Queen was still in the dress she had worn at Chantilly, which was most considerate of her since they, of course, had had no opportunity to change. The cup for the Prix de Diane was on the dining-room table, and they had a wonderful evening. After dinner a car took them back to Newbury racecourse, where they had left their cars, and they drove home. For the Herns it was the end of a perfect day. Racing is full of ups and downs but, Dick reflected, this was the kind of day that makes it all worth while.

The distance of the Prix de Diane was ideal for Highclere, and Dick believed that a mile and a half was a bit beyond her. Although she ran a good race to be second to the great Dahlia, who was winning the race for the second time and had a lot in hand, in the King George VI and Queen Elizabeth Stakes over that distance, it left its mark and she was never the same afterwards. She was unplaced in her two remaining races, the Benson and Hedges Gold Cup and the Prix de l'Arc de Triomphe. Fortunately her prospects for stud were unaffected by her exertions and she bred two good horses, Milford and Height Of Fashion, of whom the latter was to have an extremely beneficial influence on the later years of Dick's career as a trainer.

The year, 1974, that Highclere was gaining her Classic victories another filly destined to win two Classic races for the Queen was foaled. This was Dunfermline, a tough bay filly by Royal Palace out of Strathcona by St Paddy. Although there have been Derby winners that have been greater failures as stallions than Royal Palace, and he sired a few other decent performers on the flat plus the triple champion hurdler See You Then, he certainly did not come up to expectations at stud and Dunfermline was his only Classic winner. Stroma, the granddam

189

of Dunfermline, had been recruited to the royal bloodstock band for only 1150 guineas at the Doncaster St Leger Sales as a yearling. She did not win a race but had proved her worth at stud by breeding the Eclipse Stakes winner Canisbay. It was hardly a pedigree that promised a filly of such exceptional merit as Dunfermline. Throughout her two-year-old and three-year-old seasons she showed class, stamina and consistency, and never finished out of the first four in nine racecourse appearances.

She was placed in each of her three races as a two-year-old, two of which were important races over a mile – the Group 3 May Hill Stakes at Doncaster and the Group 1 Argos Fillies Mile at Ascot. At Doncaster she was beaten by half a length by Triple First. They met again at Ascot, where Dunfermline turned the tables but again suffered a ½-length defeat, this time by Miss Pinkie. As Triple First and Miss Pinkie had both been carrying 7lbs more when beating her, it looked as if she needed either to make exceptional improvement or longer distances to be in the Classic picture the next year.

That year, 1977, was the Queen's Jubilee Year, and Dunfermline made sure that Virginia Wade's victory in the women's singles at Wimbledon was not the only cause for British jubilation on the sporting scene. Her first race was the Pretty Polly Stakes over 1¼ miles at Newmarket at the end of April, when she served notice that she was going to be a force in the longer distance fillies' races by winning by 4 lengths from Freeze The Secret, who was to prove a more formidable opponent at Epsom. The Oaks came next, and it was an occasion of drama before and during the race. The drama started when the favourite Durtal was overcome by nerves and bolted with Lester Piggott on the way to the start and crashed through the fence at the bottom of the paddock in a horrific accident which might well have been fatal for the champion jockey. Fortunately that man of steel escaped with a shaking, and actually rode a winner later in the afternoon. Then in the race Dunfermline got badly boxed in on the descent to Tattenham Corner and seemed to be in a hopeless position as they straightened up for home, with Vaguely Deb and Freeze The Secret forging clear into an apparently unassailable lead. Then Willie Carson got Dunfermline into overdrive, and began to make relentless progress. *The Bloodstock Breeders Review* gave a graphic account of the final stages:

> Two furlongs out, it was still hopeless. A furlong later it was only improbable. With a hundred yards to go, it was real; it was all happening as Dunfermline carved into Freeze The Secret's precious lead with merciless determination that no force on earth could deny.

At last Dunfermline got her head in front close to home and worried Freeze The Secret out of it to win by ¾ of a length. This thoroughly appropriate victory to mark the Queen's twenty-five years on the throne was rapturously acclaimed by the crowd, but sadly the Queen herself was not present owing to a political engagement. The Queen Mother was there and her delight was plain for all to see.

Dunfermline's next race was the Yorkshire Oaks. She started a hot favourite, but the way the race was run did not bring her stamina into play and she was only third behind Busaca and Royal Hive. Dick took the precaution of providing her with a pacemaker, Gregarious ridden by Alan Bond, in the St Leger the following month. Nevertheless her task looked extremely difficult, if not impossible, against the Vincent O'Brien-trained colt Alleged, who was unbeaten and had won the Great Voltigeur Stakes at York in impressive style. Alleged started at 7–4 on, with Dunfermline at 10–1. Gregarious set a good pace, but Alleged settled close behind him, going easily with Lester Piggott on his back obviously brimming with confidence, while Dunfermline was in fifth place. Alleged cruised into the lead on the last turn, and for a few moments the race seemed to be over. However, that was far from being the case. Dunfermline moved up in the straight with far less hard driving from Willie Carson than had been necessary at Epsom, and headed Alleged a furlong and a half from home. Alleged rallied gamely and fought every yard of the way, but Dunfermline was the better stayer and ran on to beat him by 1½ lengths. So great was the superiority of the first two that the third horse Classic Example was 10 lengths back.

That was not the end of the matter. The first two had come close together in the closing stages and, although there was no objection from the rider of Alleged, the Stewards called an enquiry and there was an agonising wait of twenty minutes before Dunfermline was confirmed as the winner. The head-on patrol camera showed that, while Dunfermline had ducked to her left towards Alleged, they had not touched and Alleged, indeed, had moved off a straight line to his right at the same moment. Dunfermline was the undoubted winner on merit.

The pacemaking role of Gregarious had been vital, and the outcome fully justified Dick's belief in the value of pacemakers which had been put into practice effectively in the case of Bustino. He expressed it in these words: 'If you've got a good horse and you know he stays, you want to have a pacemaker for him. For one thing you don't get a false run race and, for another, it gives the jockey confidence. He knows there will be a bit of pace on!' He regretted bitterly that no pacemaker had been provided for Dunfermline when she and Alleged met again in the Prix de l'Arc de Triomphe three weeks later. Alleged was drawn on the extreme outside and Dunfermline was near the inside. Lester Piggott jumped Alleged off into the lead and, as soon as he was able, tacked across to the inside where he was able to dictate the pace. He gradually quickened the pace as he approached the last turn, and as soon as he was in the straight he went for home as hard as he could go. For most of the race Dunfermline was locked in behind a wall of horses on the inside rail, and in the circumstances she ran an excellent race to be fourth. 'A filly like her who really stayed had no chance the way the race was run,' said Dick, who gave generous praise to Piggott for riding one of the brainiest races of his life. 'His tactics won it,' he summed up.

Four weeks later Dunfermline returned to Longchamp for the Prix Royal Oak, then the French equivalent of the St Leger. She ran another good race, but was somewhat past her best and had to be content with third place behind Rex Magna and Trillion. She was kept in training for another season, but never thrived in the spring and summer. As Dick put it: 'She didn't look ready, she didn't look the part, and her four-year-old career was a disaster.' The best of her three efforts was when she was second to Montcontour, with the good New Zealand horse Balmerino, who had been second in the 'Arc', and Rex Magna behind her, in the Hardwicke Stakes at Royal Ascot. She was unplaced in the King George VI and Queen Elizabeth Stakes and a remote fourth of seven behind Ile de Bourbon in the Geoffrey Freer Stakes at Newbury. In September it was decided that she would not run again, but she had to remain at West Ilsley because she was to go to Kentucky to be mated with Nijinsky and the regulations decreed that she must not have been on a stud. From the moment of that decision she began to thrive, but by then it was too late and she had no engagements. Fillies often improve when they go out of oestrus and this may have been what happened in her case. Her stud career was equally disappointing: she was barren in each of her first three seasons and she bred only three minor winners. Dick thought that there was a masculine element in her make-up which detracted from her capacity as a matron. Other great racemares have been similarly affected; Allez France, the brilliant winner of twenty-one races, including the Prix de l'Arc de Triomphe, was an example.

Although the career of Dunfermline ended in anticlimax, she had made a major contribution to the Queen's fortunes on the Turf. In Highclere's three-year-old season, 1974, the Queen had been no higher than eighth in the list of winning owners because one of her two Classic victories had been gained abroad and was not included in the British statistics. Both the Classic victories of Dunfermline had been gained at home and lifted her to third place in the list of winning owners, with twelve winners of seventeen races of £135,038, and she was one place higher in the list of winning breeders. This was a return almost to the heady days of the 1950s, when the Queen was leading owner twice: in 1954, when Aureole won the King George VI and Queen Elizabeth Stakes, and in 1957, when Carrozza won the Oaks. It was Dunfermline's glory that she inflicted on Alleged, who gained a second 'Arc' victory in 1978, the only defeat of his career, and that she did so in a manner that contained no hint of a fluke.

The 1977 season was Willie Carson's first as Dick's stable jockey and the Classic victories of Dunfermline gave the best possible start to an association which was to last for twelve seasons. The year ended on a glorious note when Dick was appointed Commander of the Royal Victorian Order (CVO). The honour was all the more welcome for being unexpected. He had had no prior warning when he heard of it as a news item on his car radio while he was driving up to Leicestershire for a day's hunting.

The golden age for fillies continued with Dunfermline's year-younger half-sister Tartan Pimpernel, who won the Group 3 May Hill Stakes and was second in the Group 1 Argos Fillies mile as a two-year-old and, after failing to make the grade as a Classic filly the next season, returned to form and won the Galtres Stakes at the York August Meeting. It had its final flowering with Height Of Fashion, whose breeding had a double connection with West Ilsley because she was by Bustino out of Highclere. She was a big bay filly, but she was an exceptionally good two-year-old. She made her debut against seven colts in the Acomb Stakes at the York August Meeting. Willie Carson could not ride her because he had taken a crunching fall when Silken Knot broke both cannon bones at the turn into the straight in the Yorkshire Oaks two races beforehand, but fortunately Lester Piggott was available. Dick noticed Lester eyeing her somewhat dubiously in the parade ring and told him: 'I know what you're thinking – that she is a big rangy filly and must be backward. Actually I fancy her a lot, and she should go very close. Whatever you do, don't be hard on her because I think she is a good filly in the making.' She won nicely from two good colts in Ashenden and Count Pahlen, and went on to win two important fillies races, the May Hill Stakes and the Hoover Fillies Mile, and retire unbeaten at the end of her first season.

Her three-year-old campaign opened with an eventful race for the Lupe Stakes at the Goodwood May Meeting. There were only four runners, one of whom was her pacemaker Round Tower, a useful filly who won her next two races. She looked such a certainty that she started at 5–1 on. One of her rivals was Devon Air, trained in Devon by Jack Cann, but she slipped up and fell at the top of the hill turning into the straight, and Height of Fashion had to jump over her as she lay prostrate. This left Round Tower many lengths in front, and for a long way it looked as if she would not be caught. Ernie Johnson was riding away on Round Tower, hoping desperately that Willie Carson and Height Of Fashion would come. In the end they did, passing Round Tower inside the last furlong to win by 2 lengths.

Height Of Fashion did not run in the Oaks but waited for the Princess of Wales's Stakes, one of Dick's favourite races, which he won seven times, at the Newmarket July Meeting. Ardross, the top-class stayer who also had the class and speed to finish second in the 'Arc', was preferred to her in the betting. She was equipped with a pair of blinkers, and Willie Carson rode a most enterprising race to make all the running. Ardross could never get in a blow and finished only third, with Amyndas in second place.

Immediately after the Princess of Wales's Stakes Height Of Fashion was sold privately to Sheikh Hamdan for a sum reported as £1 million. Sales of valuable fillies and mares are always matters of nice judgement. The advantage of a quick improvement of cash-flow has to be balanced against the possibility of long-term losses in the breeding department. The imponderable factor was that, at the end of the twentieth century, the prediction of the breeding value of individual horses and mares was still wrapped in impenetrable mystery. A filly may be culled on the grounds that she is too big, or too small, or too temperamental, or too badly bred, or too unsound in wind and/or limb, and with any one or more of those flaws she may still turn out to be a high-class broodmare. The sixth Earl of Rosebery, one of the most successful breeders of the first half of the twentieth century, summed it up when he recalled that he culled Indiscretion because she was excitable, had very little athletic ability and declined to use such ability as she did possess. She became the dam of Imprudence, winner of the 1000 Guineas, the Oaks and the French 1000 Guineas. The royal entourage considered Height Of Fashion too big for a broodmare. At the time Dick was bitterly disappointed that she was to be lost to the Royal Stud, because she was so talented, with precocious speed and top-class middle-distance ability, and was a daughter of a dual Classic winner. The decision to sell proved a disastrous misjudgement, but in the end it turned out greatly to Dick's advantage because she was the dam of the two top-class colts Unfuwain and Nashwan, both of whom were sent by Sheikh Hamdan to be trained by him.

Before producing Height Of Fashion Highclere bred a good colt called Milford, her first foal, named after Lord Porchester's house near Highclere. Milford had a pure Classic pedigree, as he was by the Derby winner Mill Reef. He looked a live candidate for the Derby when he won his first two races as a three-year-old, the White Rose Stakes by 8 lengths and the Lingfield Derby Trial by 7 lengths, and he was not far behind his stable companion Troy in the betting on the Derby. He was ridden by Lester Piggott at Epsom and was disputing the lead at Tattenham Corner, but then faded to finish tenth. He returned to winning form in the Princess of Wales's Stakes, and at the end of the season he was sold as a stallion to stand at the Greenmount Stud in Ireland.

Whereas Highclere, Dunfermline and Height Of Fashion were prominent at the level of top-class racing ability, another filly of the Queen's, Light O' Battle, was prominent at the level of farce. She was by Queen's Hussar out of Highclere's dam Highlight and so very closely related to that Classic filly, but she had a devilish temper. She was so averse to discipline that it took three times the normal period to break her, and she was so free with her heels that she was never shod behind. She was taken to the racecourse for the first time at the end of October to run in the Radley Stakes, for which she started at 33–1 while Dick's other runner Bluebell, owned by Lord Porchester, was favourite, having won a nursery under a big weight at the previous Newbury meeting. Willie Carson was on Bluebell, and Light O' Battle was ridden by Dick's principal work rider Brian Proctor. Dick's instructions to Proctor were to do his best but not to be hard on her, never dreaming that she was good enough to trouble Bluebell. Bluebell took up the running about a furlong from home, and Dick switched his glasses to Light O' Battle to see how she was getting on. To his astonishment she was going easily. She cruised up to Bluebell, with Proctor sitting stock still and looking across at Willie, and they crossed the line together. The judge at first announced Bluebell as the winner, which was an appalling result as it was obvious that Light O' Battle must have won if Proctor had moved a muscle. There was some booing from the stands. Dick met Light O' Battle as she came off the course. Proctor's face wore the expression of a man who was going to be hanged the next morning. 'Look happy,' Dick told him. Fortunately the judge had made a mistake, which he quickly corrected and declared Light O' Battle the winner. Dick and Proctor were saved from a situation of extreme embarrassment. 'Never do that to me again,' Dick admonished Proctor.

The result was one of the extraordinary flukes that occur occasionally in racing. Light O' Battle afterwards became completely uncooperative, and finished a distant fourth in the Lupe Stakes the only other time she ran. Proctor rode few fancied horses, and his mounts in public were mostly backward horses that needed a run, though he did ride Cabin Boy when that game little horse gained his only success on the flat at Bath. He had one brush with authority after he had ridden Dunfermline's daughter Red Shoes into third place at Salisbury on her first outing as a three-year-old. The local Stewards stood him down on the grounds that he had not ridden her with sufficient vigour. Dick thought that the verdict was so manifestly unjust that he appealed, and his appeal was upheld and the verdict overturned at Portman Square. Red Shoes ran in nine more races that season without winning, so it is unlikely that she would have done any better in the Salisbury race if she had been ridden with all the vigour in the world.

Proctor had been apprenticed to Sir Gordon Richards and came to West Ilsley when Gordon retired. His value as a work rider was not only that he was a good horseman but that he obeyed instructions and could give useful information about the animal after the work. He was totally unlike Boyce and Heffernan, Dick's two chief work riders when he was training for Major Holliday; Boyce wanted to win every gallop, while Heffernan always wanted to hold back and gain information about the horses which, no doubt, he passed on to his punters. Proctor stayed with Dick until he retired and then got a good job with the Maktoums, which involved spending his winters in Dubai.

The successful racing performances of Height Of Fashion and her sale marked the end of the golden age of fillies owned by the Queen and trained at West Ilsley. Success in breeding thoroughbreds usually moves in cycles, and the passing of the golden age was followed by the descent of the Royal Studs into a deep trough from which there was no real recovery for years. In 1984, when the Queen had a total of twenty-seven horses in training (fourteen with Dick and thirteen with Ian Balding), she won six races worth £25,070. Three years later the returns were even worse, as in 1987 she had thirty horses in training (thirteen with Dick, twelve with Ian Balding and five with William Hastings-Bass) and she won seven races worth £22,974. These deplorable results must have involved deficits of at least £300,000 on the training account in each year, and inevitably there were audible flutterings in the dovecotes of the comptroller's department. It was a sad sequel to the purchase of West Ilsley Stables.

The Queen's enthusiasm and commitment to racing and her horses never wavered. Although Dick discussed running plans with Henry Porchester from the time of his appointment as racing manager in 1969, he also communicated regularly with the Queen by telephone to give her news of the well-being of her horses and how they had worked. He found her a very easy and charming person to train for, because she understood horses, never wanted to rush them or hurry their development, knowing that they were immature animals always prone to injury. Having had a stud for so long, she had a thorough knowledge of all the families, their characteristics and what could be expected of them.

The enjoyment she derived from her visits to West Ilsley was unmistakable. She usually went in April and once or twice more during the summer to see the work, and when she was at Windsor she went over occasionally for evening stables. Dick would drive her up to see the work in the Land-Rover, with Porchester sitting in the back. Downlands on fine spring and summer mornings are magical places; the horizons are hazy, the air pure and clear and the landscape suffused with a golden dawn glow. Moments of utter silence may be broken by a sudden flurry of wings or pierced with thrilling bursts of bird song. The Queen is a country person and Dick always tried to draw her attention to aspects of the natural world that would interest her: golden plover and, on one occasion, a baby leveret lying in its form which he had noticed the previous day. One morning when she was out a filly got loose at the top of the starting gate canter on the winter gallops. She was a green two-year-old and very hard to catch. After a number of attempts had failed, Dick decided to walk the string home, hoping that she would follow them, and the Queen went ahead to the crossing of the West Ilsley to East Ilsley road to control the traffic in case she took it into her head to gallop down the track towards the stables. Afterwards Dick speculated that some passing motorist may have driven home and told his family: 'There was a woman holding up the traffic on the West Ilsley road this morning and, do you know, she looked exactly like the Queen.' In fact, her services on point duty were not required, as the filly attached herself to the string and walked quietly home.

After watching the work the Queen would go back to The Old Rectory, where the party for breakfast would also comprise Porchester, the Herns and, if he was riding in the south that day, Willie Carson. Mrs G's cooked breakfasts were famous, and the Queen would go up to the hot plate on the sideboard and help herself sparingly: a little scrambled egg, perhaps, with a rasher of bacon and some tomato. The conversation would be about what they had seen on the gallops that morning and future plans for the horses.

Mrs G cooked for the Herns for thirty years and, thanks a good deal to Sheilah's tuition, became a very skilful cook. She was born in West Ilsley, and at the beginning of the Second World War married Jock Gillot, who was apprenticed to Eric Stedall at Hodcott House, when she was twenty and he was one day short of his twentieth birthday. Jock was called up and served with a mule pack company of the Royal Army Veterinary Corps in the Italian campaign. After the war he had a job at the depot at Didcot until the call of racing became too strong and he returned to work for Dick. He was an excellent stableman. Mrs G, long widowed, still lives in retirement in one of the Fir Tree Cottages donated by Sir Michael Sobell.

At the end of the decade of the 1980s there were signs of a modest revival in the Queen's racing fortunes. In 1989 she won fourteen races and £68,269, though less than a third of the total, £21,410, was contributed by the eleven horses trained by Dick. Of the three-year-olds, All Saints Day won a maiden race at Brighton, Hall Of Mirrors won a handicap at Newmarket and Trying For Gold won a maiden race at Salisbury and a graduation race at Wolverhampton. The best and most promising of her horses at West Ilsley was the two-year-old Marienski, a superbly bred colt by Nureyev out of Highclere, who won a maiden race over 7 furlongs at Newmarket in August. By then time for Dick as a trainer at West Ilsley in charge of some of the Queen's horses was running out. The 1990 season was his last in that capacity. The number of horses he trained for the Queen was reduced to five, and Marienski had not improved in the manner hoped for. He did not win a race, though he was third in a Listed race at Haydock. Dick's only winner for the Queen was Full Orchestra, successful in a maiden race at Windsor. It was a tame ending to an association that had known the triumphs of great fillies like Highclere and Dunfermline.

NINE

HUNTING, A FALL, AND RECOVERY

MENTION OF JOHN MASEFIELD'S *Reynard The Fox or The Ghost Heath Run* is calculated to draw a recitation from Dick Hern, accompanied by an impish grin, because it is one of his favourite poems. Not the whole of it; at 2500 lines in rhyming couplets it is the longest narrative poem about hunting ever written and defies even Dick's prodigious ability to memorise songs and verses – but certainly a considerable sample. A great deal of the charm of *Reynard The Fox* lies in the fact that at the end of the day, after the excitement, the tribulations and the fluctuating fortunes of the chase, all the species involved – human, equine, canine and vulpine – are weary but at peace. Tom Copp, the farmer of Cowfoot's Wynd, remarks to the huntsman Robin Dawe:

> There've been runs longer but none more hot,
> We shall talk of today until we die.

and the poem continues:

> The stars grew bright in the winter sky,
> The wind came keen with a tang of frost,
> The brook was troubled for new things lost,
> The copse was happy for old things found,
> The fox came home and he went to ground

And the hunt came home and the hounds were fed,
They climbed to their bench and went to bed,
The horses in stable loved their straw,
'Good night, my beauties,' said Robin Dawe.

There is nothing cruel or bloodthirsty about *Reynard The Fox*, and its appeal to an animal-loving hunting man like Dick Hern is plain. His Jorrocks-like devotion to hunting, kindled first during his West Somerset boyhood before the Second World War and taken up again enthusiastically at Porlock after the war, culminated in twenty wonderful seasons from 1964 to 1984 that brought him some of the greatest pleasures of his life. Most of his hunting during that period was in Leicestershire; but no hunting man would consider his experience complete without a number of days in Ireland, where the broad expanses of unspoiled countryside, mostly grass, and varied obstacles provide ideal conditions for the sport. Dick had days with the Meath, the Limerick, the Scarteen, the Wexford and the Kilkenny. He recalled a day with the Meath when he and George Rich were staying with Liz Burke, the Joint Master, owner of the successful Stackallan Stud and mother-in-law of the ground-breaking breeder Tim Rogers; hounds put up a fox in a churchyard, and they had a tremendous hunt. For the Wexford and the Kilkenny he stayed with Victor McCalmont, the Master of both packs, at Mount Juliet, one of the greatest Irish country houses. The McCalmonts were one of the most prominent families in hunting and racing – Victor's father had owned that byword for speed The Tetrarch before the First World War – and everything at Mount Juliet was done in style. Looking from his bedroom window, Dick observed with approval sixteen hunt horses at exercise, each ridden by a groom in bowler hat, leggings and boots. Dick marvelled at Victor's stamina. They did not sit down to dinner until eleven and went to bed in the small hours, yet Victor was up fresh for hunting in the morning.

Dick enjoyed a less conventional day's hunting with his old

Newmarket friend Fergie Sutherland near Blarney in County Cork. The hounds were nominally harriers, but hunted foxes on weekdays and ran a drag on Sundays. Dick was out on a Sunday, when they had a fast drag hunt over grassy, stone-faced banks. Fergie had given up training at Newmarket and moved to Ireland, where his maverick ways fitted readily into rural society. He had lost a foot when he trod on a mine while serving in the Korean war. Fortunately he retained the knee, and had an artificial leg, and with practice had learnt to ride well enough to continue hunting with relish. He had a small stable of jumpers at Kilinardrish on the estate of his mother, whose second husband was that intrepid and eccentric soldier Carton de Wiart. He gained a major triumph when he won the Tote Cheltenham Gold Cup with Imperial Call in 1996.

Dick's acquaintance with Fergie Sutherland had begun in Porlock days, when Fergie had spent a month there and Dick had taught him to ride. While at Newmarket Fergie had kept horses in rented stables behind the Crown Hotel in Oakham and had hunted regularly with the Cottesmore. Dick used to go out as often as possible, riding hirelings and borrowed horses. Dick found the Master, Bob Hoare, not only a capable huntsman but a man of much charm. One day Dick and Fergie arrived late, and were standing inadvertently on the line while hounds were running. Bob Hoare galloped past and they expected an earful of abuse; but, in response to their raised hats and apologies, he merely turned towards them with a beaming smile and waved his whip in acknowledgement. However, after a time Dick decided that too much of the Cottesmore country was coming under the plough and moved to the adjacent Quorn, keeping his horses at livery with George Rich at Thorpe Satchville, 5 miles south of Melton Mowbray. Melton, situated at the convergence of three of the most famous hunting countries – the Quorn, the Cottesmore and the Belvoir – was Mecca for the hunting fraternity. Dick became a subscriber solely to the Quorn, but was a member of the Melton Hunt Club, which entitled him to an occasional free day with the other two packs.

Dick's practice was to hunt two days a week, on Mondays and Fridays. He would leave home at 7 a.m., drive up to Leicestershire to have breakfast with George and Barbara Rich, and then go on to the meet. After hunting he would go back and spend the night at the Richs and drive home early the following morning, when the roads were reasonably quiet, in time to go out second lot. He usually had two horses out and they were needed, because the Quorn used to try and roll two days into one by wasting no time. If the hunted fox went to ground, they would leave it and draw for another, so a horse got no respite.

The Quorn country is gently undulating and almost every kind of fence is encountered from the easiest to the barely jumpable. A fast, bold horse is essential. After Dick had won the St Leger for him with Provoke in 1965 Jakie Astor offered to reward the feat by buying him a hunter, and Dick acquired a horse from George Rich. He was a good hunter, but on the slow side for the country and Dick had difficulty in keeping up with hounds. This confirmed his belief that thoroughbreds, properly schooled, make the best hunters. He liked to get hold of a horse in spring and spend the summer schooling it in elementary dressage and jumping timber. He had a succession of good thoroughbred hunters, including Hardbake, a more than useful middle-distance handicapper whose victories included the Bessborough Stakes at Royal Ascot. However, the two best were Harper's Ferry and Kilcoran. Dick trained Harper's Ferry for Jakie Astor, but he was too big and backward for the flat; afterwards Jakie himself trained him to win six races over fences, ridden in three of them by John Oaksey. Kilcoran had the speed to win over 6 furlongs on the flat, and afterwards jumped well enough to win over hurdles and fences when trained by Fred Winter. He was eleven years old when Dick acquired him. There had been little time to school him before Dick took him out hunting for the first time and he nearly pulled Dick's arms out. The second time he settled and did not pull, because he had learnt that hunting was not the same as racing. He was a very strong horse with plenty of bone, and a brilliant jumper.

One season, for variety, Dick switched to the Meynell, which adjoins the Quorn on the north-west side, and kept his horses at livery. The Meynell is mostly grass, with small enclosures, so there is plenty of jumping. For most of the season Dick's second horse was lame and he had to rely on Kilcoran, who was such a strong horse that he could often do two days a week if he did not keep him out too long. Following the same practice as with the Quorn, Dick used to leave home at 7 a.m. on hunting mornings, stop for breakfast at The Belfry, the site of a championship golf course north-east of Birmingham, and then drive on to the meet. After hunting he would go to the Richs, spend the night there, and drive home the next morning.

Reflecting on his twenty years of hunting in Leicestershire, Dick would quote the passage from Whyte Melville which was the motto of the magazine for all kinds of equine sport: 'I freely admit that the best of my fun I owe it to horse and hound'.

Nevertheless those halcyon days were to come to an abrupt and brutal end. Like a number of the leading provincial trainers, Dick had a small house in Newmarket which he occupied for race meetings and the principal bloodstock sales. On Friday 7 December 1984, the last day of the December Sales, Dick left his house at 45 Lowther Street and drove to Thorpe Satchville to have breakfast with Barbara Rich – George had died in tragic circumstances some time beforehand. After breakfast he rode his first horse to the meet, which was at Twyford, only a mile down the road. According to the *Badminton Library*, a gallop over the Twyford Vale in the late nineteenth century was the earthly parallel of going straight to heaven, but in Dick's time much of it had been ploughed up. Certainly there was nothing celestial about Dick's last morning there. 'It was quite busy, but not spectacular. My horse went well,' he recalled. Second horses were at Thimble Hall, where Dick changed on to Badger. Owned originally by Bill (Lord) Harrington in County Limerick, Badger had been bought for Dick by Barbara Rich. By a thoroughbred out of an Irish draught mare, he was a very good hunter who would jump anything his rider was brave enough to point him at. Out of the hunting season he served as Dick's hack and was very good at that too. He had just one strange characteristic: he could not bear the rustle of paper and if he heard it he would take off and bolt out of control. Dick adopted the expedient of carrying his work list in a polythene sleeve; in that way the paper did not rustle and Badger remained perfectly calm.

On the day in question Barry Hills, one trainer who shared Dick's love of hunting, and his wife Penny were at Thimble Hall. Barry was on his feet because he had had a fall and could not ride. He gave Dick a glass of port, and in consequence Dick missed hounds moving off. However, he quickly followed, turned off the road, jumped a little fence into the next field, and soon caught them up. The Quorn hounds were not hunting that day because there was an outbreak of coughing in kennels, and the Fitzwilliam were having an invitation day. In later years Dick speculated that if the Quorn hounds had been out his accident would probably not have happened, because it was unlikely that they would have taken precisely the same line. Anyhow they found and started to run. They were passing a farm called Whites Barn and Dick pointed Badger at a fence that would have taken him into the same field as hounds; instead he had the fall which meant the end of his hunting career.

Afterwards Dick believed that he may have had a blackout as Badger took off. Eyewitnesses testified to two aspects of the fall. Firstly, that Badger swerved in the air, probably to avoid a water trough on the landing side; secondly, that Dick made no attempt to break his fall with his arms, but shot straight ahead out of the saddle to plunge head first into the ground. He broke his nose and it was obvious at once that he was severely injured. At the time he was not in a great deal of pain, but was chiefly aware of the unpleasantness of swallowing a lot of blood from his broken nose, especially when he was turned on his back. Tom Connors, a hunting doctor, jumped the same fence further along and was quickly on the scene; indeed he had a marvellous knack of being the first to attend stricken riders. He was a much-loved local character, combining horse-dealing with hunting and his medical practice at Long Clawson a few miles north of Melton Mowbray. His brother used to find horses in Ireland and send them over, and his two sons Derry and Nicky used to show them in the hunting field. On this occasion he suspected immediately that Dick had broken his neck, summoned an ambulance and travelled with him to Leicester Royal Infirmary, where his suspicion was confirmed. The news was conveyed to Sheilah at Newmarket, who immediately motored to Leicester and spent the night with him. Like the good friends they were, Barbara Rich and Barry Hills also visited the hospital the same evening. The next day he was transferred to the Spinal Injuries Hospital at Stoke Mandeville, Sheilah travelling with him in the ambulance.

After Dick had been at Stoke Mandeville a day or two, the staff were mystified when he vomited and brought up large quantities of dried blood, but he had no doubt that it was the result of all the blood he had swallowed from his broken nose. He was fortunate to be in the care of Dr Hans Frankel, one of the foremost spinal injuries specialists in the world. The most urgent requirement was the Dowell operation to peg his neck in position, which necessitated the removal of a piece of bone from the hip and implanting it in the neck. This was performed successfully in London and Dick then returned to Stoke Mandeville for further treatment. In January the prognosis was optimistic and Sheilah issued a statement: 'My husband will be able to resume riding but I don't know whether he will go hunting again. He won't be 100 per cent for several months, but the progress is good. Doctors have told me that he should make a full recovery.' This optimism soon evaporated as the extent of his injuries became apparent. Dick was doomed to the life of a tetraplegic, a condition of partial paralysis with little movement in the bottom half of his body and restricted movement in his arms.

While he was at Stoke Mandeville there were visits from the Queen, whose evident concern was a real morale-booster, and Mrs Thatcher, who came primarily to see Norman Tebbitt, injured in the IRA bombing of the Queen's Hotel at Brighton. The miners' strike was in progress and the weather was unseasonably mild, thus reducing the demand for electricity. Mrs Thatcher stood by the window for a few moments looking out at the warm winter sunshine, and then remarked: 'Well, it looks as if the Almighty is on our side, but I'm afraid I cannot say the same for the bishops.' Henry Porchester was a regular visitor, and also paid weekly visits to the stables at West Ilsley for the purpose, as he put it later, of 'keeping up morale'. In fact, Ian Cocks, the assistant trainer who was standing in for Dick, found his visits time-wasting and finally restricted him to seeing his own and the Queen's horses.

Dick went home in the middle of March. Dr Frankel was very much opposed to releasing him so soon as he thought that Dick would become too dependent on other people. However, Sheilah insisted that he must take charge of the training as soon as possible else the owners would begin to get edgy with the opening of the flat season approaching, and Dick entirely agreed with her. At first he had nurses night and day, and had very little movement in his body. As Dick himself expressed it: 'I was as weak as a robin.' Then they had a great stroke of luck. They heard about a spinal injuries physiotherapist called Ruth Goodchild who worked at the Royal Buckinghamshire Hospital, a rehabilitation unit at Aylesbury. She agreed to treat Dick, and her help proved a crucial factor in his recovery. At one time she used to come every day after doing a full day's work at the clinic – it was an hour's drive from Aylesbury – and would sometimes go on to London afterwards to see another patient. Dick never knew how she managed it, but was eternally grateful to her for everything she did for him. She got him going, taught him to stand up, use arm crutches and a walking frame, gave him various exercises and took him in the swimming pool. She continued to come and see him whenever he had any worries about his condition. He summed up: 'The whole thing about our relationship is that I have supreme confidence in what she says. If she tells me I can do a certain thing, I know she is right and try to do it.' She used to accompany the Herns on their winter holidays to Antigua and Dubai, helping Dick with his swimming regime and sometimes giving Sheilah a much needed break so that she could go on expeditions to the Nile or Petra.

The swimming pool which they had installed in their early days at West Ilsley then really proved its value. Sheilah had applied to Jakie Astor for permission to build the pool, which he granted immediately. At the time an earthmoving machine was doing a job at the yard, and Sheilah went down and asked the driver to come up and excavate the pool for them when he had finished work for the day. This was duly done. Some days later Jakie telephoned and said that he had had second thoughts about the pool. 'I am afraid you are too late,' she replied. When Dick began the water treatment he would sit on the edge of the pool and then slide down into Ruth's arms in the water. Later a hoist was installed which lowered him into and lifted him out of the water. A greenhouse-like structure was erected over the pool so that it could be used in all weathers and at all seasons. He would be in the water for forty minutes a day, and the treatment was enormously beneficial for exercise and for improving his movement.

Tetraplegia and confinement to a wheelchair brought fundamental changes to the way in which Dick had to practise his profession of training racehorses. The racing journalist Ivor Herbert described the problem succinctly: 'Training is tactile. There is a paramount need to feel a thoroughbred's delicate forelegs for the first signs of strain; to feel neck muscles, to check the crest; to feel the loins for tenderness; and anywhere along the back for pulled muscles.' Ivor knew what he was talking about, because he had been a successful trainer of jumpers, winning the 1957 Cheltenham Gold Cup with Linwell and training a very fast chaser called Flame Gun for Michael Sobell. Dick countered his inability to touch the horses in two ways. Firstly, Geordie Campbell became his 'hands', schooled to feel the horses' legs under his watchful eyes and detect any signs of trouble; and secondly, he developed an exceptionally keen eye for detecting physical problems, illustrating the phenomenon that when one human sense is defective, another is enhanced in order to take over its function. Willie Carson described it aptly: 'They say blind people learn to see through their fingers. Well, this was the same thing in reverse.' He watched the horses go out in the morning, he watched them trot, canter and gallop, and he watched them as they came in, and he was able to detect any little differences in their movements that might indicate trouble. Every fine evening he would have the horses brought out into the yard one by one and have another searching look at them. He dictated letters to his secretary and kept in touch with owners by making telephone calls, usually on Sunday mornings.

The routine, of course, could never be precisely the same as it had been before. Dick remarked to Mikey Seely: 'The thing I miss most is riding with the horses before and after their work. You can see how they are and how they feel, and if one of them is beginning to think a bit.' Nevertheless Dick was not the first man to train horses successfully from the seat of a car, and a hack is not always an indispensable tool of the trainer's trade.

Dick had a reliable assistant in Ian Cocks, who postponed his intended retirement in view of the stable's predicament, but in the restricted circumstances of his wheelchair-borne existence he felt the need for someone to act as a combination of PA and ADC. Some years earlier the racing journalist and failed former trainer Tim Fitzgeorge-Parker had telephoned Dick and asked him whether he could give his nephew Marcus Tregoning a job. Dick felt no obligation to do Tim a favour, but agreed to see Marcus if he came to the next Newbury meeting. They met

211

accordingly and Dick took an instant liking to the young man and agreed to employ him as a pupil assistant, doing his two or three horses to gain experience. He stayed for a season and then left to go to New Zealand, where he worked for Jim Wallace, a vet who kept three stallions and also had twenty horses in training at Masterton in the North Island. During the Southern Hemisphere winters he moved to Virginia and worked on the stud of Danny Van Cleef. When Dick came out of Stoke Mandeville Sheilah telephoned him and offered him the special post they had in mind. He accepted, with results which turned out most happily for both parties.

Marcus became Dick's right hand, taking notes, running errands and making himself useful in a hundred different ways. In 1986, when Dick resumed attendance at race meetings at which he had runners, Marcus drove him – Sheilah had done so in the past, but getting the wheelchair in and out of the car was too much for her – and accompanied him throughout the day. Nor were the benefits of the association entirely one-sided; Marcus was obtaining invaluable experience from hearing Dick's conversations and telephone calls, studying his methods and preparing himself for the day when he would become Dick's successor.

A smoothly successful start to the 1985 season would have raised the spirits of everybody connected with the West Ilsley stable – the trainer, his wife, owners, stable staff and jockeys – but in fact, two serious setbacks intervened. As if his physical rehabilitation did not involve enough trouble, Dick lost his balance when trying to walk in the house, his companion was unable to save him and he fell, breaking his femur. He was taken to the John Radcliffe Hospital in Oxford, where he was fortunate to find himself in the care of the eminent Professor Duffy. After examination Duffy told him: 'The alternatives are these: either you have it plated and screwed, and you can go home in ten days, or you go into traction for three months.' For a busy trainer there was only one choice. Not too much time was lost, but the other problem was less easy to solve. Dick began the season with a string of 120 horses, including fifteen belonging to the Queen, but the virus had returned and until it had blown itself out there could be few runners. Winners were even rarer, and it was not until Longboat, owned and bred by the solemn and elderly Dick Hollingsworth – who was invariably described by the press-room wit Roger Mortimer as Hertfordshire's most eligible bachelor – won the Group 3 Sagaro Stakes at Ascot at the beginning of May that a success of any substance came the way of the stable. The stable's Classic hope, Lady Beaverbrook's Petoski, a bright bay colt of superb physique and presence, was beaten into second place in the Guardian Classic Trial at San-down and the Chester Vase, and finished only eleventh behind Slip Anchor in the Derby.

Dick was not going to the races, but not because he was unwilling to be seen in public while results were disappointing. He was preoccupied with getting himself fit with daily physio-therapy sessions and with the details of running the stable. He kept himself well informed about the performances of his runners through the reports of jockeys and staff, television and videos obtained from the International Racing Bureau. At home he was on the gallops every day, supervising the work. Looking at those days in retrospect, he remarked: 'Often a trainer is better employed at home than wasting time travelling to meetings or socialising on the racecourse, as long as the owners understand the situation.' Dick had sympathetic owners.

The turning point came in the Group 2 Princess of Wales's Stakes at the Newmarket July meeting, when Petoski came into form with a hard-fought victory, with the odds-on favourite Lanfranco, the easy winner of the King Edward VII Stakes at Royal Ascot, beaten into third place. That was a good effort, but it hardly prepared the racing public at large for his majestic performance in the King George VI and Queen Elizabeth Stakes eighteen days later. The field of twelve was well up to the stan-dards of that championship race, including the brilliant filly Oh

213

So Sharp, the winner of three Classic races that year, the subsequent Prix de l'Arc de Triomphe winner Rainbow Quest, the
Irish Derby winner Law Society and the top-class Australian
horse Strawberry Road, who had recently won the Grand Prix
de Saint Cloud. Oh So Sharp enjoyed such a tall reputation that
she started at slight odds-on even in such august company, and
she looked like adding to her laurels when she took the lead more
than a furlong from home. Then Willie Carson pulled out Petoski
to make his challenge. The handsome colt, trained to the peak of
perfection, answered his rider's urgent calls with zest and wore
down the filly relentlessly to win by a neck. If there was sadness
that Dick was not present, the victory gave him enormous satisfaction and, following the fraught start to the season, provided
the ultimate vindication of all the painful endeavour that had
gone into rehabilitation from his fall seven months earlier.

Two weeks previously Dick had sent Helen Street over to win
the Gilltown Stud Irish Oaks for Sir Michael Sobell, and the week
after the Ascot meeting five winners at Goodwood, including
the two-year-old colts New Trojan, Gitano and Wassl Touch,
confirmed that the stable was really back on track. By the end
of the season Dick had turned out the winners of fifty-three
races worth £370,761 and was sixth on the list of winning
trainers, only one place lower than in 1984. That represented a
signal triumph over adversity, and demonstrated that expertise,
good organisation, hard work and team spirit could steer the
stable to heights of achievement of which any trainer or training
establishment could be proud.

Dick had always been a man who was readier to count his
blessings than his misfortunes, and this admirable trait was much
in evidence at this period. Years later he observed philosophically:
'If I had made a proper job of breaking my neck, and killed
myself, I would have missed a lot. I have enjoyed my life since
my accident and I have had quite a few thrills. I would not have
trained two great horses, Nashwan and Dayjur.'

Petoski was kept in training as a four-year-old, but was unable to recover the form which had brought him his resounding Ascot victory in 1985 and was beaten in all his three races. He was retired to the National Stud, but he was one of the nine out of ten horses that fail to fulfil the sanguine expectations with which they enter stud. As a stallion he did not stamp his progeny with either his striking good looks or his athletic ability. He was relegated to Chris Sweeting's Conduit Stud in Oxfordshire as a National Hunt stallion and did much better in that role, siring a number of good jumpers including Dick's George Bull.

Although Petoski disappointed, older horses gave the main impetus to the fortunes of West Ilsley in 1986. Bedtime, having missed the previous season, returned to form and won the Group 3 Brigadier Gerard Stakes. However, the real hero of the stable was the five-year-old Longboat. He had been one of the best stayers in the country in 1985, when he was second to Gildoran in the Ascot Gold Cup after winning the Sagaro Stakes. Now he had matured into an outstanding stayer and won the staying Triple Crown of the Ascot Gold Cup, which he won by the decisive margin of 5 lengths, the Goodwood Cup and the Don-caster Cup. This feat placed him in the august company of such past great stayers as Alycidon, Le Moss and Ardross. With only moderate help from the younger horses, Dick finished the season with a total of forty-five victories worth £339,010, which gave him seventh place on the list of winning trainers.

It was the other way round in 1987. The older horses were undistinguished and the three-year-olds, apart from Dry Dock who won the Group 3 Chester Vase and was third in the St Leger, and Port Helene who won the Listed Lingfield Oaks Trial, contributed little that was significant. The two-year-olds, on the other hand, included several bright prospects. The princi-pal achiever of that age was Emmson, who won four races and ended the season by winning the Group 1 William Hill Futurity over a mile at Doncaster. Charmer, Minster Son and Unfuwain showed plenty of promise for the future.

Charmer and Minster Son were both owned by Lady Beaverbrook. Minster Son was bred by Willie Carson, and two of Dick's owners, Lady Beaverbrook and Lord Chelsea, wanted him when he was offered at the Newmarket October Yearling Sales. Lady Beaverbrook wanted him because he was by Niniski, who had carried her colours and was the sire of Petoski; Lord Chelsea wanted him because he had been to see him on Dick's advice and liked him. Dick saw that there was a potential conflict. It was arranged that Lord Chelsea should bid up to his limit of about £20,000 and that, if the bidding continued, Lady Beaverbrook should then come in. Actually Lady Beaverbrook came in long before the agreed sum; she loved to do the bidding on her own account, sitting in her favourite place to the right of the auctioneer's rostrum. From the far side of the ring Dick could see what was happening and that they were bidding against each other, but there was nothing he could do about it. Eventually the colt was knocked down to Lady Beaverbrook for 36,000 guineas. Dick commented: 'Lord Chelsea was entitled to be annoyed, and he was annoyed; but, considering what a nonsense we had made of it, he took it extremely well.'

Minster Son and Unfuwain both ran for the first time in the Yattendon Stakes, a race which often reveals a high-class colt, at Newbury in August. Unfuwain was superbly bred, by Northern Dancer out of Height Of Fashion, whom Dick had trained to win the Princess of Wales's Stakes for the Queen before she was sold to Sheikh Hamdan. He started favourite in the field of twenty-seven. Minster Son had shown little at home, was ridden by Brian Proctor who seldom rode a fancied horse and started at 20–1. It proved to be yet another case of the stable neglected upsetting the apple cart, as Minster Son outpaced Unfuwain, ridden by Carson, in the last furlong to win comfortably. A month later Unfuwain came out again in the Hanson, Haynes and Clark Stakes, another race which often reveals a good colt, on the same course and made amends for his defeat. Charmer won yet another race apt to provide useful pointers for the future, the Westley Stakes at Newmarket in October.

Dick finished the 1987 season at eleventh on the list of winning trainers, the first time he had had a placing in double figures for eighteen years. This lowly position was compensated for by the fact that he had one two-year-old colt who had already proved himself top class, and three others with top-class potential. The outlook for the next year's Classic races looked very promising. As things turned out, 1988 was to be not only a traumatic year for Dick, but also one of the most controversial years in the history of the British Turf.

TEN

THE LEASE CRISIS

HENRY GEORGE REGINALD MOLYNEUX HERBERT (also known as 'Porchey' from his title of Baron Porchester), 7th Earl of Carnarvon, is one of the most public-spirited aristocrats of the last half century. In this respect he differs from his father. The 6th Earl, 'Old Porchey' as he was known, was relaxed about everything not directly concerned with his own interests. He was an indifferent amateur rider on the flat, socialised with the rich and famous and loved a game of bridge. He had a certain charm and was a bit of a rake, a bit of a card. Although he owned many racehorses and was a successful breeder, he was never elected to the Jockey Club and resented the fact that his son was elected to the Club at the age of forty – incidentally his grandson Harry Herbert was elected at the same age, but that was twelve years after his death.

What the 6th and 7th Earls had in common was love of shooting and thoroughbreds. They inherited their interest in breeding from the 5th Earl, the famous Egyptologist and discoverer of Tutankamen's tomb, who founded the Highclere Stud at the turn of the nineteenth and twentieth centuries. The 6th Earl bred Blenheim, winner of the Derby in 1930, though he sold him to the Aga Khan as a yearling. The 7th Earl owed much of his success as a breeder to his famous grey mare Jojo and her descendants. He had many good horses to carry his colours including Tamerlane, who was narrowly beaten in the 2000

Guineas, Smuggler, Town And Country, and the brilliant fillies Roseate Tern, Niche, Lemon Soufflé and Lyric Fantasy – a number of them trained by Dick.

Henry Carnarvon undertook many public duties both in racing and in the wider world of local government and politics. In racing he served one term as Chairman of the Council and two terms as President of the Thoroughbred Breeders Association; for many years he was Chairman of the Jockey Club's Race Planning Committee and was a prime mover in the introduction and development of the Pattern race system that became the model for the classification of quality races all over the world; and he was also a long-serving Chairman of the Levy Board's Stallion Advisory Committee. He sat on the Parliamentary All-Party Racing Committee. Outside racing he was a Deputy Lieutenant of Hampshire, served two terms as Chairman of the Hampshire County Council, and was Chairman of Serplan which had wide-ranging responsibilities for overseeing planning in the south-east. He chaired the All-Party Chamber Committee whose report came down in favour of a Royal commission before a decision about the future of the hereditary peers was made – the recommendation was accepted in principle, but the Government decided to do things the other way round. He was so well regarded by his peers that he was elected as a crossbencher to be one of the seventy-five hereditary members of the House of Lords to stay on, pending full reform of the House.

As manager of the Queen's horses and an owner of horses in the stable himself, he formed a warm professional and personal relationship with Dick. The Porchesters – Henry was Lord Porchester until the death of his father in 1987 – and the Herns went on holiday together several times, once renting Jeremy Hindley's spacious house on Barbados where they were joined by Sir Robert, then assistant private secretary to the Queen, and Lady Jane Fellowes. On 28 May 1988 *The Racing Post* published a feature on Dick consisting of an article by Paul Haigh, an atrocious caricature which made him look like a First World War profiteer by Richard Wilson, and appreciations by four of his associates – the former owner of the West Ilsley stables Jakie Astor, the stable jockey Willie Carson, the assistant trainer Alex Scott and Henry Carnarvon. Carnarvon's contribution was fulsome:

> I think I've trained with some of the greatest trainers in the world, including Fred Darling, and Dick must be one of the best of them all.
>
> He's an incredible horseman who understands the make and shape and handling of a horse better than anyone I can think of. He is absolutely meticulous in stable management and inspires incredible loyalty and admiration from members of his staff.
>
> I thought he was immensely brave after his accident. Every time I went to see him I was struck by the marvellous way in which he handled it. Sheilah was quite marvellous about it too.
>
> Although he couldn't move, he wanted to know everything about the yard and would assimilate in his mind everything we were telling him. He would know every horse, every box and every detail as described to him.
>
> He's a wonderful raconteur and tremendous fun, as is Sheilah, and they are both marvellous company.

Henry had more to say in the same vein in an interview with Michael Seely published in *The Times* on 31 May, the eve of the Derby:

> I sometimes feel that he sees more now than when he was riding horses, being able to touch their skins and feel their legs. He's always had an extraordinary ability to concentrate. And now when the lads ride the horses round him, he can see how they're breathing and how they've taken the exercise. He'll see if a horse is trotting right or if it is not relaxed. And he's always had this knack of being able to notice things that might go wrong.

There could hardly be stronger evidence of a relationship of intense mutual regard than was signified by these two interviews. Clearly Henry had enormous faith in Dick's ability to train horses to the highest possible standard in spite of his physical handicap. Their friendship seemed unbreakable. Astonishingly, within a couple of months of the publication of those interviews the relationship of Carnarvon with the Herns was to lie in tatters, and there was hardly an epithet too harsh for them to apply to him.

––––––––––

The four two-year-old colts that had shown so much promise in 1987 all trained on and achieved top-class status as three-year-olds, though only one of them won a Classic race – and that victory, owing to exceptional circumstances, was not attributed to Dick as trainer. Charmer was the first into action. He ran in the Ladbroke European Free Handicap at the Newmarket Craven Meeting, and looked like winning when he took the lead more than a furlong from home, only to be beaten for speed by Lapierre up the final hill. He ran again in the 2000 Guineas two weeks later. He was with the leaders at half way, then lost his place, but came again strongly in the last furlong and failed to catch the winner Doyoun by only half a length. In spite of his defeat, he had proved himself a top-class miler.

Unfuwain came next. He ran in the Warren Stakes over the Derby course and distance at the Epsom Spring Meeting and outclassed his opponents to win by 15 lengths. It was much the same story in the Chester Vase, the oldest of the Derby trials, which he won by 8 lengths. Minster Son also had a smooth Derby preparation, winning two Listed races over 1¼ miles, the Newmarket Stakes and the Predominate Stakes at Goodwood. Michael Seely made a habit of telephoning Dick at 9 a.m. every Sunday, and when he rang on the Sunday morning before the Derby Dick, playing up to his reputation for being shy of publicity, answered the call: 'Howard Hughes here,' and added with characteristic reticence in reply to Seely's query: 'My Derby horses are okay, I think, but I can't tell you about anyone else's.' Dick's former stable jockey Joe Mercer was more forthcoming.

'I know Dick thinks a lot of Charmer,' he told Seely. However, Willie Carson chose to ride Minster Son, in whose favour he was prejudiced because he bred him, while Paul Eddery was on Charmer and Steve Cauthen on Unfuwain.

On the day none of Dick's three runners was concerned in the finish. Unfuwain got to the front early in the straight, but would not let himself go on the firm ground and dropped back to finish seventh behind Kahyasi. Neither Minster Son nor Charmer was ever in the race with a chance and they finished eighth and eleventh, respectively. The latter pair both came back with injuries; Minster Son pulled his longissimus muscles and Charmer was jarred up.

Emmson was the last of the quartet to re-appear. He finished fourth in the Mecca-Dante Stakes, the most reliable of the modern Derby trials, and then finished third behind Hours After and Ghost Busters in the French Derby. It was probably not the strongest field to have run for the premier French Classic race, but he had done enough to prove himself a high class colt over 1½ miles.

Unfuwain ran next in the Group 2 Princess of Wales's Stakes, a race which Dick liked very much because he thought that the weights favoured an improving three-year-old. Unfuwain got the soft ground he needed on that occasion and won convincingly. There were then hopes that he would complete the Princess of Wales's Stakes and King George VI and Queen Elizabeth Diamond Stakes double achieved by Petoski three years earlier. He went to the front more than 2 furlongs from home and hopes ran high, but Mtoto had the better finishing speed and pegged him back in the last furlong. Mtoto had recently won the Coral-Eclipse Stakes for the second year running, but his connections were doubtful about his ability to stay the extra 2 furlongs at Ascot and instructed Michael Roberts to drop him out in the early part of the race and save him for a late run. Dick thought that he might not have caught Unfuwain if Willie Carson had gone flat out for the line after taking the lead, instead of cruising. It is true that Mtoto repeated his superiority over Unfuwain when they met again in the Prix de l'Arc de Triomphe two months later, when they were second and fourth behind Tony Bin, but the ground was very fast and it was only a last-minute decision to let Unfuwain take his chance.

Minster Son showed that he was well on track for the St Leger when he won the Group 3 Gordon Stakes at Goodwood the following week, beating the well thought-of Assatis by 2 lengths.

The four Classic colts had thus made an important contribution to a reasonably satisfactory start to the season, but their summer campaigns were interrupted by events that were both dramatic and traumatic for the Herns. On Monday 13 June Sheilah recorded in her diary: 'Had to get up to Dick in the night. He had had a terrific sweat. He looked and felt rotten all morning.' An appointment was made for him with Dr John Costello, a general physician whose particular field was the respiratory tract, at the Cromwell Hospital in West London. Sheilah and Marcus Tregoning took him to London, and Marcus pushed his wheel-chair into the lift to deliver him to his room. An Arab gentleman got into the lift with them and Dick said to Marcus: 'What time is it we are meeting Hamdan?' Marcus realised that he was making no sense and that something was seriously wrong. He took Dick to his room and went to look for Costello. Fortunately he soon found him, because when they got back to the room Dick was lying on the floor unconscious.

Dick was examined by the heart specialist Dr Jewitt, who diagnosed a leaking heart valve. Sheilah was told that the alterna-tives for a replacement were a pig's heart valve, with an estimated life of ten years, or a steel valve, which should last indefinitely. She wisely chose the steel valve, which was still working well twelve years later. The operation was performed by Mr Keats on 16 June, the Thursday of the Royal Ascot Meeting. The same evening Sheilah telephoned Neil Graham in California and asked

223

him to come home as soon as possible and take over the post of assistant-trainer.

Alex Scott had been assistant trainer at West Ilsley, but in the early summer he had been invited to succeed Olivier Douieb, who was terminally ill with cancer, at Oak Stables in Hamilton Road, Newmarket. Douieb's principal patrons were Maktoum Al Maktoum and the fabulously wealthy American Allen Paulson. Scott offered to stay at West Ilsley until the end of the season, but Dick insisted that it was too good an opportunity to miss and that he would risk losing it if he delayed. Dick wanted to appoint Marcus Tregoning as assistant, but Carnarvon insisted that he was too inexperienced and strongly advocated Neil Graham. Dick reluctantly agreed. Graham arrived at West Ilsley, and Scott stayed on for one week to see him settled in.

Dick was released from the Cromwell on 24 July, the day after Unfuwain had run at Ascot. He was not to be at home for long. In the early hours of Friday 5 August he was rushed back to the Cromwell, and underwent an immediate operation to relieve fluid on the heart. At that time he was immensely grateful for the devoted attention of the physiotherapist Nicky Brown, who stayed with him all night while he was in intensive care.

The following day Sheilah wrote to the Queen:

> With humble duty to Your Majesty, I feel constrained to write to you to let you know that Dick had to undergo heart surgery on Friday morning. He is now in intensive care. His surgeon, Mr Keats, assures me that Dick will be stronger as a result of the operation than he has been for some years, and is confident of a good recovery.

It seems certain that Henry Carnarvon must have been made privy to the contents of this letter, which makes his subsequent actions all the harder to understand.

For the next six weeks Sheilah lived under conditions of incessant hard work and constant stress almost too much for a single person to bear. She got up early every morning and went out on the Downs to watch the work. She took the dogs for a walk, went down to the yard to supervise matters there and then spent hours in the office attending to all the business of the stable. In the afternoon she would go to London with Marcus or Nigel, a young New Zealander who was helping out generally around the stables, often taking a home-cooked meal for Dick. She used to get home late for a short night's sleep before repeating the same programme the next day.

On Sunday 14 August she decided not to go to London because Dick was to be sedated in preparation for tracheotomy the following day. Instead she was summoned to Milford Lake House, Henry Carnarvon's residence a mile north of Highclere Castle, for an interview at 12.15. That evening she went to see Willie and Elaine Carson, who were living in West Ilsley. She was distraught and inconsolable. 'Dick has been sacked and we have got to get out of the house,' she told them. When she had protested that they had nowhere else to live, Carnarvon had said that they had their house at West Wittering, an impractical suggestion since it was only a seaside cottage and in any case was owned jointly with Pamela Holliday, Sheilah's old friend who had been so helpful in suggesting that Dick should apply for the job of private trainer to Major Lionel Holliday thirty years earlier. All the Carsons could do was to listen sympathetically and do their best to comfort her. Before going to bed she wrote in her diary: 'The worst day of my life.'

Sheilah's diary fixed the date of the interview, and the evidence of Willie Carson confirmed its drift. When Carnarvon was asked in 1999 when the information was first conveyed to Dick that the lease, which was due to expire in November 1989, would not be renewed, he replied: 'I can't remember.'

Sheilah's diary recorded the sequence of events in the next few weeks. On 16 August she wrote: 'Henry (Carnarvon) is forcing my hand and pulling the plug.' On 22 August she wrote that there had been a meeting of doctors to discuss the case – Costello, Jewitt, Frankel from Stoke Mandeville, the Queen's physician Sir John Batten and the Jockey Club Medical Officer Michael Allen. It was significant that the three doctors who had been treating Dick – Costello, Jewitt and Frankel – gave their opinion that Dick should be able to continue to train, while the two outsiders – Batten and Allen – expressed reservations.

The result of the meeting thus was inconclusive, but Carnarvon evidently accepted the judgement of Batten and Allen. Three days later Sheilah wrote in her diary that she had typed a letter to the owners, on Carnarvon's instructions, and taken it up to the Cromwell where Dick, with great difficulty, had managed to sign it. The letter stated:

> You may imagine how painful it is to have to write this letter in order to let you know that on the advice of my doctors I have decided to relinquish my Trainer's Licence and have asked the Licensing Committee to grant a temporary licence to Neil Graham. Lord Carnarvon acting for Her Majesty the Queen is making arrangements for another trainer to train at West Ilsley for the 1989 season. Neil Graham will hold the licence for the rest of the current season and a new trainer will then be appointed.

Sheilah concluded her diary entry: 'Another really nasty day.'

The responses of the owners were varied and revealing. Some, like Arnold Weinstock, seemed to accept the finality of the situation: He wrote:

> Because it comes as no great surprise, your letter of 25 August 1988, is no less a cause of sadness . . . We have worked together as friends and colleagues for many years, in agreement and disagreement, but always with goodwill and without rancour. I can only hope that whatever happens in the future, we will be able to remain in contact and that you will continue to take an interest in our bloodstock in one form or another.

Others, like that from Dick Hollingsworth, all of whose horses were given nautical names in honour of Felucca, the foundation mare of his Arches Hall Stud, looked forward to the day when Dick would be training for them again. Hollingsworth wrote:

I was very sorry to receive your letter and learn that on medical advice you have decided as a temporary measure to relinquish your trainer's licence. I am more than grateful to have had the benefit of your long experience and knowledge which have resulted in many victories culminating in the 1980 Oaks (Bireme). I most sincerely hope that you will soon recover your health and that you will be able to resume what has been a very happy association.

Another painful duty was to inform the staff. A notice was typed and read to them by Geordie Campbell. It stated:

> The Major has asked me to see you all today to tell you that sadly he has had to decide, on the advice of his doctors, to call a temporary halt to his career as a trainer. He has asked me to thank you all for the way you have worked and supported him over the years, especially just recently when he has been so ill. He bitterly regrets having to let you all down.

The statement added that the Jockey Club had been asked to grant a temporary license to Neil Graham, and that Lord Carnarvon was making plans for another trainer to go to West Ilsley. Thus the fiction that Dick's doctors had advised him to give up his licence and consequently leave West Ilsley was conveyed to both the owners and the staff. The news was a crushing blow to the members of staff, some of whom had been working at West Ilsley for more than a quarter of a century and now faced an uncertain future and a possible loss of their jobs.

The next day Matthew McCloy, the Newbury solicitor who became a director of the British Horseracing Board, went to lunch with Sheilah at The Old Rectory. McCloy pointed out that the lease automatically became null and void if the trainer relinquished his licence to train issued by the Jockey Club. The letter to owners had stated that Dick would relinquish his licence, so the lease would terminate immediately instead of running until November 1989 as the contract stated. 'I have been set up,' Sheilah commented. Her feelings were exacerbated by the news that Costello was pleased with Dick's progress.

227

On August 29 Sheilah recorded that she had had 'a nasty interview with Carnarvon – one of the nastiest sessions I have ever had', though she did not record any details of the interview. She returned home shaking. The pill was sugared to some extent by a letter from the Queen saying that they could go on living at The Old Rectory. Nevertheless the letter revealed plainly that the Queen had been misinformed, as she wrote: 'I have heard from Sir John Batten, who has spoken to Dick's doctors, and Dr Michael Allen and they are unanimous in stressing that Dick should give up training now for his own sake, to enable him to recover and even "enjoy" some retirement.' The unanimity, of course, was confined to Batten and Allen. The misunderstanding was underlined four days later by Costello's emphatic denial that he had ever said that Dick would not be able to train again.

In reply Sheilah wrote a letter to the Queen which conveyed her thanks and at the same time flatly contradicted the assumption that Dick must give up training. She wrote:

> We are all so very grateful for the wonderful kindness Your Majesty has shown in allowing Dick to remain at The Old Rectory for as long as he needs it. We are both at the moment suffering from shock at the speed of events, but we are trying to adjust. Dick is so much improved that the doctors are amazed. He is a very unusual man and his powers of recovery astound everyone. I know he would very much like to continue to train until his dying day. Sitting in a wheelchair, more or less unable to use his hands, would, I think, drive him dotty.

It must have been at about this time that Sheilah wrote to Dr Frankel at Stoke Mandeville, though her draft of the letter is undated. Frankel had kept in touch with Dick since his fall and regularly monitored his progress. Dick believed that Frankel regarded him as a kind of exhibit A, an example of how a tetraplegic could carry on his career that he could use to encourage other tetraplegics among his patients. He had made a special

effort to attend the medical meeting at the Cromwell on 22
August. She wrote in her letter:

Dear Dr Frankel,
I apologise for not having written to thank you very much indeed
for first going to visit Dick once again at the Cromwell, and
more especially for being 'in' on the medical meeting. It was
exceedingly good of you to give the time and it is much appreciated by both of us.

What the outcome of it all will be I just don't know. It is a
very final decision to hand in your licence, and it has obviously
upset Dick very much. It also means from a legal point of view
that he relinquishes all right to remain at West Ilsley, which
has inevitably put us in a weak position for bargaining over the
hand-over.

However, it is now done, and as Dick has always said it is no
good crying over spilt milk. But I think the powers that be could
have left it all to the end of the season, which would have given
him time to get stronger to face his decisions and would have
given us time to put our house in order. As it is, it is most painful
and difficult to understand. In my opinion he deserved better.

These two letters lay bare the sense of defeat and despair prevailing in the Hern camp in the last week of August.

On 1 September Carnarvon telephoned and Sheilah recorded
in her diary that he said that owing to the letter to owners it
was not possible for Dick to continue training in 1989. 'So he
has got us,' she commented, adding: 'I *must* pull myself together
and make Dick keep going.' She had a powerful incentive to do
that. She had become an experienced and perceptive work-
watcher, and what she had seen on the gallops in the last month
had convinced her that in Nashwan they had a colt of true Classic
potential.

For the Herns the early days of September were the darkest.
Neil Graham had taken over and they were close to despair. Ian
Balding, who trained at Kingsclere only 5 miles from Milford
Lake House, knew Carnarvon well and was a close friend of the

Herns, was incensed. Thinking things through, he reasoned that no decision to oust Dick would have been taken unless they had someone in mind to replace him; and that person could only be his brother-in-law William Hastings-Bass – Ian's wife is William's sister Emma. William was very well liked by Carnarvon and already trained eight horses for the Queen. He picked up the telephone and dialled William's number in Newmarket. 'So you're going to West Ilsley,' he said when William answered. 'How did you know?' asked William. 'I guessed,' said Ian. They agreed to go together to visit Dick at the Cromwell and on the evening of 5 September Ian rang Sheilah to tell her that he was going to see Carnarvon and try to make him see reason. 'But I doubt it,' she commented in her diary.

Of 6 September Sheilah wrote in her diary: 'What a day. Dick rang to say Henry (Carnarvon) had rung saying he couldn't get anybody else while he was still at West Ilsley. Dick took it he meant he could stay on – luckily he rang to confirm it – no such thing! Dick had to move from West Ilsley! Talk about flesh and blood.' However, elsewhere the ice was breaking. That morning at the Cromwell Ian and William found Dick with a tube still in his throat, obviously a pretty sick man; but the bed was strewn with copies of *The Racing Calendar*, entry forms and form books and Dick was clearly actively engaged in managing his stable and, moreover, was fighting mad. When they left the hospital Ian and William had lunch together. Years later Ian recalled their conversation. 'We agreed that there was no way he was going to die and that the idea of turning him out of West Ilsley was outrageous. William said that he would telephone the Queen that evening and tell her that he was uncomfortable about the idea that he should go to West Ilsley at the end of the year, and I said that I would put the case to Carnarvon.' After lunch Ian telephoned Carnarvon and asked to see him as a matter of urgency. 'Come here at six o'clock this evening,' he replied.

Punctually at six Ian turned his car off the road, down the drive of Milford Lake House winding between banks of rhodo-

Gordon Richards on Pip and Dick on Chiltown on the winter gallop. Chiltown was given to Dick by
salie Culver, mother of Charlie Fenwick who won the 1980 Grand National on Ben Nevis. From the
nting by Mara McGregor, c1980.

Michael Sobell with the trophy after Troy had won the 200th Derby in 1979. Joint-owner Lord
instock is on the left.

Cabin Boy, ridden by Hywel Davies, on his way to victory at Warwick, 1981.

Sun Princess, ridden by Willie Carson in the winner's enclosure after the St Leger in 1983.

...oski (*nearest camera*) coming to win the King George VI and Queen Elizabeth Stakes from Oh So ...arp (*number 15*) and Rainbow Quest (*number 6*) at Ascot, July 1985.

...dy Beaverbrook with Petoski after he had won the 1985 King George VI and Queen Elizabeth Stakes.

Dick in cheerful conversation with the Queen's Racing Manager Lord Porchester (later Lord Carnarvon) ten years before the lease crisis.

Dick's close friend Ian Balding on his way to saddl up at Epsom.

Lord Weinstock and his son Simon in anxious conversation with Willie Carson as they await the verdict that their Prince of Dance has deadheated for the Dewhurst Stakes, October 1988.

Sir Michael Sobell, joint-owner of West Ilsley stables and the Derby winner Troy.

...narth, ridden by Willie Carson, gives Dick his last Group I victory in the Generous Dewhurst Stakes at ...vmarket, October 1995.

...ayir, ridden by Richard Hills, gives Dick his last Classic victory in the 1000 Guineas at Newmarket, ...' 1995.

The Queen's Racing Manager, Lord Carnarvon, a protagonist in the lease crisis 1988/89.

Sheilah (at the apex on top of the gun) at a reunion of the Women's Auxiliary Service (Burma) – WASB, May 1990, a year after the resolution of the lease crisis.

Dick and Sheilah with jockey Richard Hills, in the paddock at Newmarket before his last runner Ghalib
October 31st, 1997.

dendrons, parked at the side of the house and walked to the front door along a path with the expanse of the tree-girt lake on the left and the single-storey facade of the house on the right. He was shown into a small sitting-room, where he found himself confronted by Henry Carnarvon and his Countess Jeanie, who must have resembled a Flemish burgher and his wife depicted by Van Eyck. Henry was as stony-faced as Giovanni Arnolfini, and Jeanie as fetching as his Giovanna Cenami. 'Poor darling Jeanie,' Henry declared. 'I am being called a murderer, and that is not at all a nice thing for my wife to hear.' Ian explained that he – he did not mention William – had been to see Dick that morning and had come away with the strong impression that he had no intention of dying. He was fighting very hard to recover and could not wait to get back to West Ilsley. He begged that no precipitate action should be taken to terminate his occupation of West Ilsley stables. Henry retorted that he had received letters from the doctors giving a very pessimistic prognosis; moreover, the owners were pressing for a resolution of the doubts surrounding the future of the training operation at West Ilsley, and with Dick in such poor health it would be impossible to attract new owners to the yard. Ian warned that the popularity of the Queen in the racing world would be seriously undermined if there was a perception that Dick had been badly or arbitrarily treated, and that it would be unfair on anyone who was appointed to succeed him because he would have to face a wave of animosity from the public. 'There is no question of a new appointment at the moment,' said Carnarvon, obviously unaware that Ian had seen William Hastings-Bass that day.

The final entry in Sheilah's diary for that day, after recording that Ian had been to see Carnarvon, ran: 'Dick rang again' (presumably the call was to Carnarvon) 'saying it would be less messy and much happier all round if things were left as they should be and, after talking all round the point, it seems as if this may happen'.

The tide had turned, but to what extent the change was due

to Ian's intervention and to what extent it was due to a question of law it is impossible to tell. In Brian Holmes, Dick had a secretary of multiple talents. He had been appointed to the job in December 1978 after spending twenty years in the Royal Army Pay Corps, and therefore was well qualified to keep the stable accounts as well as performing all the normal duties of a trainer's secretary, doing the entries and dealing with correspondence. Also, providentially, he had a contact in Weatherbys and from that source he ascertained that there was no need for Dick to relinquish his licence; it could simply remain in suspension – 'on the back burner', as he described it – until he was fit to resume, while a temporary licence could be granted to Graham as an employee on a monthly salary. Accordingly, on 31 August Dick had written to Sir John Barlow, the Jockey Club Licensing Steward: 'Further to my letter of 25 August, on reflection I now think it is better not to officially relinquish my licence for the current year, but merely to request that you grant a temporary licence to my assistant, Mr Neil Graham, for the period during which I have been advised to rest' – which was two months. Since Dick did not relinquish his licence, the attempt to terminate his lease at the end of 1988 was effectively scotched. Carnarvon tacitly admitted that fact when he telephoned on 7 September. 'Thank God it now looks OK for next year,' Sheilah wrote in her diary that evening, but added significantly: 'But I wonder at what cost.' This reversal of fortune provided the most dramatic twist of the whole story of the final phase of Dick's tenancy of the West Ilsley stables.

By the end of September Dick was recovering fast. On the 25th Costello gave an optimistic report and Dick was sent to Stoke Mandeville, where he was examined by Frankel who, Sheilah recorded, was 'very positive and cheerful'. On the 30th he was released and returned to West Ilsley, where he went straight down to the yard to catch up with developments. 'It's lovely to have Dick home,' Sheilah recorded. He returned to Stoke Mandeville on 3 October, and went to the Cromwell for the day on the 5th for an X-ray, the results of which pleased Dr Jewitt very much. He went home for good two days later. Sheilah drove Dick to Stoke Mandeville on 7 November for a check-up by Frankel, who was entirely satisfied with his recovery. Two days later Dick's licence was delivered to him by special messenger. The 1988 flat season had come to an end at Doncaster the previous Saturday and Neil Graham's temporary licence expired.

The future for the Herns at West Ilsley, however, remained obscure. Later in November an offer was made that Dick could share the stables and yard with William Hastings-Bass for the 1990 season, but it specified that he could train only the older horses that he had left at the end of 1989 and should take in no yearlings. Dick had little hesitation in declining it, but made a counter-proposal in a letter to the Queen: He wrote:

> I hope that you will consider the following suggestion, that at the end of my lease in 1989 Your Majesty will be prepared to grant me a two-year extension. At the moment I feel that I shall be quite capable of training the horses and it is the work that I love. I am quite prepared to have a medical examination whenever required during the time I am training next season and suggest 1 July to be an appropriate time.

This suggestion was not accepted. The Queen visited West Ilsley with Carnarvon for evening stables on 9 December. She wrote to Dick on the 27th: 'I am sorry we did not reach a clear understanding about the future of the stables when we met recently.' Willie Carson believed that the refusal to extend the lease was a serious error. 'If Dick had been given another two years, he would probably have retired quietly at the end of that period. The refusal put his back up. He is a fighter and very competitive, and he became determined to carry on,' he said.

1988 had been, in meteorological terms, a year of extraordinary turbulence for the Herns. The worst scenario, to be ousted at the end of the year, had been avoided, but renewal of the lease when it expired in November 1989 had been ruled out.

There was an urgent need to find new training quarters and means to finance them, and it was fortunate that Lord Halifax stepped forward to take charge of the search for funding. Halifax had had horses in training with Dick for many years, but their association began to bear fruit abundantly in 1981 when he asked Dick to take a big backward colt called Bedtime that had failed to fetch his reserve at the yearling sales. When Bedtime came to West Ilsley Dick found that he made a noise, so he had him hobdayed and gelded and put him aside to mature. When he began to train him as a three-year-old Bedtime soon showed signs of ability. He won his first two races, minor events at Windsor, and then the valuable handicap the Magnet Cup at York in July, a race which Halifax was particularly pleased to win because he was on the York Race Committee. He ended the season with four victories from five races, and went from strength to strength the next year when he won five of his six races in Europe, including Group 3 races at Deauville and Ascot. These fine efforts produced an invitation to run in the Japan Cup in November, which the Japanese were eager to promote as their passport to the stage of international racing. Their promotional effort involved free air travel for the owner and his wife, the trainer and his wife and the jockey and his wife, with accommodation in a first-class hotel and free transport for the horse. 'The only drawback,' Dick recalled, 'was that we had to sing for our supper by answering innumerable questions at a mammoth press conference.' Bedtime did his stuff nobly, dividing two Japanese horses at the finish to be second. The Herns and the Halifaxes travelled and stayed together, and by the time the expedition was over their friendship was greatly enhanced.

Halifax visited Dick in the Cromwell during July, and when the crisis over Dick's future was revealed by the letter to owners of 25 August he decided that the time to act had come. In view of the fact that the Maktoums had twenty-five horses in the stable, he thought that they were the best people to approach. At the Newmarket October Sales he spoke to Sheikh

Mohammed, who gave him a sympathetic hearing but told him that he must put the case to his brother Hamdan. Hamdan, the owner of Unfuwain and his promising half-brother Nashwan, at once agreed to help and assigned his racing manager Angus Gold to the task of finding a suitable place for Dick to train. In the next few months many training establishments were inspected and finally Kingwood, on top of the hill south of Lambourn, was selected. An immense amount of work needed to be done to the gallops and the stables to make them fit for a large string of high-class horses and it was evident that, allowing for the time to be spent obtaining planning permission, the place could not be got ready for Dick to move in until the end of 1990.

The details of the traumatic events which overtook the Herns in 1988 happened out of sight and outside the knowledge of the public, who received no more information than that Dick was seriously ill and that Neil Graham had been granted a licence to train at West Ilsley from 1 September to the end of the season. All the manoeuvres, all the attempts to secure an early termination of the lease, left the Herns with a bitter sense of grievance. Nor were they alone in feeling aggrieved. Neil Graham had been assistant to Ian Balding for five and a half years, and during that time got to know Carnarvon and dined in his house. He left Kingsclere in 1987 and went to work for John Gosden in California. He came home for Christmas, and early in January 1988 was with Harry Herbert at Highclere one morning to see Sharrood, who was about to take up stallion duties there after being trained by Gosden to win two Grade 2 races in the United States. While he was there Carnarvon telephoned from his house to speak to Harry, who told him of Neil's presence. Carnarvon then asked him to go round for a talk and a cup of coffee.

Carnarvon told Graham that Dick's assistant Alex Scott was likely to leave at some point during the year because he had purchased Fitzroy House stables at Newmarket. Would Neil be willing to take his place? He gave him to understand that what was contemplated was a long-term relationship like that of Jeremy Tree and Roger Charlton, and that ultimately he would take over from Dick. It may be observed that Carnarvon was exceeding his authority by offering him the job of Dick's assistant, though the matter of Dick's successor was of concern to him as racing manager of the owner of West Ilsley stables.

Years later Graham gave an account of what followed:

> I heard nothing more until the Thursday of Royal Ascot when I had a telephone call from Sheilah explaining the situation and asking me to go to West Ilsley as assistant. When I reached England I was asked to go to Milford Lake House for an interview. Carnarvon explained his concerns over the long term future of West Ilsley and, obviously, its immediate problems. He confirmed that it would be his wish to see me take over from Dick on his retirement. My job was to make West Ilsley a success and gain the support of the other owners. I must fulfil three conditions: firstly, I must establish a good working relationship with Dick: secondly, I must gain the owners' respect so that they would see me as his obvious successor: thirdly, the yard must continue to be successful at the highest level.

Neil became the nominal trainer with a temporary licence at the beginning of September and had his first runners at the Doncaster St Leger meeting. Ironically enough, the first horse he saddled was Carnarvon's high-class filly Roseate Tern, who finished second in the Group 3 May Hill Stakes on the opening day. Two days later he saddled Prince Of Dance to win the Group 2 Laurent Perrier Champagne Stakes and Nemesia to win the race named after Sun Princess, the brilliant filly with whom Dick had won the St Leger in 1983. He rounded off a good week on a note of triumph when Minster Son won the St Leger. Sheilah had accompanied Neil to Doncaster, but felt that Minster Son's chances were remote when the weather turned nasty and rain fell intermittently. Diminuendo, who had won the Oaks, the Irish Oaks and the Yorkshire Oaks, was considered almost a certainty and started at long odds-on, but Minster Son fairly outstayed her after taking the lead early in the straight and beat her by a length. Watching from their usual place on the roof of the weighing room, Sheilah thought he had won with great courage. He was ridden of course by Willie Carson, who was adding a page to racing history as the first jockey to win a Classic race on a horse he had bred himself.

Things continued to go well for the stable. Although he was beaten into fourth place, Unfuwain ran an extremely creditable race on unsuitable ground in the Prix de l'Arc de Triomphe. Prince Of Dance dead-heated with Scenic for the Group 1 Dewhurst Stakes and Al Hareb won the Group 1 Racing Post Trophy. By the end of the season Neil believed he had fulfilled at least two of Carnarvon's conditions, by winning races at the highest level and gaining the respect of the owners, who had been, as he put it, 'a bit twitchy' when he arrived but seemed perfectly happy when the autumn turned out so successfully. He was officially the trainer of eight winners of eleven races with earnings of £278,232 which, added to Dick's previous winnings, gave the stable a total of forty-one races and £516,433 for the whole season, a sum exceeded by only six other stables. There had been no opportunity to establish a working relationship with Dick, and he did feel that Sheilah and some members of the staff tended to resent him as 'Carnarvon's man'. However, Sheilah never showed any open hostility and, as Neil remarked, 'the system had been shown to work'.

He heard no more about being Dick's successor, but attached no significance to that until early the following February when the Herns were away in Dubai for a holiday and Dick's convalescence. Simon Weinstock had come down to see first lot canter and afterwards, during breakfast at The Old Rectory, remarked: 'Isn't it terrible about Dick?' Neil had no idea what he was talking about, but decided to temporise in the hope that Simon's meaning would emerge in the course of conversation. It did. What Simon was referring to was the fact that Dick's lease was not to be renewed when it expired the following November and that he had got to leave West Ilsley. So there would be no appointment for him as Dick's successor at West Ilsley, and he had been given no inkling of the impending change. 'I was absolutely gutted,' Neil recalled. In spite of his deep disappointment and sense of being let down, he did stay on as assistant trainer until the end of the 1989 season.

When the details of the events surrounding the proposed termination of Dick's lease in 1988 are studied, it is impossible to resist the conclusion that he was shabbily treated. A number of questions suggest themselves. Firstly, with whom did responsibility for that treatment lie? In a regiment the ultimate responsibility for error or failure of duty rests with the commanding officer, but in matters affecting the Crown responsibility rests by traditional usage with the Crown's representative. It may be argued that the Queen's racing interests constituted a special case; the Queen and Henry Carnarvon had been close friends since childhood, and for that reason responsibility was seamless. On the other hand there is ample, albeit anecdotal, evidence that in respect of the Turf Carnarvon has exercised a degree of influence over the Queen that has often been decisive. There is every indication that he was the driving force in the tactical battle to secure the early termination of the West Ilsley lease, though it is apparent, from her prompt concession over the occupation of The Old Rectory, that the Queen was in close touch with developments at all times.

The second question requiring an answer is whether it is credible, plausible even, that a man with Carnarvon's unimpeachable record of disinterested public service would act maliciously or capriciously in a manner prejudicial to the interests of someone with whom he had been on terms of warm friendship and professional confidence for fifteen years. The answer must be that it *is* incredible, it *is* implausible. So the conclusion is unavoidable

238

that in so far as there was mistreatment of an old friend and professional associate it was due not to malice or caprice, but to other failings – to error, misjudgement, impetuosity, insensitivity, even lapse of memory. He must have forgotten, for example, that he had told Neil Graham in the first few days of July that he could look forward to succeeding Dick as trainer at West Ilsley provided he fulfilled certain conditions, since some time between then and the middle of August he engaged William Hastings-Bass to take over as trainer at the end of the year.

It is right to acknowledge that Henry Carnarvon was faced with a very delicate situation in the summer of 1988. Dick had major operations and spent time in intensive care, and he would have been guilty of reprehensible irresponsibility if he had not made contingency plans for the horses belonging to the Queen and other owners if Dick were to die or be permanently incapable of controlling the stable. When that has been said it remains true that he made a premature decision to consign Dick to the scrapheap and that it was grossly insensitive to summon Sheilah at a time when she was under enormous stress, and working practically round the clock, to inform her that Dick was to have his lease terminated at the end of the year and lose his accommodation. In any case that 'sacking', which was how Sheilah described it and which in effect it was, was based on an incorrect appreciation of the terms on which an assistant trainer could be appointed to hold a temporary licence. Recollecting the events of 1988 years later, Willie Carson made an apt comment: 'It was a business decision. Carnarvon, in his wisdom, thought he was acting in the best interests of the Queen. But few agreed. It was a bad decision.'

In 1999 Carnarvon, looking back on the critical days of 1988, blamed Sheilah for 'stirring up trouble'. It was just as well for Dick's sake that she did, and it would have been more generous to admit that she fought fiercely, passionately and effectively to protect her husband's rights and interests and that she did so at grave cost to her own health in the long run.

Whereas Carnarvon had visited Dick regularly when he was at Stoke Mandeville after his crippling fall, he never visited him at all while he was in hospital during the summer and early autumn of 1988. That omission was surely a mistake. The opinion of a layman who has intimate knowledge of the patient is often worth as much as the opinion of medical experts, and if Carnarvon had visited him he might well have seen his prospects of recovery in the same light as Ian Balding. This view is reinforced by the fact that the doctors were not unanimous – indeed a majority believed that Dick would be able to train again – and that those who were pessimistic were those that knew him least.

Fair-minded observers were in no doubt that Henry Carnarvon on behalf of the Queen was engaged in, idiomatically speaking, the thoroughly un-British practice of kicking a man when he was down. Carnarvon appeared to place excessive emphasis on serving what he conceived to be the interests of the Crown, and to believe that the end justified the means employed. Ian Balding, Dick's noblest ally in the whole unpleasant business, spoke from the heart when he called it 'the saddest, nastiest, episode in racing history'.

At the last Henry Carnarvon was outfought and outmanoeuvred on the issue of the early termination of Dick's lease, and his efforts to achieve that termination were proved to be premature and ill-judged. There was no prospect of a renewal of the lease when it expired in November 1989. That was how matters stood during the winter of 1988–1989; the issues had not been aired and public opinion had nothing on which to bite. When news about Dick's future broke in the early spring of 1989 the position was instantly transformed and public opinion rapidly hardened in his favour.

The Herns arrived home early in February with Dick refreshed and recuperated after their holiday at the Hyatt Hotel in Dubai.

They had spent much of their time on the roof of the hotel where there was a swimming pool and lunch was available. Thanks to the good offices of John Wallis, who was highly placed in the Hyatt hierarchy and was the elder son of Dick's great friends Tommy and Viv Wallis, the pool was kept at the temperature of 90 degrees F suited to Dick's needs; there were a few, but not many, complaints from other hotel guests that it was too hot.

When they had left, Nashwan had been throwing a splint and Dick was relieved when he got home to find that it had come right out and hardened up and he was completely sound. Nashwan was a big, handsome, powerfully built, chestnut half brother to Unfuwain by Blushing Groom. He stood 16.2 hands and looked every inch a Classic colt. He had won both his races as a two-year-old. His reputation preceded him to the racecourse, and he started quite a hot favourite in a field of twenty-seven when he made his debut in the EBF Yattendon Stakes over 7 furlongs at Newbury on 13 August. Willie Carson had to push him out, but he won convincingly in the end by three-quarters of a length. His second race was the Listed Red Oaks Autumn Stakes over the Old Mile at Ascot in October. This time he started at odds-on and showed that he had learnt a lot from his first run, making light of his task to beat Optimist by 4 lengths. He certainly had not been overfaced in his first season and had had just the right amount of experience to set him up for a Classic programme as a three-year-old. Dick decided to train him for the Derby.

A new, and for the first time, public phase in the chronicle of Dick's tenancy of West Ilsley stables intervened before the flat season opened at Kempton and Newcastle on 25 March, the Saturday of the Easter weekend. On Monday 13 March a statement was issued from Buckingham Palace:

> The Queen has appointed Mr William Hastings-Bass to take over the West Ilsley stables when Major Hern's lease runs out in Nov-

241

ember this year. Major and Mrs Hern will continue to live at The Old Rectory and Mr Hastings-Bass will train from Hodcott House, previously the home of the late Mr Jack Colling, Major Hern's predecessor at West Ilsley.

Rumours that Dick's lease would not be renewed had been circulating for some time, but this was the first official disclosure of the fact. The news prompted an outburst of criticism. Willie Carson was quoted as saying: 'It's terrible news,' and he added: 'They've made a bad decision. I've nothing against Hastings-Bass, but there's no way he's going to fill the yard like Major Hern did. He'll be a hard act to follow.' Willie's comments earned Carnarvon's undying hostility. However, if the jockey, as an employee, had stepped out of line, he was not alone. The former assistant trainer Alex Scott was equally outspoken. He stated: 'It is quite clear to me that Major Hern's health is more, not less, likely to deteriorate if he's taken away from all those things which have always been his *raison d'être*. I'd sum it up by saying that the loyalty and bond between himself and his staff does not seem to have been reflected in the relationship between landlord and tenant.'

These sentiments of insiders were echoed stridently in the press. Dick had never had a great deal of time for the members of the press outside a small circle of friends. At the same time they respected him as a dedicated professional, a man of unswerving probity, whose character was a shining example to the whole racing community. They found universally that he was a man wronged in the spring of 1989, and their reaction was to rally unanimously to his support. Criticism fed on criticism. Pressman bid to outdo pressman, and journalism interacted with public opinion to breed ever-more extreme views. Pejorative words like 'eviction' were in general use. To speak of eviction was of course entirely inappropriate and loaded, because 'eviction' and 'refusal to renew a lease' are in no way synonymous.

At last Sir Robert Fellowes, by then promoted to Deputy

Private Secretary to the Queen, decided that the time had come to intervene. He was well aware of the delicate nature of the issue, because Ian Balding had sought him out when they were both on holiday in Barbados in February and warned him of the likely impact on the Queen's popularity. On 29 March he wrote a letter to Dick from Windsor Castle. He began by saying that he was writing not as one of the Queen's advisers but in a private capacity. He went on to describe the anguish recent events had caused the Queen, Porchey and Jeanie and their family – Geordie (Lord Porchester), Carolyn (Lady Carolyn Warren, married to the bloodstock agent John Warren) and Harry. He wrote:

> I believe that the sort of stuff being written and said about the West Ilsley lease is bad for racing, bad for the Queen and by extension the country, and not, in fact, in your real interests. It certainly is in no one's interests for the business to fester on throughout the season, with the press feeding off a story each time one of the principals runs a horse or appears on the racecourse. So, my conclusion is that you and Sheilah are the only ones who can help matters. Were either of you to bring yourselves to tell a respected journalist or two two things, the situation could yet be greatly improved. The two are: (a) that you have always been treated with generosity and consideration by the Queen, and (b) that you respect and understand her decision not to renew your lease. At all events, I do know that, whatever the rights and wrongs of the past months, your health and your future have been the prime considerations for the Queen throughout.

Although some eyebrows might be raised at the use of the word 'prime', Dick, a life-long royalist who had always been profoundly appreciative of the privilege of training for the Queen, was not slow to be persuaded by Fellowes's arguments or to adopt his suggestion. Five of the best disposed racing journalists – Michael Seely of *The Times*, Brough Scott and John Oaksey of *The Racing Post*, Peter Scott of *The Daily Telegraph* and Monty Court of *The Sporting Life* – were invited to lunch at The Old Rectory on 10 April, and all accepted except John

Oaksey, who had a previous engagement. Sheilah arranged an excellent lunch and wrote in her diary that evening: 'It went well, and Brough, who I thought might be the most difficult, was the most helpful. Dick also carried it off very well and was good about our plans for the future.'

Besides having the five journalists to lunch, Dick issued a statement to the press the same day. It was worded:

> While I very much appreciate all the support and encouragement which I have received, I hope the recent correspondence which has appeared in the press about the fact that I shall not be training at West Ilsley in 1990 will now cease. For the last twenty-three years I have had the honour of training for Her Majesty the Queen and during that time she has always been extremely kind and understanding about the problems involved in training race-horses.
>
> Although I am planning to continue training, I feel sure that the only reason the Queen and her advisers decided to terminate my lease was concern for my health. I am extremely grateful to Her Majesty for allowing me to continue to live in The Old Rectory at West Ilsley for as long as I wish to do so.

Most of the newspapers printed the statement the next day. It immediately became clear that feathers were still ruffled. The same day Sheilah attended a demonstration of breaking a horse at the Royal Mews, Windsor, by the amazingly skilful American horsemaster Monty Roberts, and afterwards wrote in her diary: 'It was a revelation how he did it without any whip or strength, and in twenty-five minutes he had a man on his back walking, trotting and cantering. Patrick (Beresford, an old friend) thankfully was there, as Henry (Carnarvon) arrived and didn't acknowledge me. The Queen was there – nothing was said.'

Moreover it quickly became clear that Dick's pious wish 'that the recent correspondence. . . .will now cease' would not be granted.

Meanwhile the racing season was hotting up. Ten days after the issue of Dick's statement Al Hareb, who had been earmarked for the 2000 Guineas since his victory in the Racing Post Trophy, ran so abysmally in the Charles Heidsick Champagne Craven Stakes, finishing last by 10 lengths, that all thought of a Classic programme for him had to be abandoned. It was then that Sheikh Hamdan said to Dick: 'Why don't you run Nashwan?' Nashwan was well forward and Dick had planned to run him in one of the Derby trials, and he proceeded to do a most impressive bit of work on the trial ground. 'I have never seen a horse work better over 7 furlongs and he left his lead horse a long way behind as he quickened up,' Dick said. There was no doubt that he must run in the 2000 Guineas and when they got back from first lot all the lads were rushing to the phone to back him.

Guineas day, 6 May, was sunlit, balmy and breezy and the going was good to firm. Nashwan proved, as Brigadier Gerard had done before him, that Dick was perfectly capable of preparing a colt to win without a preliminary race. Nashwan took the lead 2 furlongs from home and, although strongly challenged by Exbourne up the final hill, held on to win by a length, with two other very good colts, Danehill and Mark Of Esteem, in third and fourth places. A huge crowd gathered round the winner's enclosure and burst into spontaneous applause as Nashwan, his chestnut coat gleaming in the sunlight and ridden by a beaming Willie Carson, came in. Dick, in his wheelchair, and Sheilah were waiting for him. Somebody called for three cheers, which were rendered deafeningly. It was a moving tribute to a man that the racing fraternity had taken to their hearts because, rightly or wrongly, they saw him as a victim of injustice. Dick recalled the occasion years later: 'I was so thrilled that, after all that had happened and getting the sack, I should have been given such a star on that particular day. The reception Nashwan got was fantastic. Everyone was right behind me, and I could feel the pleasure they were expressing in their cheers and applause.' He summed up his feelings in eight words: 'It was the sweetest moment of my life.'

———

Expectations that Dick's entertainment of the select few journalists and press statement would eliminate, or even damp down, criticism were quickly disappointed. Even the select few were not silenced. For example Michael Seely wrote:

> This is a time for plain speaking. The sustained applause from thousands and the calling of three cheers for the sixty-nine-year-old trainer as he came forward in his wheelchair to receive his trophy signalled not only recognition for an outstanding professional feat. It also showed sympathy for the man they considered to have been badly treated. Unfortunately the whole business has become a matter of public concern, and it is being discussed and debated outside the narrow confines of the world of racing.

As Peter Halifax put it: 'After the 2000 Guineas the press really went into overdrive.' There was even speculation that if the Queen won a race at Royal Ascot, the horse would be booed into the winner's enclosure. The pressures were extreme: from the press, from public opinion and from men of integrity and independent judgement like Ian Balding, who had nothing to gain from their intervention – indeed, Ian had a great deal to lose, as he was training nine horses for the Queen that season and his attitude showed tremendous courage.

Whether it was as a result of these pressures or of a spontaneous internal re-assessment of the issues, a dramatic change of mind produced a statement from Palace sources on 17 May:

> In November 1988, with the knowledge of the officials of the Jockey Club, Her Majesty the Queen made an offer to Major Hern whereby at the end of his present lease, which expires in November of this year, he could share the West Ilsley stables for 1990 with William Hastings-Bass.

Although at the time Major Hern felt unable to take up this offer, the Queen has now improved it and Major Hern has gratefully accepted the offer in principle.

The details of the arrangement to create two yards are under discussion between the trainers and will be subject to final approval by the Stewards of the Jockey Club.

The final terms, which were set out in a letter written by Carnarvon from Milford Lake House on 22 June and approved by Dick, contained two significant improvements on the original proposal: one was that ten boxes would be erected for Dick's use on the Old Stud field, an area close to the stables, and the other was that no limitations were to be imposed on the ages of the horses he could train. Dick was also to have the use of the eastern half of the divided stables and the twelve boxes known as the eastern boxes, together with the joint use of certain facilities such as the covered ride, the lunging ring and the gallops. The letter contained a further offer that the Queen would have a total of fifty boxes erected at the Old Stud which would be available for Dick's use for as long as he wished to continue training there. In his reply Dick said that he was most grateful to the Queen for her kind offer of the fifty boxes, but that he did not wish to accept it because he felt that 'it would not be in either of our best interests'.

In the meantime Nashwan had added the Ever Ready Derby to his 2000 Guineas victory, taking the lead 2 furlongs from home and running on strongly to win in most emphatic style from Terimon, who started at 500–1 and was the longest-priced horse to be placed in the history of the race. He was owned by Lady Beaverbrook, but trained by Clive Brittain. Nashwan had started a hot favourite at 5–4. Dick reported that much as he enjoyed the Derby and Nashwan's subsequent races, nothing was quite as sweet as the Guineas.

In *Private Eye* Jeffrey Bernard, describing the circumstances of Derby Day and the conduct of the royal party, descended to depths of scurrility exceptional even by his standards. However, when the scurrilous comments were pared away, an accurate reflection of the public mood remained. He wrote:

> It's Carnarvon's unique achievement that he's managed to unite the whole spectrum of racing people against him, from staunch Royalists on the one hand to bounders and riff-raff of the worst sort on the other. Public opinion has in no way been appeased by the ludicrous and hastily stitched-up compromise whereby he (Hern) is staying on for an extra year during which time he will have to share the yard with Hastings-Bass.

The second sentence quoted reveals ignorance of the way the compromise had been reached. In any case, the storm had practically blown itself out and Bernard's was one of the last blasts from the press, though the underlying sentiment of hostility to the Queen's advisers remained. Perhaps fortunately, the Queen had no winner at Royal Ascot. If she had done, there is little reason to suppose that its return to the winner's enclosure would have been booed, but it would not have been rapturously applauded.

The triumphal progress of Nashwan continued, and he added victories in the Coral-Eclipse Stakes and the King George VI and Queen Elizabeth Diamond Stakes to the Guineas and the Derby, thus becoming the first horse to win all those four races as a three-year-old. He had done enough to consolidate his reputation as a great racehorse and his defeat in his last race, the Prix Niel, in unsuitably soft ground at Longchamp in September, involved no loss of face. Nothing was found the matter with him, but it was considered inadvisable to send him back to Longchamp for the Prix de l'Arc de Triomphe. Instead he was to run in the Champion Stakes, but that plan had to be abandoned when he became a victim of the coughing epidemic which was playing havoc with the stable. He was retired to Sheikh Hamdan's Nunnery Stud at Thetford at a covering fee of £45,000 and he proved himself a high-class stallion. Although Dick admitted the difficulty of comparing one generation with another, he was firmly of the opinion that he was the best horse he had trained over 1½ miles.

Nashwan's half brother Unfuwain also added to his laurels, winning the Group 3 Lanes End John Porter Stakes at Newbury and the Group 2 Jockey Club Stakes at Newmarket. Of the other top-class colts of 1988, Emmson did well enough to win the Group 3 Prix Gontaut Biron at Deauville, but Charmer failed to win a race and Minster Son never got to the racecourse.

Nashwan was in a different class to any of the other three-year-old colts, but Roseate Tern, the property of Henry Carnarvon but still in the stable despite his differences with Dick, was a top-class filly, finishing third in the Oaks and going on to win the Group 3 Lancashire Oaks and the Group 1 Aston Upthorpe Yorkshire Oaks. Elmaamul was the most promising of the stable's two-year-olds and looked a genuine Classic prospect when he won a maiden race over 7 furlongs as Newmarket in July and the Reference Point Stakes over a mile at Sandown in September, his only two races. Dick ended the season in fourth place on the list of winning trainers, with forty-four races won and £1,096,219 earned in stakes; it was the only time that his stable earnings passed the £1 million mark.

The ambivalence of Dick's attitude to the crisis of his fortunes in 1988–1989 lay in the fact that he was torn between unquestioning loyalty to the Queen on the one hand and disillusioned resentment at what he interpreted as the baneful influence of Henry Carnarvon on the other hand. Compared with the desperate scenario that emerged from Sheilah's interview with Carnarvon on 14 August 1988, which dictated departure from West Ilsley stables and The Old Rectory at the end of that season, the final settlement was neither unfavourable nor ungenerous. That settlement gave Dick the right to lifelong rent-free occupation of The Old Rectory, together with the gardener's cottage, the garage and the flat over the garage, sole occupation of the stables until the end of 1989 and occupation of half the stables for 1990, creating breathing space for him to make arrangements to continue his training career elsewhere. Even if the assertion that the sole consideration of the Queen and her advisers was Dick's health is discounted as a palpable exaggeration, and it is accepted that ensuring smooth continuity of the training operation was a consideration of probably equal importance, Dick did not come out of it at all badly. His plea for renewal of the lease after November 1989, for a term of two years, was doomed to be refused because a commitment to Hastings-Bass had been made early in the summer of 1988, when the Queen's advisers wrongly assumed that Dick's days as a trainer of a large string were numbered. The commitment to Hastings-Bass was premature at best. Dick continued to train high-class horses successfully for a period longer than a seven-year extension of the lease of the West Ilsley stables would have covered. That is the great irony of the whole dispute, but to have foreseen it would have required a degree of prescience which the Royal party could hardly be expected to possess.

ELEVEN

LAST YEARS OF TRAINING

WILLIAM HASTINGS-BASS moved his horses from Newmarket to West Ilsley at the end of 1989. The partition of the yard worked amicably. The division gave William the main yard, while Dick occupied the ranges of boxes on the north-east side. No serious problems arose from the sharing of the joint facilities. William and Dick got on well enough together and the Herns invited the Hastings-Basses to dinner, but they did not develop a close friendship.

Even with the new boxes at the Old Stud, Dick did not have enough room for all his horses at West Ilsley and had to rent ten more boxes at James Bethell's yard at Chilton. Although Chilton is only 3 miles away, it is on the far side of the busy dual carriageway of the A34, and it was not feasible to bring horses from there to work on the West Ilsley gallops. The horses stabled there had to work on the Chilton gallops, which inevitably complicated the stable's training schedules.

The numbers of horses trained by William and Dick were almost identical. William began the season with seventeen horses belonging to the Queen and forty-seven for other owners, a total of sixty-four: while Dick had five horses belonging to the Queen and fifty-eight for other owners, a total of sixty-three. With regard to success, there was no comparison. At the end of the season William had mustered twelve individual winners of sixteen races with earnings of £107,681, while Dick had had nineteen individual winners of thirty races with earnings of £502,902 – nearly five times as much. These results left no room for doubt about Dick's ability to continue as a trainer of a large string of horses about which Carnarvon had been so doubtful in the summer of 1988. They might have been better still if many of William's horses had not arrived from Newmarket with runny noses. Dick's horses inevitably were infected, and he was convinced that some of them did not recover full health the whole season.

Two top-class three-year-olds – Elmaamul and Dayjur – were the main contributors to the earnings of Dick's stable. Elmaamul's performances as a two-year-old had hinted at a Classic future and the hint materialised when he finished third to Quest For Fame and Blue Stag in the Derby after battling for the lead all the way up the straight. He proceeded to gain Group 1 victories in the Coral-Eclipse Stakes and the Phoenix Champion Stakes and was second to the filly In The Groove in another Group 1 race, the Juddmonte International Stakes.

At the end of the season Elmaamul was allotted 125 in the International Classifications, a rating well within Classic parameters. Ratings-wise, however, he was inferior to his stable companion Dayjur, who was allotted 133, which made him the champion three-year-old of all the distance categories and was the highest rating ever for a horse in the sprint category.

Dayjur was a medium-sized brown colt bought as a yearling by Sheikh Hamdan at the Keeneland July Sales. He had a pedigree replete with speed. His sire Danzig and his maternal grandsire Mr Prospector were two of the strongest influences for speed in the world at that time, and his dam Gold Beauty had been a top-class sprinter in the United States. When Dick began to work him in the spring of his two-year-old season he soon realised that he had plenty of potential. However, he looked as if he was becoming too free, so Dick concentrated on getting him to settle and worked him in behind, just coming up to the leaders at the finish of the gallop. He won his first race at Newbury in June, but when he returned to Newbury the next month for the Listed Manton Rose Bowl he faded a little in the closing stages and was beaten into second place. When he came in Willie Carson said: 'This horse makes a slight noise, and that probably stopped him.' He could not run again that season because he sustained a nasty cut at the back of his pastern, but luckily it only bruised the tendon badly and did not sever it. It took a long time to get right and while he was recovering from the injury Dick decided to have the Hobday operation on his wind. This was performed by the great expert Geoffrey Brain and was a complete success.

When he went back into serious training in the spring of 1990 he again worked very well, but in his first race, the Ladbroke European Free Handicap over 7 furlongs at Newmarket, he failed to stay and finished only seventh. He won a minor race over 6 furlongs at Nottingham two weeks later, but next time out was narrowly beaten in a race over the same distance at Newbury. Watching the race on the video, Dick noticed that Willie was sitting still on him for most of the race while the other jockeys were riding vigorously, but that he had found nothing when he came off the bridle. He concluded that he would do better if he were allowed to run along from the start. His next race was the Group 2 Temple Stakes at Sandown and Dick instructed Willie to use his speed. Willie was not too confident that these tactics would be successful, but Dick insisted. In the event Dayjur jumped off in front, made all the running and won comfortably. His next race was the Group 2 King's Stand Stakes at Royal Ascot. It rained heavily on the morning of the race and the ground became soft. Dick advised Sheikh Hamdan that Dayjur should be pulled out, but the Sheikh decided to run and his decision was justified when Dayjur handled the ground well and won easily. The plan was to run him next in the Group 1 July Cup over 6 furlongs at Newmarket, but he did not seem quite himself in the meantime. Every day when he came back from exercise and had a pick of grass he would stale, and his urine was very pale. Dick was certain that he was not right and did not run him. Subsequently he won the Group 1 Ladbroke Sprint Cup at Haydock and the Group 1 Prix de l'Abbaye at Longchamp on his first trip abroad. It was a sunny day at Longchamp and there was a small shadow across the course just before the winning post, thrown by a lamp post. Dayjur lost some ground by pausing to jump it, but fortunately he was well clear and won impressively by 2 lengths from Lugana Beach. Dick thought little of the incident at the time, but it was to prove prophetic.

The race in which he was expected to set the seal on his reputation as the top international sprinter was the Grade 1 Breeders Cup Sprint at Belmont Park, New York, on Breeders Cup Day, 27 October. Belmont, with a dirt track 12 furlongs and an inner turf track 10½ furlongs in circumference, is the fairest galloping course in the United States. It has many other assets. This is how it was described in *Horse Racing*, under the advisory editorship of Ivor Herbert, published by Collins in 1980: 'Although it is not situated in scenic surroundings such as the Bois de Boulogne [site of Longchamp] or the Sussex countryside [site of Goodwood], the beauty of Belmont Park lies within its own confines. Here, quietly nestled away from neighbouring avenues and highways, is a world truly apart. With its magnificent grandstand and tree-shaded paddock, Belmont ranks as one of the most picturesque racetracks in the world.' That is all very well, but from Dick Hern's point of view it has one overriding drawback: the judge's box on the roof of the grandstand throws tapering shadows across the final stages of the straight on sunny late afternoons in the autumn. Dayjur was just getting the better of the filly Safely Kept, who had made all the running, when he encountered the first of the shadows and, though he jumped it in his stride like a high-class hurdler, forfeited his hard-earned lead. He jumped another shadow right on the finishing line and, as a result, was beaten by a neck. Even in defeat Dayjur covered himself with glory. His task had been gigantic. Safely Kept had won eighteen of her previous twenty-three races, had been narrowly beaten in the corresponding race and been voted champion sprinter of the United States the previous year. Once in front, she was the very devil to pass. Dayjur was running on dirt and round a bend for the first time in his life. Considering that that misadventure alone deprived him of victory, his performance was that of a true champion.

The defeat of Dayjur was disappointing, but the information that Sheilah gave Dick after they had flown back to England on Concorde was devastating. Before leaving home she had been diagnosed with cancer and needed to go into the Chelsea and Westminster Hospital immediately for an urgent operation. She had not told Dick about it because she did not want to spoil the trip and only Liza Brown, one of her oldest friends who accompanied them to New York, had been let into the secret. Dick had no inkling that anything was wrong; he did not even know that she had been to the doctor. It was a terrible blow, and a blow that was all the more cruel in view of the battles she had fought on Dick's behalf, indeed on behalf of them both, during the previous two years. Her health was terminally undermined. During the years between the autumn of 1990 and her death in March 1998 she had six more major operations; yet such was her will to live, such was her defiant spirit and her determination to carry on with her normal life as long as it lasted, that very few people outside a small circle of intimate friends had any idea how ill she was until the final few months.

Sheilah's convalescence from her first operation coincided with the upheaval of their lives caused by the move of the horses to Kingwood. Work on building the stables which replaced the old yard there had not begun until August as a result of delays in the granting of planning permission, but when completed the new training complex was magnificent. There were two yards of thirty boxes each, a covered ride with a circuit of nearly a furlong, a lunging ring, two all-weather gallops and two large horse-walkers which are so useful for horses that have just run and are a bit stiff. Dick had plenty of experience of woodchip gallops and recommended hardwood chips, which have a life of about three years and then need to be replaced. He had also been to the Royal Ascot Polo Club where there was a big arena surfaced with a substance called Polytrack. It seemed excellent but, as he did not know anyone who had made a gallop of it, he confined it to the lunging ring. Later the two all-weather gallops were converted to it. Dick considered it the best artificial surface he had seen. Horses do not slip on it and it is usable in all conditions, because it does not freeze and does not become too soft in wet weather.

Dick and Sheilah exercised their option to remain at The Old Rectory at West Ilsley, where they had lived already for twenty-eight years. It was a solid red brick, early Victorian house, built originally in 1842, with later additions. They had made it very comfortable, and equipped it to meet Dick's needs. Moreover, they had it for Dick's life-time, an important consideration when they did not know how much longer Dick would continue to train. Sheilah had another powerful reason for being reluctant to leave; she was a passionate gardener and had moulded the grounds to her own design, while her two greenhouses were very precious to her. All these arguments militated against a move to Kingwood, which was 10 miles away as the crow flies, but 15 miles and twenty minutes by car through the winding Berkshire lanes. It meant some inconvenience for Dick, but they decided it was worth that for the pleasure of staying in their old home.

Dick commuted to Kingwood every morning in time for first lot. Sometimes he stayed for evening stables, but at other times he would go home at lunchtime and leave Marcus Tregoning, who had succeeded Neil Graham as Dick's assistant, and Geordie Campbell to look round in the evening. One of the difficulties that Dick encountered at his new base was getting to know the gallops. It is easy for a trainer who can ride, because he can take out a hack in the afternoon and canter over them, familiarising himself with every detail of the lie of the land. 'At West Ilsley,' said Dick, 'I knew every blade of grass on both the winter and summer sides. It is very different when you are confined to a car.' Fortunately he was able to keep Les Boucher, the gallops man who had been there for years and knew the gallops like the back of his hand. He was an enormous help to Dick.

Dick trained at Kingwood for seven seasons, but had only two really top-class horses during that time, Harayir and Alhaarth. Harayir, by Mr Prospector's exceptionally fast son Gulch, was a very good, uncomplicated filly, and so consistent that she finished out of the first three in only two of her fourteen races. As a two-year-old in 1994 she won the Group 2 Lowther Stakes at York, beating the favourite Gay Gallanta by 3 lengths, but Gay Gallanta turned the tables in the Group 1 Cheveley Park Stakes two months later, which she won with Harayir in third place. Harayir wintered exceptionally well. For her reappearance in 1995 Dick had to choose between the Group 3 Nell Gwyn Stakes and the European Free Handicap over the same 7 furlongs at Newmarket two days later, and opted for the latter race because the Nell Gwyn Stakes would have brought her face to face with some of the same fillies that she would be meeting in the 1000 Guineas in two weeks time. Although she was beaten she proved that she had trained on by finishing second to the French-trained colt Diffident. Sheikh Hamdan had two fancied fillies in the Madagans 1000 Guineas, the favourite Aqaarid and Harayir. Willie Carson was no longer retained by Dick, whose reduced stable at Kingwood was not large enough to justify the retention of a leading jockey, and was retained by Sheikh Hamdan instead. The choice was his, and he preferred Aqaarid, while Richard Hills was on Harayir. Hamdan's fillies filled the first two places, but it was Harayir who prevailed to give Dick his final Classic victory. Harayir won three more races – the Group 3 Hungerford Stakes, the Group 2 Tripleprint Celebration Mile and the Group 2 Challenge Stakes. She had proved herself wonderfully tough by keeping her best form from mid-April to mid-October.

Alhaarth was a two-year-old of 1995, and that season was not far advanced before the rumour began to circulate that he was something out of the ordinary and precocious to a degree unusual in the progeny of Unfuwain. For once racecourse rumour did not lie, because he was unbeaten in his five races, which included four Pattern races. His first appearance was in the Strutt and Parker Maiden Stakes over 7 furlongs at Newmarket in July. Maiden races on the Newmarket July course are often contested by two-year-olds destined for high rank, but it is usually difficult to identify them at the time. Alhaarth's race was a typical example. He won by only a neck from another debutant, Mark Of Esteem, and it was impossible then to predict that Mark Of Esteem was to develop into a Classic miler or to appreciate that it had been an excellent performance to beat him. From Newmarket Alhaarth went to Goodwood for the Lanson Champagne Vintage Stakes, a Group 3 race which is the first two-year-old Pattern race of the season over 7 furlongs. The race has a fine record for producing stars of the future. It had been won by the subsequent Classic winners Troy, Don't Forget Me, Dr Devious and Mister Baileys; Dick had won it five times, his winners including Troy and Petoski, and in beating Allied Forces by a length Alhaarth was judged to be well up to their standard. Alhaarth proceeded to win the Group 3 Solario Stakes at Sandown, the Group 2 Laurent Perrier Champagne Stakes at Doncaster and the Group 1 Dewhurst Stakes at Newmarket. He made rather heavy weather of winning at Doncaster, but was impressive in the Dewhurst Stakes, the most reliable Classic pointer among the two-year-old Pattern races.

Dick's other notable horse in 1995 was Cuff Link, who was the subject of his only experiment with interval training. Cuff Link had a tendency to break blood vessels which rendered him unsuitable for Dick's normal training methods. Dick reasoned that if Kim Bailey could win the Cheltenham Gold Cup with a horse, Master Oats, that was interval trained, then the same might work with a stayer on the flat. Dick recalled: 'When I took him to Royal Ascot I had no idea whether he was fit enough, but he won the longest flat race in the Calendar, the Queen Alexandra Stakes.' What made the day unforgettable for Dick was the fact that Cuff Link's owner, Lord Weinstock, expressed his delight by bending down and kissing him on the back of the neck as he sat in his wheelchair in the winner's enclosure!

Alhaarth was allotted 126 in the International Classifications, a rating which made him clearly the best of his age in Europe. Dick, never a man to err on the side of over-optimism, felt that he 'would train on into a real live 2000 Guineas contender'. His pedigree was satisfactory. He was the best two-year-old sired by Unfuwain, and if Unfuwain had shone over longer distances than a mile Alhaarth sprang from a family renowned for first-class speed which had produced the French 2000 Guineas winner Green Dancer, a very close relative of Alhaarth. In any case Alhaarth had shown ample speed as a two-year-old. Sadly, things just did not work out right. His first outing as a three-year-old was in the Group 3 Craven Stakes over the Guineas mile in mid-April. He was a horse who had to be up with the leaders and Dick had made a plan with Willie to let him go on. Then, as Willie was getting onto his back, Hamdan told him that he would prefer him not to make the running. As a result he ran terribly free and was fighting for his head throughout the first half mile; that, as Dick remarked, 'really cooked his goose'. He finished in second place, a neck behind Beauchamp King.

Circumstances conspired against him in the Pertemps 2000 Guineas a fortnight later. There had been a spell of dry weather and the course had been watered. There had also been high winds and most of the water had blown onto the far side of the course, making the ground there much slower than the ground on the stands side. Alhaarth was drawn on the far side, number twelve in the field of thirteen. 'He might as well have stayed at home,' said Dick. Although he ran a creditable race to finish fourth, he was more than 6 lengths behind the winner Mark Of Esteem, whom he had beaten the previous July.

Dick felt afterwards that it was a mistake to train and run him in the Derby and the Irish Derby. He resented the waiting tactics that were used in an attempt to enable him to stay the distance and he simply lacked the necessary stamina. It was apparent that the speed elements in the dam's side of his pedigree were dominant. He did not recover his best form until he went to Longchamp in October to run in the Group 2 Prix du Rond-Point over a mile. Allowed to take the lead from the start, he made every yard of the running to win in the style he had made familiar as a two-year-old. He was given a rating of 121 in the International Classifications which, if below his rating for the previous year, was still well within the parameters for Group 1 status, for which the minimum is 115.

The 1997 season was Dick's last as a trainer. There were various reasons for his decision to retire. One was the progressive deterioration in Sheilah's health; he wanted to be able to spend more time in her company in the short time that remained. Another was that training at Kingwood was simply not an economic proposition for him. Years later he explained: 'With hindsight I realise that I should have been much better off if I had never gone to Kingwood and had retired at the end of 1990. At a place like Kingwood where you are paying a high rent, with only sixty boxes you face a big loss if you do not have a good season. Training fees do not cover the overheads, and you are in trouble unless you have some good horses to make up the deficit.'

The fact was that the good horses were not there in sufficient numbers. The 1995 season was his best at Kingwood, when he was sixteenth in the list of winning trainers thanks to the victory of Harayir in the 1000 Guineas and the two-year-old campaign of Alhaarth. However, in 1992 he had not been in the top fifty for the first time since the disastrous virus-stricken season of 1966, and he was out of the top fifty in three of his remaining five seasons. The biggest earner for the stable in his final season was Sarayir, who was credited with £12,230 for her victory in the Pertemps Virginia Rated Stakes at Newcastle, but she was not in the same class as her elder half-brothers Unfuwain and Nashwan and was out of her depth when she ventured into the Classic company of the 1000 Guineas. Falak won the Rosehill Conditions Stakes at Doncaster and Right Wing, who was afterwards to win the Lincolnshire Handicap when trained by John Dunlop, won the Triumvirate Limited Stakes at Ascot. However, the biggest earner for the stable after Sarayir was Ghalib, who won a maiden race at Newbury and a conditions race at Ascot. It would have made a big difference if Alhaarth had still been in the stable, but he had been transferred to Saeed Bin Suroor at Newmarket. He won two Group 2 races, the Budweiser American Bowl International Stakes at the Curragh and the Prix Dollar at Longchamp, but he was not offiicially considered to have made any improvement as a result of the change of stables and was put on exactly the same mark, 121, in the International Classifications.

Many of Dick's old patrons had followed the flag to Kingwood. In 1991 they included Arnold Weinstock, with seven horses, Dick Hollingsworth, Bunny Rotherwick, Jakie Astor and Kirsten Rausing, but by 1997 their numbers had been reduced by the death of Rotherwick and the illness of Astor, while Weinstock's team had been cut to four. During his seven seasons at Kingwood Dick became increasingly reliant for horses on the Maktoum family, with Sheikh Hamdan far the largest supporter. In 1991 the Maktoums contributed thirty-three, or forty-nine per cent, of the sixty-seven horses, but in 1997 they contributed thirty-seven, or sixty-four per cent, of the fifty-seven horses in the stable. Despite their support, the total number of horses trained by Dick had declined alarmingly.

Dick was extremely grateful to Sheikh Hamdan for providing such a superb training centre at Kingwood, but if he had had a better understanding of the economics of the situation he would have thought seriously about whether it was sensible to move there. The fundamental problem was that he was unable to obtain a firm advance quotation of the rent he was to pay. In the late autumn of 1990 Angus Gold, Sheikh Hamdan's racing manager, and Bobby Dolby, his manager at Shadwell Stud, invited themselves to come and see Dick at his house in Lowther Street in Newmarket. They told him that they did not know what the annual rent at Kingwood would be, but they did not think it would be very big – probably in the region of £15,000. Dick had already moved his horses into Kingwood stables before he was informed that the rent was £60,000. He protested, but by then the whole business was in the hands of faceless accountants. The rent, he was told, represented only 1 per cent of Sheikh Hamdan's investment in the place and could not be reduced.

As Dick's financial situation at Kingdown deteriorated, his secretary-accountant Brian Holmes worked hard to find ways of saving money, but in a high-class racing stable the scope for economies is limited and the main items of expenditure, like forage, wages and transport, are irreducible. Dick's losses mounted rapidly. He was forced to sell a cottage that he owned in West Ilsley to reduce his overdraft, but by 1997 retirement was inevitable. His successor, his former assistant Marcus Tregoning, was on a much better wicket, because he became a salaried employee.

Sheikh Hamdan used to visit Kingwood occasionally for evening stables, never in the morning to see the work. He usually arrived in the white Mercedes that he kept for years because he thought it was lucky. He was never accompanied by the large retinue that often surrounded other members of the family on the racecourse, but was often attended by his friend and adviser Hadi Al Tajir, a banker who spoke excellent English and was an agreeable companion. At other times Dick kept Hamdan informed of the wellbeing of his horses sometimes by telephoning him direct in Dubai, and sometimes through his racing manger Angus Gold. He always kept Angus in touch with developments.

Dick's last runner, Ghalib, dead-heated with Proper Blue for third place behind Saafeya and Sandmoor Chambray in the Listed James Seymour Stakes at Newmarket on 31 October. Sheilah had accompanied him in the paddock. Three weeks earlier she had worked on Vivian Wallis's bottle stall at Ascot's charity race day, playing her part as energetically as ever though nobody could fail to notice how distressingly thin she had become.

The day Ghalib ran at Newmarket was Sheilah's last on a racecourse. She was was re-admitted to the Chelsea and Westminster at the beginning of February because she was in such pain that she needed regular doses of morphine. After that her decline was relentless. Her last venture outside the hospital was on 14 February 1998. George Bull, bred by Dick and owned jointly by him and Sheilah, was running in a hurdle race at Newbury and Sheilah was determined to see the race in the William Hill betting shop 500 yards down the road. Her cousin Giles Blomfield, Liza Brown and Vivian Wallis's daughter Nona Baker, who worked wonders in giving her encouragement, went with her. She refused the use of a wheelchair, insisting she could walk, a frail, pathetically thin figure still imbued with the dauntless spirit that had sustained them in the darkest days of 1988. George Bull had won at Windsor in December after a ding-dong battle with Better Offer from the last hurdle, and he won twice more later in the season. At Newbury he could finish only fifth. Sheilah was undismayed. She always talked to everyone everywhere, in public places, trains and planes, and she now made no exception of Hill's betting shop. On the way back to the hospital she tired visibly and had to take Giles's arm. She paused for a few moments in front of a well-stocked pavement flower stall, gazing intently at the colourful blooms that she loved so much. Then she entered the doors of the hospital for the last time. It was St Valentine's Day, and that evening she gave a party for the nurses in the passage outside her room, where sofas were placed for the convenience of visitors. There was champagne and a cake and she made it a happy occasion.

She died at 3.30 a.m. on 8 March. Only her strong heart and invincible spirit had kept her alive so long. 'It was terrible to see her wasting away in front of our eyes,' said Dick. On the 16th she was cremated at Oxford Crematorium after a service attended only by Dick and a few close friends. A Service of Thanksgiving followed at West Ilsley in the quaint parish church of All Saints, with its flint walls and red-tiled roof without tower or spire, only a stone's throw from The Old Rectory. Over five hundred people came to pay their last respects to a woman who had inspired such abundant love and admiration. There was not room for them all in the church and those excluded were accommodated in a marquee in the garden of The Old Rectory, where the service was relayed. Afterwards all the mourners were sustained with champagne and smoked salmon. Services of Thanksgiving are not meant to be occasions of great solemnity, and Sheilah would certainly have approved of the conviviality with which her many friends lovingly commemorated her.

EPILOGUE

DICK HERN IS NOT THE ONLY MAN to have trained racehorses successfully from a wheelchair. Mikey Heaton-Ellis, who had been partially paralysed in a racing fall, did so from Barbury Castle in Wiltshire for much of the 1990s. Seventy years earlier Captain Dick Gooch, one of Dick's predecessors at West Ilsley – Eric Stedall and Jack Colling intervened – was similarly afflicted. By the strangest of coincidences Gooch, like Dick, broke his back in a fall when out hunting with the Quorn; for a time he was confined to the front room of Hodcott House and supervised the training of his horses by having them led round on the lawn where he could see them from the window. He had the reputation of being one of the ablest trainers of stayers of his generation, and won the Goodwood Cup with Old Orkney and Kinchinjunga. Old Orkney was the great rival of the immortal Brown Jack, whom he beat in the Ascot Stakes and the Goodwood Cup. For all that special skill, Gooch never attained the distinction of Dick as a trainer of Classic horses.

Retirement from training, followed only four months later by the death of Sheilah, left enormous gaps in Dick's life. Sheilah had been his devoted companion, and also an integral part of his professional life, for more than forty-one years. She had also been one of the last surviving members of his immediate family, as she had been predeceased by his parents, his brother Michael and her parents. They had no children. His mother Winifred was the longest-lived of the family and had reached the great age of ninety-three when she died in 1986. When she became too frail to live by herself in a cottage with a steep flight of stairs, Dick moved her from Devon to The Malthouse, a house on the eastern fringe of West Ilsley which he had converted so that she could live entirely on the ground floor. While she was living in Wales soon after the Second World War she went down with pneumonia, and was prescribed an overdose of antibiotics which so damaged her aural nerves that she became completely deaf; for the last thirty years of her life she existed in a totally silent world. If that had occurred half a century later, she could have sued and would surely have been awarded heavy damages for medical negligence, but in those non-litigious days action was not even considered. Her chief joy was playing Scrabble and Sheilah often used to go down to The Malthouse in the evenings and play the word game with her.

What Dick missed most in retirement from his profession, apart from Sheilah's company, was being out with the horses. He was essentially a practical horseman who empathised with his horses, loving them for their limitations as much as for their virtues. 'Horses have good memories but no power of reasoning,' he once remarked. 'If a horse could say to himself: "I'll rub this tiresome fellow off on the next gatepost", we should be in trouble.' Office work never appealed to him. He enjoyed planning the entries for his horses, because this necessitated solving the fascinating problem of matching opportunity to ability and fitness; but the humdrum routine of paper work repelled him and he was fortunate to have in his secretary Brian Holmes a competent and reliable man who relieved him of most of that burden. He was also fortunate in having as his successor at Kingwood Marcus Tregoning, who had been his assistant and with whom he had a relationship of deep mutual trust. Marcus was pleased to have Dick's advice and long experience to call on whenever he felt it was needed, and for his part Dick derived tremendous enjoyment from going out regularly on the King-wood gallops and seeing the work during the first year after Sheilah's death.

In 1999 Dick had increasing pain in his back, from which sitting perfectly still provided the only relief. He had to suspend his visits to the Kingwood gallops, which was a major depri-vation, and his exercises in the swimming pool. Lack of exercise does no favours to the other functions of the body. He made an appointment with John Costello, who referred him to an Australian surgeon, Mr Crock. Crock examined the X-rays and told him: 'I know what's the matter with you – narrowing of the spine.' Alternate vertebrae had become displaced, causing pressure on the nerves and intense pain. The next visit was to the anaesthetist, a middle-aged lady who, after ten minutes study of the X-rays, pronounced the verdict that he was not a fit enough subject for a general anaesthetic. Dick went home crest-fallen, but a week later Crock rang to say that, after careful thought, he had decided that he could do the operation under a local anaesthetic if Dick agreed. Dick did not hesitate. The operation was performed at the Cromwell in November. For two hours Dick lay flat on his stomach, feeling nothing, but hearing a dreadful cacophony of sounds from his back. When it was all over he said to the surgeon: 'It sounded as if you were using a large hammer and chisel.' 'I was using a small chisel and a large hammer,' Crock replied.

The operation was successful, but it had involved cutting through a lot of tissue, and it left Dick terribly weak. When he was discharged from the Cromwell he went to the Royal Buckinghamshire Hospital at Aylesbury for rehabilitation, where he was once again in the care of Ruth, who had married one of her patients and become Mrs Obetan. He finally went home on 18 December. During the next few months he was gradually recovering his strength, struggling to walk on the Zimmer frame at home and making weekly visits to Aylesbury for work in the gym, walking on arm-crutches with a physio on either side and another behind him in case he fell over backwards. April 13 2000 was a day of significant progress: he walked from the front door to the hall, a distance of half a dozen yards, three times on the frame.

Life at home settled into a regular pattern. He did exercises in the morning, had lunch and then spent the afternoon watching racing on the Racing Channel, or the BBC or Channel Four if they were screening it. He did more exercises in the evening, had dinner and afterwards settled down to watch films on video. Westerns were his favourite viewing, especially Westerns starring John Wayne or Clint Eastwood. He always got a thrill from watching John Wayne debouching from a frontier fort at the head of a detachment of the 7th US Cavalry, with the reliable Victor McLaglen as the sergeant, to scour the plains for the raiding Apache.

His small breeding operation, with the mares kept at Willie Carson's Minster Stud – the stud had supplied the name of the St Leger winner Minster Son – was a constant source of interest. The foundation mare was Tinted Venus, the dam of Fortune's Darling with whom Dick had won the Lowther Stakes for Major Holliday. Jakie Astor had bought Tinted Venus at Holliday's dispersal sale but, although she bred ten winners altogether, she never produced anything else as good as Fortune's Darling. When she was twenty-three years old he gave her to Dick, who decided to send her to Seaepic, a horse he had trained for Lady Beaverbrook and who would have been more than useful if he had not had breathing troubles, at Philip Young's Three Gates Stud at Moreton Morrell in Warwickshire. Dick called the resulting colt foal Cabin Boy after the cabin boy Agrippa in the popular ballad *The Good Ship Venus*. Being by Seaepic out of Tinted Venus, he was a strong candidate for the title of best-named horse in the *Stud Book*.

As he was out of such an old mare, Cabin Boy was predictably backward, though he was declared the winner of a race at Bath in September of his two-year-old season. He actually finished

second but Sovereign Lane, who beat him by a neck, had interfered with him a furlong from home and was relegated to second
place after a Stewards Enquiry. He was gelded at the end of that
season. He did not win as a three-year-old, although he was
placed three times. It was when he was schooled over hurdles
that his true vocation became apparent as, although he was only
a little horse, he jumped brilliantly. He won fourteen races
altogether, trained by Tim Forster for thirteen of them. He was
very sound and very game. He did win a steeplechase but, on
account of his size, he found jumping fences terribly hard work
and was happier over hurdles. He gave the Herns enormous
pleasure and, when his racing days were over, he went back to
West Ilsley as a hack.

Another of the mares, Hors Serie, also was a gift. Miss Eulalie
Buckmaster, a daughter of the former Master of the Warwick-
shire Hounds, polo player and founder of Bucks Club in
London, lived at Moreton Morrell where the leading breeder
Bob McCreery had his stud before moving to Stowell Hill in
Somerset, and Dick got to know her through the McCreerys.
She was very hospitable and always had a bottle of Bollinger
ready for drinking when they went to lunch with her. As a result
she sent her horses to be trained by Dick and these included
Hors Serie, who won as a two-year-old and had the class to
finish second in the Ribblesdale Stakes at Royal Ascot the next
year. When she decided to give up having horses on the flat
because she felt too old to go and see them run, she gave Hors
Serie to Dick. Dick sent her to be covered by his former charge
Relkino who, after a spell at the Barton Stud near Newmarket,
was sold to the National Stud and stationed at Chris Sweeting's
Conduit Stud in Oxfordshire as a National Hunt stallion. When
Relkino arrived at Conduit Sweeting told one of his sons to take
him round the stud. He put a saddle on him and rode him
round. Although he had not had a saddle on his back since he
ran in the Champion Stakes, Relkino never batted an eyelid. He
got several good jumpers like Relkeel and Arctic Kinsman, but

died of a twisted gut at the age of sixteen before his potential as a specialist sire could be realised.

Bespoke, the produce of the mating of Hors Serie with Relkino, was very versatile, and won on the flat and over hurdles and fences. After that Marcus Tregoning won three point-to-points on him, and when Dick retired he became a hack for Marcus's head lad Vic Chitty. He always lived on racehorse rations and looked extremely well on that diet. There are encouraging signs that Hors Serie has founded an on-going family. Her daughter Moon Spin bred, to a mating with another former Hern charge Bustino, the useful staying filly Rosa Canina. Leased to John Dunlop, Rosa Canina won five races as a three-year-old in 1999, one over 1¾ miles and four over 2 miles. At the end of that season she retired to Minster Stud as a broodmare.

On March 30 2000 George Bull, the horse that Sheilah had gone to the betting shop to watch running on her last outing from hospital, had his first race for seventeen months when he made his debut over fences in the Peter and Sybil Blackburn Memorial Challenge Trophy Novices Chase at Taunton. It was an unusually valuable race for the Somerset course, worth £5390 to the winner. After Sheilah's death Dick had formed a partnership to own him, called the Hopeful partnership, which included Sheilah's cousin Giles Blomfield. George Bull jumped like a stag, made all the running and won by 10 lengths. His trainer Henry Daly, who had succeeded Tim Forster at Downton Hall, thought very highly of him and believed him capable of going to the top of the tree as a chaser, but disaster struck when he ran again at Bangor a little over two weeks later. He was cantering in front with the race apparently won when he completely misjudged his jump at the last open ditch and fell heavily, breaking his shoulder.

Dick's interest in breeding does not end with his mares and their produce. He also has annual breeding rights in the half-brothers Unfuwain and Nashwan, and the sale of nominations brings in a nice income – in 1999 £10,000 in the case of Unfuwain and £45,000 in the case of Nashwan. There are, of course, certain hazards associated with the sale of nominations. Dick's are sold on 1 October terms, which means that the mare must be in foal on that date for the fee to be payable. The first year that Nashwan was at stud Dick sold the nomination to Sheikh Mohammed, who sent his brilliant mare, the 1000 Guineas winner Ravinella. She got safely in foal, but two days before the end of September she went down with colic and died. The pregnancy was not insured, and that taught Dick a lesson for the future.

The nomination income was welcome, because the household of a tetraplegic involves heavy expense, not least on staffing. Russell and Irene Brown had been with him since 1995. Russell, who had spent most of his life in the steel industry in the north-east, did the driving and the heavy work involved in attending to Dick's needs, and Irene looked after the housekeeping Another helper was needed. For some time Dick engaged single men, but they all found life in a small village too slow, with no entertainments except the pub, and it became obvious that another married couple was the answer; as Marcus Tregoning had moved out of the flat over the garage which he had occupied as assistant trainer, the necessary accommodation was available. Patricia had taken over the job of cook when Mrs G retired.

Liza Brown played a vital role. She had been a close friend of the Herns for so many years, accompanying them sometimes on holidays, that she was uniquely qualified to look after the pressing business matters which Dick found difficult to cope with. She was tidy, painstaking and meticulous. He referred to her jokingly as 'my dame d'affaires'. Liza was, above all, a very loyal friend, and loyalty is a quality by which Dick sets great store. All his life he has given and received loyalty – from jockeys, stable employees, owners and friends. Dick has never been a religious man. 'I am not an atheist,' he declares but, unlike Sheilah, he is not a regular churchgoer. Nevertheless he personifies many Christian virtues which include, besides loyalty, truthfulness, a steadfast adherence to principle and single-minded observance of duty. His word is his bond. One of the most striking aspects of his character is total absence of self-pity. In the face of set-backs, like his hunting accident and his life-threatening heart problem, which would have spelt the end of an active career for most men, his resolution to carry on has never faltered, nor has his sense of humour failed. It was that steely resolve, that refusal to be beaten, as much as his sublime training skill, that earned him the respect of the whole racing community.

Dick's simple philosophy and his lack of self-pity are reflected in his own words:

> When I look back on my life I realise how lucky I have been. I was always mad about horses, and I have always been with them throughout my life except for the war years. I have also been very lucky to have trained some high-class horses, some of the best horses in the world. I have always had a love affair with the thoroughbred ever since, at the age of sixteen, I first rode Happy Days. I have been able to live in the country all my life. Every time I have been to London I have thought how lucky I was not to have to commute with a hard hat and a brolly, travelling up and down in overcrowded trains.

'Some of the best horses in the world' was not a phrase that he used lightly. Among the fillies that he trained, Sun Princess, Highclere and Dunfermline all gave world-class performances; among the colts, Brigadier Gerard was supreme at a mile, and Troy and Nashwan showed glimpses of greatness over middle distances. The comparison of horses of different generations is an inexact science, and even the authors of the International Classifications, the official annual ratings of the best horses worldwide, admit that for technical reasons they do not provide an accurate measure of the relative merits of horses ten years apart, as Troy and Nashwan were. If the International Classifications were to be believed, Troy, with a rating of 136 (allowing for a 40lb all-round increase in the ratings introduced in the meantime) was superior to Nashwan, with a rating of 131. However, when it is accepted that the Classifications are fallible in this respect, the nuances provided by a trainer's intimate knowledge of individual horses must be a more accurate guide. This is what Dick had to say about his three Derby winners:

> Henbit could never have lived with Nashwan or Troy, who were both exceptionally good horses over a mile and a half. I believe that Nashwan was the better because he had the speed to win the Guineas as well as the Derby. Troy could never have won the Guineas. Indeed a mile and a quarter was hardly far enough for Troy, and he was not as impressive when he won the Benson and Hedges Gold Cup over that distance as he had been when winning the Derby and the King George VI and Queen Elizabeth Stakes. Nashwan was equally good at all distances from a mile to a mile and a half.

At the end of his racing career in 1989 Sheilah had a video compiled showing all Nashwan's races, with interpolated comments from various people able to throw light on specific aspects of the horse. His most commanding performances were in the Guineas and the Derby. Although he won the Eclipse Stakes by 5 lengths in the end, he had an unnecessarily hard race because Willie Carson gave him so much to do after allowing Opening Verse to go 6 lengths clear early in the straight. The race may have taken the edge off him for the King George VI and Queen Elizabeth Stakes only two weeks later, when he had to struggle to win by a neck from Cacoethes, whom he had beaten by 7 lengths in the Derby.

What the video reveals with breathtaking clarity is the power and beauty of his stride – the leading leg stretched far out in front of him, the rippling movements of his shoulders, the thrust of his quarters. He was described as moving like a panther. The phrase 'poetry of motion' is often used loosely. This was it. Mikey Seely, the racing correspondent of *The Times*, was asked by the interviewer where he would place him among the great horses of modern times. Mikey measured his words carefully. He said that there had been greater individual performances, citing the Derby victory of Shergar and the 'Arc' victory of Dancing Brave. But he concluded that the quadruple triumph of Nashwan (the 2000 Guineas, the Derby, the Eclipse Stakes and the King George VI and Queen Elizabeth Stakes) was unique, and placed him on a pedestal no other horse could share.

It was Dick's privilege to have had such a horse to train, and Dick's crowning achievement was that he was able to bring his talents to a peak and keep them there long enough to gain a series of Group 1 victories.

Good horses require good jockeys to ride them, and in his two long-serving stable jockeys Joe Mercer and Willie Carson Dick had precisely the right men to do justice to his equine stars. Joe was Brigadier Gerard's regular partner and Willie rode Troy and Nashwan. They were both skilful, sympathetic horsemen, expert race riders and entirely reliable in their personal relationships. Joe was the more serious and was an excellent timekeeper. Willie was more light-hearted, with an impish sense of humour and a cackling, infectious laugh, but he was notoriously unpunctual on work mornings. On one occasion he and Dick were discussing the wonderful judgement of pace of the American jockey Steve Cauthen, then riding with outstanding success in Britain and giving virtuoso performances when making every yard of the running on Reference Point in the 1987 Derby and King George VI and Queen Elizabeth Stakes. 'He's got a clock in his head,' said Dick. 'I've got a bit of a clock in my head too,' said Willie. 'What you need is a good alarm clock,' Dick retorted. Dick's relationships with Joe and Willie were as trusted friends as well as employees. 'Not that I didn't get an occasional rollicking,' Willie recalls. 'The worst was not for anything I had done wrong in a race, but for being too friendly with the press.' That reveals, perhaps, as much about Dick's prejudice as it does about Willie's habit of spontaneous and unguarded comment.

One of Dick's favourite poems, *The Man from Snowy River*, written by the Australian A. B. Paterson in the last decade of the nineteenth century, might, mutatis mutandis, have been written about Dick. The Man from Snowy River, which flows from the flanks of Australia's highest mountain Mount Kosciusko, volunteered to join the hunt for 'the colt from old Regret', who had got away and joined the wild bush horses; and, after a desperate chase across terrible terrain, outstripped the other riders, captured the colt and brought him back The final stanza runs:

And down by Kosciusko, where the pine-clad ridges raise
Their torn and rugged battlements on high,
Where the air is clear as crystal, and the white stars fairly blaze
At midnight in the cold and frosty sky,
And where around the Overflow the reed-beds sweep and sway
To the breezes, and the rolling plains are wide,
The Man from Snowy River is a household word today,
And the stockmen tell the story of his ride.

In his time Dick Hern overcame obstacles just as formidable as, and much longer lasting than, those of The Man from Snowy River, and his name too will be a household word in racing circles as long as professionalism, strength of character and the will to win are held in honour.

One question is outstanding. In the few years that have passed since Dick retired, the evolution of international racing has proceeded at such a furious pace that the Breeders Cup, which was the wonder of the thoroughbred world when John Gaines announced it in the spring of 1982, is in danger of becoming old hat. Races of enormous value contested by horses from many different countries have been staged in the Middle East, where the Dubai World Cup at Nad Al Sheba was the richest race in the world in 2000, and the Far East, where races like the Japan Cup at Fuchu and the Hongkong International Bowl at Sha Tin are the principal magnets. Itinerant stars such as Singspiel and Jim And Tonic glamorised the new races. Australia looms ever larger on the racing stage, attracting an increasing number of runners from Europe, and Taufan's Melody, from the small stable of Lady Herries, became the first British-trained winner of a Grade 1 race in the Antipodes when he captured the Caulfield Cup in 1998. Whatever next? It surely cannot be long before South America, particularly Argentina which has produced so many horses that have distinguished themselves on the track or at stud in the United States, makes a move to get in on the act.

The question about Dick is this: how would he have reacted to this changing international scene and how would he have adapted his planning to its opportunities if he had still been training at the beginning of the new millennium? It is possible to give an unequivocal answer. Astonishingly for a Somerset-bred countryman, he has an outlook devoid of parochialism, and he has always shown ingenuity and imagination in devising programmes for his horses. It should not be forgotten that he demonstrated the way forward for his British professional colleagues in exploiting the opportunities for top-class horses abroad by winning the Prix Vermeille with Highest Hopes and the Prix de Diane with Highclere; further afield, he took Bedtime to be second in the early days of the Japan Cup and Dayjur to be the unluckiest of losers in the Breeders Cup Sprint. Significantly, his last Pattern race winner was Alhaarth in the Prix du Rond Point at Longchamp. Given the right ammunition, he would have relished the challenge of the ever-broadening scope of international racing and taken unerring aim at the most lucrative targets wherever they were offered.

———

The household of a widower may be well-ordered, but order alone does not bring contentment. Sheilah's death left a void at The Old Rectory, and inevitably Dick was oppressed by a deep sense of loneliness after a long happy marriage to such a loving and dynamic personality. In the circumstances he accounts himself very fortunate to have found a solution to this pervasive dilemma. In the old days at Porlock he had been in love with Pat Wykeham-Fiennes, but they had lacked the financial means to set up a home and get married. They had drifted apart and lost touch, while Dick married Sheilah and Pat married Richard Shedden MC, a brother of the top-class horseman John Shedden. When Richard died she reverted to her maiden name, and at the time of Sheilah's death she was living at Iwerne Minster in Dorset. As a widow she shared Dick's problem of loneliness.

Exchanging letters of condolence put them in touch again. After some months they began to see each other. Dick went down to have lunch with Pat several times, and she began to visit West Ilsley regularly. Their characters were easily compatible. They shared their memories of Porlock, their love of horses and their sense of humour. Pat even grew to enjoy 'Westerns'. Dick found her a wonderfully restful person to be with. In the new millennium she was spending half her time at The Old Rectory, staying there for a week or ten days at a time and then returning to Dorset to look after her own house and garden. They settled into a relationship of gentle and affectionate companionship that assuaged their loneliness and is profoundly rewarding for both of them.

INDEX